C000143436

Globalization, Americanization and British Muslim Identity

The Department of Research and Publications at the Islamic College for Advanced Studies (ICAS) is an academic and cultural centre, concerned with general issues of Islamic thought. The idea of an Islamic institution of higher learning grounded on Islamic normative values and historical heritage, yet fully capable of responding to, and guiding Muslims in meeting the demands of modern Western epistemological, cultural, socio-political and economic ideas, are based on years of experience and contemplation, all of which now form conceptual history of ICAS. The Department provides a meeting point for the Western and Islamic worlds of learning. At ICAS it contributes to the multi-disciplinary and cross-disciplinary study of the contemporary world. Beyond ICAS, its role is strengthened by developing international academic contacts. It is an intellectual forum working from an Islamic perspective to promote and support research projects, organise intellectual and cultural seminars and publish scholarly works. It tries to establish a distinct intellectual trend in Islamic thought which relates to the vivid legacy of the Muslim nation and its continuous efforts for intellectual and methodological reform. This involves a large number of researchers and scholars from various parts of the world.

ICAS' publications fall into the following categories: *Theology, Philosophy, Mysticism, Islamic Legal Theory and Islamic Law, hermeneutics and Qur'anic studies, Hadith methodology, Social Sciences, and Languages.*

Since ICAS is an academic college promoting intellectual debate, and scholarship, the views expressed in the books published will always reflect independent views and diverse approaches to the problems being dealt with.

ICAS Press

Saied Reza Ameli

Globalization, Americanization and British Muslim Identity

ICAS Press

British Library Cataloguing-in-Publication Data
A catalogue record for this book is available from the
British Library

ISBN 1 904063 02 0 (pb)

© Saied Reza Ameli, 2002
This edition first published 2002

*The right of Saied Reza Ameli to be identified as the author of this work has been asserted by him
in accordance with the Copyright, Designs and Patents Act of 1988*

Published by
Islamic College for Advanced Studies Press (ICAS)
133 High Road, Willesden, London NW10 2SW

Cover photograph by Muhsin Kilby

Contents

Tables and Figures

Tables

7

Figures

Acknowledgements

First I would like to thank Dr K. H. Ansari whose invaluable guidance and knowledge has helped me to gain a deeper understanding of the profound conceptual, theoretical and empirical aspects of my research. I was also privileged to benefit from Dr V. Martin, who helped me throughout and contributed greatly by reading my book, and further by her wise suggestions on my work. She undertook this task with high amiability and sympathy. Further comments made by Dr R. Prokhovnik on the first draft of this study, which I hope has informed the direction of my subsequent research.

I need also to thank Ms June Jackson for her tireless editing of my English, and to extend my gratitude to Dr John Hutnyk, Mr S. Toussi and Mr M. J. Elmi for their kind assistance. I would also like to thank Dr Reza Shah-Kazeni for his most valuable advice and constructive suggestions during the final year of my work on this book. His wife, Mrs Nurin Shah-Kazeni, was also most gracious in extending her help during the final stages of the project.

I must also thank the young British Muslims of Brent who were the subjects of my empirical research for their honest contribution in interviews and filling out of questionnaires, and for their thoughtful and deep insights into the subject matter of this research.

Finally, I must mention my family whose never-ending support has made this all possible. During the last five years my wife and my sons, Mahdi and Abbas, have patiently supported me by helping to transfer my data. For all these years I could not fulfil my proper responsibility as a husband to my wife or as a father to my children, including Saleh and Fatemeh. I am enormously grateful to them for being more than accommodating of my situation. I would like also to thank my mother-in-law and father-in-law for their kind encouragement, but my deepest appreciation is reserved for my parents whose invaluable support has helped me to finish this work.

Globalization, 9/11 and Muslim Identity

This book is going to press just a few months after the September 11, 2001 attacks on the World Trade Center in New York City, and the Pentagon in Washington, DC. A third aircraft crashed near Pittsburgh, Pennsylvania. The combined impact of these events led to the US-organized ventures into Afghanistan in order to destroy that country's Taliban regime and the al-Qaeda network allegedly led by Osama bin Laden (or the Bin Laden Brotherhood). At the time of writing, the conflict between the 'Muslim world' and the US-led West has been greatly amplified both by the expressed desire of the US government to obliterate the Saddam Hussein regime in Iraq and by Israel's incursions into Palestinian territory in response to what the US and Israeli leaderships call 'Palestinian terrorism'. In this connection there is a growing rhetorical and ideological debate about 'homicide,' 'suicide,' 'martyrdom' and 'killing.'

In the wake of 9/11, the 'war on terrorism' rapidly legitimized – at least in most of 'the West' – attacks on all manner of independence, resistance and liberation movements, including the reining in of American support for the Irish Republican Army (particularly since its involvement with the guerrilla movement in Colombia became fairly well-established); wide, if reluctant, support for Russian attempts to crush Chechnian resistance; and ambiguities such as the apparent, if temporary, American support for the overthrow of Venezuela's democratically elected President. Virtually no part of the world has been isolated from the strategic use of the theme of terrorism. Moreover, in spite of my use of the phrase 'Muslim world' in a new confrontation with the West, there have, of course, been nations with a strong Islamic culture (such as Pakistan) or, at the other extreme, secular nation-states with a strong Islamic presence (most notably Turkey), on the US-led Western side. In fact, in the years leading up to 9/11 and, especially, in its aftermath, the shifting alliances of convenience between and among nation-states have become ever more 'anarchic' and difficult to fathom.

One major feature of this restructuring of world politics and the remarkable increase in visibility of the *cultural* dimension of globalization has been the growing significance of questions concerning both the self-identity and the identification of peoples, most notably (but not only) of Muslims in Europe and America.[1] This has involved a remarkable mixture of anti-Muslim or anti-Islamic sentiment and of attempts to enhance respect for Muslims, notably in the USA, the UK and France. At the same time, there has been an almost equal ambiguity concerning Jews, with both anti-Israel and pro-Israel movements becoming evident in Europe and the USA. More specifically, some of those involved in anti-Israel movements are undoubtedly anti-Semitic – in the sense of anti-*Jewish* – and here they have much in common with what some perceive to be *Arab* or *Islamic/Muslim* anti-Jewishness. On the other hand, there are many, particularly but not only in the West, who try to make a clear-cut distinction between being opposed to the actions of the nation-state, even the constitutional form, of Israel and racist sentiment. The tragedy is that this is becoming an increasingly difficult position to sustain, insofar as the far (Christian) Right in the USA and its equivalent in Israel are systematically attempting to establish that being against Israel's policies equates to being anti-Semitic (i.e., anti-Jewish). Witness the 'Quisling' characterization of the Norwegian representative on the disputed UN commission investigating the apparent Israeli atrocity in Jenin in the West Bank region.[2] Fears engendered by the growing presence of fascist or neo-fascist movements in Europe have served only to exacerbate racist sentiments and actions.

Throughout much of the contemporary world there has, then, undoubtedly been a highly visible return of negative racial, ethical, cultural, and religious stereotypes. Indeed identity politics, as it is often called, has become more than dangerously pernicious since 9/11, this being a more complex but also more satisfactory account than the clash-of-civilizations thesis. Not that the thesis of a resurgence of Islam against 'the West,' or vice versa, is without foundation. Clearly, in spite of some attempts to prevent it in both the USA and much of Europe, on the one hand, and, in the very broadest sense, in most Muslim countries, on the other, pejorative stereotypification is fast proceeding.

What has all of this got to do with globalization? There have been numerous responses to this question, but to me the most analytically satisfactory answer is that it not merely has a great deal to do with globalization but that it is an *aspect* – be it an ugly one – of globalization itself, facilitated in large part by central features of the globalization process, such as complex and

---

1. It has to be said here that in Said Reza Ameli Renani's book careful distinctions are drawn between Muslim and Islamic identities in Britain.
2. Quisling became a Nazi puppet following the German invasion of Norway early in World War II.

extensive networks of mainly electronic communication. In the cruder, and capitalistic-economistic, view of globalization, the *jihadist* – in the sense of the secondary form of jihad – confrontation with 'the war against terrorism' endangers, for some cancels, globalization. But, in a sociologically-based conceptual respect, one of the periodic features of globalization has been encounters of various kinds – sometimes violent – between civilizations, regions, societies and so on. We have – in my view, very unfortunately – become well-acquainted with a conception of globalization that severely limits it to the idea of capitalistic Westernization. No wonder that in Islamic societies globalization constitutes a disguised version of the notion of the triumph of the (Americanized) West. This view of globalization has to be strongly resisted, and it is one of the numerous virtues of the present book that globalization is *not* used in this way.

Globalization has been a very long process extending over many centuries, a process involving cultural, political, social-communicative and, yes, economic dimensions. It has, moreover, involved much violence and many wars. It has often been said that Islam is an anti-global religioculture. But nothing could be further from the truth. Indeed, one of the causes of problems between Christianity (however secularized it may have been) and Islam over the centuries is that they involve *rival* conceptions of the 'organization' of the world as a whole.

With so much migration and the consequent creation of yet more diasporas in an increasingly compressed world, it is not at all surprising that controversies of national, religious and ethnic identities have become so prominent. The present book is remarkable for the sophistication and sensitivity of its analysis of Muslim identities in Britain. Its timeliness is obvious, being published in the unpredictable year following 9/11. The fact is that increasingly large numbers of people around the world have mixed identities and competing loyalties. Thus, the attempts of political elites to enforce loyalty to nation-states by the compulsory teaching of 'national traditions' will become ever more problematic.

Roland Robertson[1]
Aberdeen, Scotland
April 2002

---

1. Roland Robertson is Professor of Sociology and Director of the Centre for the Study of Globalization, University of Aberdeen; Distinguished Professor of Sociology Emeritus, University of Pittsburgh, Honorary Professor of Cultural Studies, Tsinghua University, Beijing, China. He has held visiting positions in the UK, the USA, Hong Kong, Sweden, Japan, the Czech Republic, Brazil, Turkey and Austria. He is also President of the Global Studies Association.

Theoretical Approach

Part I

Theoretical Approach

Introduction

My main concern in this study is to look at the impact of globalization on British Muslim identity, i.e. on the identity of Muslims born and brought up in Britain. In order to explain the main concerns of this study, as an introduction, I set out first the statement of the problem, then the framework, which will examine the whole structure of this study. Finally, some of the key concepts will be elaborated.

In the first part of this study, namely Chapters 1 to 3, the main emphasis will be directed towards the theoretical and the historical aspects of this research. In the second part, Chapters 4 to 7, the focus will be upon its empirical aspects. Concrete findings will help to assess the validity, correctness, strengths or weaknesses of the theories addressed in previous chapters.

Chapter 1 addresses the characteristics and the main theories of cultural globalization. Westernization and Americanization as an influential aspect of the process of globalization will also be discussed in this chapter. Chapter 2 assesses the consequences of globalization for religious identity and its implications for the construction of British Muslim identity. In this chapter the dichotomy of homogenization and heterogenization is discussed in reference to major theorizers of globalization.

The focal point of Chapter 3 is the development and configuration of Muslim identity throughout the history of Islam. The history of Muslims in general will be broken down and examined according to the following system of periods: the formation and transformation of Muslim identity in:

1. The prophetic period (613–632)
2. The period of the rightly-guided Caliphate (632–661)
3. The Umayyad and Abbasid Caliphate (661–1258)
4. The age of Empires: Mongol, Ottoman and Safavid (up to the hegemony of the West) (1258–1789).

From the sociological point of view, these four periods can be considered as pertaining to a 'traditional society'. Then the Muslim world within a Western-dominated globe will be studied:

5. The period of Modernization (1789–present), and its shift to
6. The postmodern/globalizing age.

This will be followed by an examination of the extent to which the forces of globalization, the local forces and also the force of history have affected Muslim identity in 'the globalization era'.

In Chapter 4, I will concentrate on the issues associated with Muslims' background in Britain and the sample group of the study, located in the Borough of Brent in London, and the construction of a typology of British Muslim identity based on the individuals who have been the subjects of this research.

Chapter 5 will examine some of the processes of globalization that have contributed to the context within which the religious identity of British Muslims has evolved. In this chapter, consideration has been given to the association between the various aspects of British Muslim identity, such as 'religious understanding', 'religious practice', 'religious belief', as well as 'social relationships' and 'day-to-day issues' in relation to the process of globalization.

Chapters 6 and 7 will concentrate on the key processes of globalization under the headings of 'homogenization' and 'heterogenization'. With respect to homogenization, Chapter 6 will first examine the views of British Muslims with regard to the 'British Muslim identity' as well as their perception on the issue of citizenship. The processes of Americanization and globalization of Muslim movements are then analysed. The heterogeneity of British Muslim identity in relation to the process of globalization is the final theme which will be critically examined in Chapter 7. Resistance, legitimizing identity and projective identities will be elaborated upon in relation to the process of globalization.

1. Statement of the Problem

During the years 1977–1979, I was studying in Sacramento. In 1979 I returned to Iran. Suddenly I realized the existence of different, to some extent contrasting, cultures in Iran. One was the product of the religious revolution while the other, prerevolutionary culture belonged to the secular political system, a clear indication of the sea-change that had taken place within the cultural ethos of Iran. What stood out with particular sharpness was the great contrast between American culture and the postrevolutionary culture of Iran. It was this contrast that provoked in me a great deal of reflection upon the reason for such a massive increase in devotion to religious values, and this at a period in human history that appeared to prove the inevitability of the process of secularization, and at a time when the global domination of capitalism and socialism seemed assured. These two ideologies, mirror images of each other within an ever-advancing global secular culture, were suddenly and decisively stopped in their tracks by the revolution in Iran.

My thoughts on these matters coincided with a series of trips to countries such as Pakistan, Senegal and Indonesia from the early 1990s. I was struck by the ubiquity of Western culture in countries thousands of miles away from the centres of Western culture. It seemed to be a phenomenon that warranted deep investigation. The presence of McDonalds or Pizza Hut in countries as diverse as Malaysia, Japan, China and Morocco, or the phenomenon of MTV Channels in the languages of those countries, demonstrated a level of homogenization, a levelling of cultures, an imposition of a uniform way of life upon diverse peoples that was startling, unsettling and provocative. This uniformity embraces different types of identities, such as strongly religious-minded people and deeply secular groups, nationalists and modernists. In Indonesia I encountered, contrary to my expectations, great segments of the younger generation who were thoroughly Westernized. Great numbers of this generation had adopted Western-style clothing, spent their leisure times not in traditional pastimes, but ones that were indistinguishable from those pursued by their Western counterparts; their favourite foods, their way of thinking and thoughts were strongly inclined westwards.

I was, therefore, hugely surprised by the tenacity shown by young Muslims living in part of London in continuing to hold on to Islamic values and their culture. Given that London is considered one of the most important centres of Western culture, the persistence of these lifestyles invited much curiosity.

If one divides globalization into two types, 'hardware technology' and 'software technology', then one can say that London is one of the most important sources of software globalization, a kind of software that is the product of liberal and secular ideology. In such a city, the emergence of a very strong religious Muslim identity, among a group of young Muslims extremely faithful to religion, and in significant numbers, was unexpected. Of course, many other Muslims have adapted to the environment and accepted the British common culture or constructed hybrid cultures combining their parent's values and traditions with those which they have experienced in wider society. The heterogenization of cultural identity within Britain, and the homogenization of culture and behaviour on the other, were the two juxtaposed observations that formed the basis of my sociological research in the field of cultural globalization. Such was the main point of departure for this study, the theme of globalization in relation to Muslim religious identity.

In today's society significant changes in terms of morality, spirituality and religious understanding are taking place. The range of religious permissiveness is also increasing day by day. This in turn modifies and shapes religious belief, values and practices – which in turn impacts upon religious identity. There is no longer a 'single collective religious identity' – a religious identity accepted by all individuals within society. The 'single identity' seems to have fragmented into several types of identity in all societies. On the other hand, since 'instantaneous communication' has been invented, individuals have come into close contact with other peoples, cultures and societies all over the world. The world has become smaller. The appearance and advancement of communication technology have played a major role in the creation of the 'network society', which seems to have been overwhelmed by the concept of 'time' and 'space'. Regardless of where you are, all individuals are living in a single space. They consume almost the same cultural, political and economic products. This process of communication, which has been facilitated by new communication and telecommunication systems, has established new conditions. Technology such as telex, telephone, fax, internet, satellite television and radio, the advances in transport and the expansion of tourism, have added a new cultural, political and economic impulse, a 'global force' to the 'local forces'.

In the arena of culture, globalization has helped to entwine different cultures, which were, previously, isolated from each other in the past. In traditional society, indigenous cultures and identities were stable, being based on local tradition, customs and religion. In the globalization era, local cultures have enmeshed with other cultures all over the world and have created a 'multicultural society'. In the process of globalization, American culture has played a significant role in the processes of the flow of information, knowledge, culture and civilization. Hollywood, Coca-Cola, Ford Motors, rock music, fashion, professional sport and many other elements of American culture have penetrated local cultures.

This trend has had a significant impact on all types of identity – national, cultural and in particular religious. To understand this tremendous change in the context of Muslim identity, one needs to look at the historical development of this identity in its own right; this shall be further evaluated in Chapter 3. At this point, the following review of some contributions to the study of globalization and religion generally, and Islam in particular, will be given as a brief introduction to the theme.

Globalization in respect of religion and culture was first discussed by Robertson and Chirico(1985). After them, sociologists like Beyer (1990), Turner (1994), Featherstone (1995) and Castells (1997) have studied it in greater detail. More specifically, Robertson (1987, 1989a, 1989b, 1991, 1992a, 1992b, 1994), Turner (1994), Ahmad (1994) and Beyer (1990, 1994, 1998) have briefly discussed aspects of the impact of globalization on religion and religious identity.

Akbar Ahmad (1994), presenting a number of articles, edited the first book on 'globalization and Islam' in which he discussed some aspects of the interaction between the process of globalization and Islam. Ahmad points out that the issue of Bosnia became a rallying point for Muslims and has shown a sharp awareness of Muslims as a 'world community', both in the West and amongst Muslims themselves. This indicates that there is a layer of a network relationship and social understanding within Muslim communities all over the world. In his previous book *Postmodernism and Islam,* Ahmad had discussed postmodernism and the Islamic resurgence as a response to it. He attempts to examine the interaction and contradiction between Islam and the west from a philosophical as well as sociological and anthropological point of view. However, he did not focus on the identities of Muslims in particular. There is no clear distinction between Islam and Muslims in his approach either.

There are some useful research findings available on the construction of Muslim identities. For instance Jacobson (1998) looked at the changes that have taken place within the religious identity of Pakistani youth in Britain. Although her study does not examine the interactions between globalization and British Muslim identity, her perspective on the dynamics of religious identity is relevant and does shed some light on the formation of Muslim identities in a globalized context.

There does not appear to be a single exhaustive study on the impact of globalization on the construction of Muslim identity, especially in relation to British Muslims. Why, one may ask, has there been so little research conducted on this subject? Part of the reason might be that theories of globalization are difficult to test through social surveys. Yet, because the theories are fundamentally future-oriented, in that they indulge in a great deal of prediction about what the future might hold, it is important to complement such theoretical exercises with both historical and contemporary empirical studies that can serve as concrete data that can either verify or falsify the theories.

In this study the impact of globalization on the British Muslim identity will be analysed. Furthermore cultural integration or any move towards a 'monocultural society' will have bearing on the notion of Muslim identity and whether Muslims have manifested a uniform or multiple response to this trend; and whether the emerging identity or identities can be analytically typologized.

The second generation of migrant Muslims, those born in Britain of Muslim migrant parents in the London Borough of Brent has constituted the study group of this research. This generation is diversely composed in terms of religious identity. In comparison to the past generations, it has changed in significant ways: their interests, their social activities, their social relationships, and their whole way of thinking and living have been subject to major alteration. There are several reasons for selecting this group in London:

1. London as a 'global city' is a unique place for this study. In countries possessing advanced communication and information technologies, the trend towards globalization seems to be more dynamic (Sasscn and Portcs, 1993; Eade, 1997b). This is because the level of involvement with electronic communication technology is greater than that in developing countries. London in particular has performed the role of a 'world city' in the emerging world system of production for over a century (King, 1990). As King has illustrated, 'London has steadily become a specialized finance and business centre and a base for cultural production in an increasingly integrated new international division of labour' (King, 1990: 71). Today, the City of London provides financial and business services worldwide. London has also come to represent a central base for Muslim leaders and elites from all over the world. For instance, the central offices of organizations such as the 'Islamic World Federation' and 'Majles Olama for Shia Community in Europe', as well as international newspapers like *The Daily Jang, al-Sharq al-Awsat, al-Ahram, al-Hayat, al-Zaman, al-Quds al-Arabi, Ettela'at International*, and several other newspapers and magazines or journals are based here. Furthermore, several satellite television channels such as the 'Muslim Broadcasting Corporation' (MBC), the 'Arab News Network' (ANN) are broadcasting from London and have come to form part of the global networking system of the Muslim world.

2. Western societies in general contain the driving forces for the globalization of the economy, culture and politics of the world. English culture plays a very important role in defining globalization in terms of the legitimization of a particular way of thinking and acting in social and political arenas. Some of the key aspects of globalization – Westernization, liberalization and democratization – are rooted in British culture. This means that London has come to play a central role in the process of globalizing a particular way of life, and thus homogenizing global culture. The Anglicization of the world is yet another part of this process of homogenization and hegemonization.

3. London is cosmopolitan and multicultural. London has become the meeting point of many cultures of the world. The presence of Muslim and non-Muslim Londoners, with their varied historical affiliation to other cultures – Pakistani, Indian, Bangladeshi, Iranian, African and others from the Arab world – has turned London into a microcosm of the globe. The social, cultural and political diversity of Muslims is also represented in London now. It is reflected in the variety of respondents to this survey who originated from more than thirty Muslim countries. According to Mlinar

(1992: 57) the 'level of globalization can be measured by the extent to which narrow territorial units are open and permit access to the wealth of diversity of the world as a whole ... therefore the higher the share of the overall global diversity, present or accessible within the territorial community, the higher the degree of globalization.' According to this definition, London as a multicultural society, which is diversely accessible to many cultures and civilizations, should be considered as one of the most important and central features of a global city in the world. The Muslim multicultural community in Britain itself is highly diverse and accessible to other nations and cultures.

To present the whole structure of this study, a theoretical framework of the research has been provided. The forces which are involved in the construction of Muslim identity in response to the process of globalization, will be elaborated more in the following section.

2. The Framework of Study

Figure 1 represents the framework for the present study, which looks at the effect of globalization on British Muslim identity. Three major factors have been identified as having the greatest impact on British Muslim identity: local factors, global factors and historic forces.

The construction of the model (Figure 1) has been influenced to a degree by Robertson's concept of 'glocalization' theory, which takes into account global and local factors. However, the model through the incorporation of historical factors, which Robertson ignores, enriches the understanding of the process of globalization in respect of the Muslim world.

Figure I.1: Construction of Muslim Identity in the 'Age of Globalization'

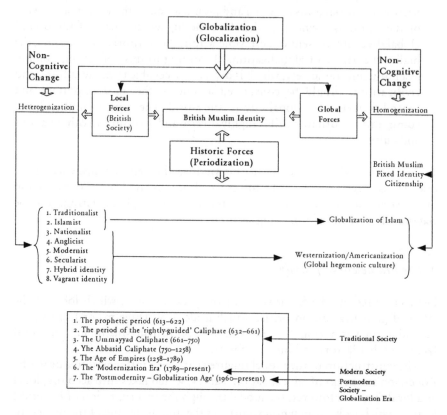

To understand the simultaneous impact of globalization and local forces on Muslim identities in particular contexts, 'glocalization' must be defined clearly. Robertson (1995: 28) pointed out that 'glocalization' describes more accurately the blending and telescoping influence of the global and the local forces. This new concept was introduced by Robertson for two reasons. First, the analysis of the processes of globalization has hitherto neglected local influence to a large degree and has been constructed on a largely trans- or superlocal basis. Nasr (1998: 20) in a very different context, makes a similar point when he argues that 'Most Western studies on Islam are completely determined by this unstated prejudice that modernism is a positive force to be taken seriously not as an adversary but as source of emulation.' Second, from the viewpoint of Robertson (1995: 26), there is little attempt to connect the discussion of time-

and-space to the thorny problem of universalism-and-particularism. For him the theme of postmodernity has involved giving too much attention to the supposed weaknesses of mainstream concern with 'universal time'; he advances the claim that 'particularistic space' be given much greater attention.

As illustrated in Figure 1, the dichotomy of homogenization/heterogenization, and universalism/particularism, are considered as two interlinked concepts, as the local in the global and the global in local. In the framework of this study homogenization and heterogenization have been considered to be two interlinked processes that are slightly different from what Robertson (1992) has suggested. In this approach homogenization is a process that is embodied at the global level; that is, local identities will themselves be globalized through global communications and relationships in the form of international organizations, or even informal global communication between those who share similar identities or outlooks, such as Islamists or Ismailis. As a result, Islamic world movements have been strengthened, and international associations of Muslim scholars, such as the Association of Muslim Social Scientists, may be seen as part of the process of homogenization of Muslim identity in the world.

Having established this claim, this study will examine how glocalization homogenizes the construction of Muslim identity at a local level. At the same time, consideration will also be given to how global forces will heterogenize Muslim identity at a global level.

It is at the local level that the fragmentation and heterogenization of Muslim identity is taking place. For it can be argued that before 1960 Muslims in most Islamic countries were organized in more uniform communities. The difference between them was based primarily on the level of the religiosity of an individual, or his/her religious affiliation, which was extensively locally based. Today, a variety of subcultures and ideologies have fragmented Muslims into several modes of identities: secular, nationalist, socialist, modernist etc., and have divided them into a number of subcultures. As Robertson (1995: 27) stated, 'It is not a question of either homogenization or heterogenization, but rather of the ways in which both of these two tendencies have become features of life across much of the late 20th-century world.'

With the processes of 'homogenization and heterogenization' in mind, I have used theoretical elements from Durkheim (1984) on the differentiation of social roles in response to modernization processes. In these processes, social differentiation, dynamically increased by industrialization, is highly influenced today by cultural exploration and diversification through global channels.

As indicated earlier, the responses of Muslims to these forces vary. Firstly, the younger generation's reaction differs from that of their elders. Secondly, gender is a theme that differs in a variety of contexts. It is made clear that to a large extent the men and the women whom I examine have different kinds of experiences, and make sense of them in different ways. Finally, the identities of Muslim youths have fragmented into different types. This could be attributed to their distinct vision of life and their unique social demands and 'historical background'. Although it is safe to assume that Muslims have a number of identities rather than a unified and singular one, the globalization process has speeded up this disintegration and has given it a global dimension. Our initial studies indicate the existence of eight different identities which are illustrated in Figure 1.

These types of identities can be viewed according to different approaches. In Chapter 1, six theories are presented on the globalization of culture and I have been inclined to accept the *transformationalist* theory (Held *et al.*, 1999) as the most relevant. This theory suggests that the process of globalization has not stabilized and, although one is witnessing the emergence and the formation of new political, cultural and economical powers, one cannot be certain of their final format. Therefore any sociological analysis in the age of globalization should take into consideration the transitory nature of the social phenomenon.

There are three other theories – *relativists*,[1] *reproductionalists*,[2] *post-structuralists*[3] that look at the globalization process, although they do not conflict with the transformationalists[4] theory. The theories of *hyperglobalizers*[5] and *scepticists*[6] have also been reviewed and rejected in Chapter 2.

3. Definition of Concepts

To understand globalization and its impact on Muslim identity, a proper understanding of the following relevant concepts needs to be clarified: 'religion', 'identity', 'religious identity' (and its composite 'Muslim identity') and 'globalization'. Since elements of Islamic belief and ritual have been examined in this survey, it is also important to discuss concepts of belief and religious ritual. A deeper look at these concepts will reveal theoretical

---

1. See Robertson (1990, 1991, 1992a, 1992b and 1995), Featherstone (1994), Turner (1994) and Beyer (1990, 1994 and 1998).
2. See Featherstone (1990 and 1995).
3. See Tiryakinan (1986) and Appardarai (1990) and works of post-structuralists in media imperialism such as Boyd-Barret (1977), Tunstall (1977), Lee (1980), Said (1981 and 1993), Tomlinson (1991) and Reeves (1993).
4. See Held *et al.*(1999) and Giddens (1999).
5. See Wriston (1992), Ohmae (1995) and Held *et al.*, (1999).
6. See Wallerstein (1991b), Hirst & Thompson (1996) and McMichael (1996).

difficulties, which must be overcome in order to use them in the analysis of the data.

3a. Religion

There is no consensus among sociologists as to the definition of religion, and there are probably as many definitions of religion as there are definers. A classic 19th century definition of religion was 'the belief in spiritual beings' (Turner, 1983: 243). 'In the West, most people identify religion with Christianity – a belief in a Supreme Being, who commands us to behave in a moral fashion on this earth, and promises an afterlife to come ... These beliefs, and many other aspects of Christianity, are absent from the significant part of the world's religions' (Giddens, 1989: 451–2).

In general one might define religion as a human phenomenon that functions to unite cultural, social and personality systems into a meaningful whole. Its components generally include a community of believers who share a common myth that interprets the abstractions of cultural values into historic reality through ritual behaviour. This experience has been recognized as encompassing something more than everyday reality, namely the holy. These elements are united into recognizable structures that undergo processes of change, development and deterioration (Hargrove, 1979). Geertz (1973: 30) argued that religion is 'a system of symbols which acts to establish powerful, pervasive and longlasting moods and motivations in men by formulating conceptions of a general order of existence, and clothing these conceptions with such an aura of actuality that the moods' notations seem uniquely realistic.'

Turner (1983: 242–3) suggested that 'the final implication of positivist reductionism is that religion is seen as primarily a cognitive activity of the individual mind, which for various reasons misapprehends the true nature of empirical and social life.'

Durkheim's work, *The Elementary Forms of the Religious Life*, first published in 1912, is perhaps the single most influential study in the sociology of religion (Durkheim, 1976). The Durkheimian perspective saw the role of religion in traditional societies lying in the 'creation, reinforcement and maintenance of social solidarity' (Durkheim, 1976: 165). In contrast to Marx, Durkheim does not connect religion primarily with social inequalities or power, but with the overall nature of the institutions of a society. He defines religion in terms of a distinction between the sacred and the profane, strongly emphasizing the fact that religions are never just a matter of belief. All religions involve regular ceremonial and ritual activities, in which a group of believers meet together as a collectivity (Giddens, 1989: 458–9).

In small traditional cultures, he argues, almost all aspects of life are permeated by religion. Religious ceremonials both originate new ideas and categories of thought and reaffirm existing values. Religion is not just a series of sentiments and activities; it actually conditions the modes of thinking of individuals in traditional cultures. Even the most basic categories of thought, including how time and space are thought of, were first framed in religious terms. The concept of time, for instance, was originally derived from counting the intervals involved in religious ceremonials (Giddens, 1989). Finally a working definition of religion for Berger (1969: 172) is 'the capacity of the human organism to transcend its biological nature through the construction of objective, morally binding, all embracing universals of meaning.'

3b. Identity

The issue of identity was initially developed in psychology and then evolved into a sociological concept. From a psychological point of view, it means the sense of self that develops as a child differentiates between parents and family and takes his or her place in society. In other words, it is an expressed sense of personal distinctiveness, personal continuity and personal autonomy. These concepts, which are more common in sociology and social psychology, tend to stress the fact that a sense of identity is formed from the dialectic between the individual and society (Evans, 1970) and, more particularly, draw attention to the ways in which membership of social groups shapes or determines individuals' perceptions of themselves (Hutnik (1985: 298).

Berger and Luckmann (1967: 174) defined identity as a phenomenon that emerges from the dialectic between the individual and society. To Erikson, the term identity connotes both as a persistent sameness within oneself (self-sameness) and persistent sharing of some kind of essential character with others (cited by Mol, 1976: 57).

Castells (1997) looked at identity construction more widely. He sees identities as a series of elements that have been constructed by materials from history, from geography, from biology, from productive and reproductive institutions, from collective memory and from personal fantasies, from power apparatuses and religious revelations. Castells points out that: 'individuals, social groups, and societies process all these materials, and rearrange their meaning according to social determinations and cultural projects that are rooted in their social structure, and in their space/time framework' (Castells, 1997:7).

Basically, the 'social interactions' perspective views an individual's identity as being the result of various social experiences intrinsically associated with all the joining and departures of social life, and such identities are social because they are sustained by a process of negotiation through interacting with others. Thus, what one means by identity, according to this perspective, is that one is situated within a series of social relations and placed as a social object. In opposition to this view is the one that traditionally regards identity as something unaltered and fixed, a kind of given potential (Kenneth Jones, 1978: 60).

Identity, as a relative concept, should be seen as a combination of individual experience with association of several factors such as historical roots, geographical environment, educational and political systems, economic consumption, religious understanding, practices and beliefs.

3c. Religious Identity

Religious identity is the outcome of a religious personality, where religious characteristics, ideas, principles manifest themselves in one's thoughts, behaviour, words and actions. Accordingly, religious identities have appended to them particular names and a relatively clear history and, normally, presuppose adherence to clearly established rules and regulations. A deep-rooted history, myths and legends, role models, rites and regulations are the traditional supports of this identity.

The use of most concepts in the sociology of religion depends on the frame of reference in which they are used. The utility of the concept diminishes when the search is directed to what lies 'behind' the term or to which sociological model would provide the best fit.

Without actually attempting to explain the identity of any particular religion, the discussion regarding the identity of religion is based on the specifications and continuity of the religion in the religious personalities and society. These in turn give form to the identity of religion arising from the fundamental message of the religion and the guidance that the respectable personalities and scholars of the religion provide. Issues such as training and education, arts, literature, a common culture of the community, political system, architecture and even experimental science also affect it. Therefore, it can be seen that religious identity can be explained as *that part of the religion that remains consistent in people and religious societies over several generations*. This definition of identity clearly separates a religious society from a non-religious one.

Needless to say, these simple and outward definitions need to be greatly refined to be meaningful in sociological terms. For it is clear that religious identity as a social phenomenon is a relative concept, which is not acquired on the basis of religious law or outward actions but has in fact altered over time and space and has to be assessed in more subjective terms, that is, as regards consciousness and self-perception. For example, an individual in traditional society was referred to as being religious when all the duties prescribed by the religion have been fully accepted and performed . However, after a period of modernization, the parameters that define one's religious identity have broadened out to such an extent that one is referred to as being religious solely on the basis of one's own self-definition, one's belief in God, attendance at church on Sundays, or participation in occasional religious ceremonies even though the individual person may not be practising all or most of the basic tenets of a religion and may be actively participating in things that are forbidden by the religion.

3d. Muslim Identity

The distinction between 'Muslim' and 'Islamic' identities is important. The discussion on Islamic identity focuses on the essence of Islam, with an emphasis on the primary sources of religion, such as Islamic jurisprudence, theology, philosophy, Islamic education or the interpretation of the *Qur'an*. In other words, the field of 'Islamic identity' is the field of theology, while specific modes and expressions of Muslim identity are discernible through the study of sociology, psychology, history and political science.

The effort to disclose 'Islamic identity' chiefly involves analysis based on the primary textual sources of the Islamic faith and the interpretation of religious concepts insofar as they influence the religious self-perception of Muslims. The formations of social structures are not considered as the main source for attempting to understand the essence of religious identity.

The main feature of discussion in the field of 'Muslim identity', on the other hand, is the cultural, social and political background of Muslims, and the transformations of religious thought at different stages of history. The distinguishing characteristics of Muslim societies among different nations, the understanding that Muslims have of their religion, motives of action and conduct, the manner in which Muslims participate in different public domains, and the expectations within Muslim society as regards the functions of religious organizations – all of these determine the field in which 'Muslim identity' will be sought.

One must bear in mind that there is a close relationship between the two identities, and certainly one cannot analyse the changing configurations of the identity of Muslims without some awareness of the relatively stable sources of Islamic identity. It is extremely difficult to arrive at a single definition of Muslim identity, given the complex interplay of factors that will determine this identity at any given time and in any given cultural context. However it is proposed in this study to gauge the identity of the respondents in the survey by paying attention to, first, his or her perceptions, values and feelings relating to membership of the Muslim minority in Britain in particular, a critical component of this identity being also the degree to which there is a sense of solidarity with Muslims worldwide. These factors will be assessed together with his or her perceptions, values and feelings relating to membership of British society, as a British citizen. The second principal means of ascertaining British Muslim identity will be derived from the perceptions of, and responses to, the global flow of culture as expressed by the respondents. Thirdly, the ways in which the processes of identity-construction and assertion of individual Muslims are the product of forces stemming from their historical background, shall be investigated and assessed.

3e. Belief

The belief dimension is defined as religious tenets that an individual internalizes. Although the content and range of beliefs might vary among different religions, or even within the same religion, every religion has a set of principles, which its adherents are expected to share. In the Islamic faith, these would include the following essential tenets: belief in God, in the Prophet Muhammad as messenger of God, in the revelation of the *Qur'an* as the word of God, and in divine judgement in the Hereafter.

3f. Religious Ritual

The ritual dimension of religious identity is defined in terms of the religious activities, practices and actions that all religions expect their adherents to perform. The major rituals in the Islamic tradition include daily prayer (*Salat*), Friday congregational Prayer (*Salat-al-jum'ah*), recitation of the *Qur'an*, fasting during the month of Ramadan, payment of Zakat, and the performance of the pilgrimage to Mecca. The range of involvement and participation of the respondents in each type of activity measures this dimension.

3g. Globalization

As Waters (1995) suggested, the word 'global' has been used for over 400 years; however the common usage of such words as 'globalization', 'globalize' and 'globalizing' did not begin until about 1960. In 1961 Webster became the first major dictionary to offer definitions of globalism and globalization. Globalization first developed as a phenomenon for analysis in the field of economics. It has become the locus for studying the interconnectedness of economies and the flow of capital and commodities across borders and between continents. More recently, the term has been taken up by sociologists and cultural theorists interested in the global flow of culture and its commodities. Robertson (1992b: 8) notices that it was not recognized as academically significant until the early or possibly the mid-1980s but thereafter its use has itself become 'globalized'.

What is meant by globalization? The review of literature for the study has determined that the term is widely used and yet diversely understood. Based on this review, at least four different interpretations of the term can be pinpointed. a. instrumental; b. cultural; c. political, and d. economical.

i. Instrumental

From this perspective, globalization is seen more as a technical revolution, which has created a new social structure. There is no specific micro-explanation here – the totality of globalization is viewed at the macro-level. Concepts such as the 'compression' of the world, overcoming time and space, growing interdependence between different global systems, are at the heart of the instrumental analysis of globalization.

Although Giddens's emphasis is more on the economic and political aspects of globalization, the main point of his interpretation refers to the significance of time and space in a global environment. For him, 'distant events, whether economic or not, affect us more directly and immediately than ever before' (Giddens, 1998: 31). Giddens (1991: 21) delineates that 'in a general way, the concept of globalization is best understood as expressing fundamental aspects of time–space distantiation. Globalization concerns the intersection of presence and absence, the interlacing of social events and social relations at distance with local contextualities.'

He also defined globalization as a general term for the increasing interdependence of world society, suggesting that 'The globalizing of social relations should be understood primarily as the reordering of time and distance in our lives. Activities and events happening well away from the social contexts, in which we carry on our day-to-day activities, increasingly influence our lives' (Giddens, 1989: 520). Globalization is also posited as a dialectic phenomenon, in which events at one pole of a distanciated relation often produce divergent or even contrary occurrences at another. Robertson (1995: 27) disagrees with Giddens when he speaks of the production of 'divergent or even contrary occurrences'. He believes Giddens remains a captive of old ways of thinking, which imply an action–reaction relationship that does not fully capture the complexities of the 'global-local' theme.

Others have defined globalization in terms of world compression, which means that events of the world are squeezed together and the world becomes a single place. Robertson (1994: 126) has continuously defined globalization as 'the process by which the world becomes *a single place*, where events in one part of the world have significant consequences for action in another part of the world.' Similarly, Waters (1995: 3) defined globalization as 'a social process in which the constraints of geography on social and cultural arrangements recede and in which people become increasingly aware that they are receding.'

Featherstone (1994: 147) explained that, for him, the globalization process means that the world is *a singular place*, which acts as a form capable of generating and sustaining various images of what the world is, or should be. From this perspective a global culture does not point to homogeneity, or a common culture, but rather it can be argued that the increased sense that we all share the same small planet and are daily involved in an increasing range of cultural contacts with others may increase the range of conflicting definitions of the world with which we are brought into contact.

ii. Cultural

Many sociologists and anthropologists have advocated a cultural understanding of globalization. Those who have suggested a cultural approach define globalization more in terms of 'cultural consumerism', 'Americanization', 'McDonaldization' or, as David Andrews (1998) has discussed, 'American Basketballization' or 'Westernization' and even 'Europeanization' of the world. Therefore, globalization in this respect means a particular culture influencing and spreading around the world. A particular or a few central regional cultures – American and European – penetrate other local and indigenous cultures through the mass communication system, distribution of economic goods, and the dissemination of information, science and knowledge.

Sociologists like Pieterse, Waters, Beyer and Featherstone have defined globalization to be in effect global Westernization mainly in terms of culture. Pieterse (1995: 46–49) says that, basically, globalization emanates from modernity. For him globalization begins in Europe and the West. Based on this theory, globalization means Westernization, which replicates all the problems associated with Eurocentrism. In this approach globalization begins with the history of the West. Waters (1995: 3) believes that the direct consequence of the expansion of European culture across the planet via settlement, colonization and cultural mimesis is globalization. Beyer points out that the globalization thesis posits, in the first instance, that social communication links are worldwide and increasingly dense. On perhaps the more obvious level, this means that people, cultures, societies and civilizations, previously more or less isolated from one another, are now in regular and almost unavoidable contact (Beyer, 1994: 2). For Beyer (1994: 7) the core hypothesis in this discussion is that, increasingly, there is a common social environment shared by all people on earth. This globality, he believes, conditions a great deal of what happens here, including how theories are formulated in relation to it.

Featherstone (1995) explains the McDonaldization of society as an economic and cultural process – in effect, economic production inducing a cultural message at the same time. He states that: 'It not only entails economic (in the form of time/money) "efficiency" gains through standardization of the product and delivery, but it represents a cultural message. The burger is not only consumed physically as a material substance, it is also consumed culturally as an icon of a particular way of life. Even though McDonald's do not go in for elaborate imagistic advertising, the burger is clearly American and it stands for the American way of life' (Featherstone, 1995: 8).

iii. Political

From the political point of view, globalization is seen by some as a process of centralization of power, leading to a more organized global system of order, which establishes more political control all over the world, and which would progressively decrease the power and authority of nation-states. In this approach, the major question is: how are the nation-states going to respond to the political globalization process[1]?

Waters (1995: 7) defined political globalization as a process which induces 'social arrangements for the concentration and application of power, especially insofar as it involves the organized exchange of coercion and surveillance (military, police, etc.), as well as such institutionalized transformations of these practices as authority and diplomacy, that can establish control over populations and territories.'

iv. Economic

In the economic arena, globalization in macro terms means a world capitalist system, which overwhelmingly dominates the world. Day-by-day nation-states become weaker and local economies slip out of the control of state policy. One of the consequences is increasing homogenization in the field of consumption. Interest and taste at the local level have changed. The processes of economic globalization have changed the consumption models of society, such transformations having been simultaneously influenced by the processes of political and cultural globalization.[2]

---

1. See views of McGrew & Lewis (1992), Giddens (1998), Lash & Urry (1994) and Mann (1996). They believe that globalization has significantly impacted the nation states.
2. Hamid Mowlana (1996) has looked at globalization from an economic angle. He defined globalization as forces of production, distribution/delivery, and consumption of goods and services. For Mowlana the consumption of goods and

(continued...)

Waters (1995: 66) and many other sociologists, in particular classical Marxists (Wallerstein, 1995, Cvetkovich & Kellner, 1998) see 'economic globalization as a vehicle for capitalism system'. They see capitalism as 'a global economic system characterized by a world market and the imposition of similar relations of production, commodities and culture on areas throughout the world, creating a new modern world system as the capitalist market penetrates the four corners of the earth.' Waters (1995) suggests that global economics are accelerated by empowering global trade organizations like GATT, which made 'network economics' first within the advanced industrial countries and then between all nation states.

In order to understand globalization as a concept, at this stage one has to analyse what globalization does not mean; this will serve as an introduction to our more extended discussion in Chapters 1 and 2.

According to Giddens (1989: 520) globalization is not a process of the growth of world unity either in the cultural arena, or in the economic and political arenas. It is not defined as a monocultural process in which people all over the world have the same moral system, religious practices, celebrations, habits, folklore and public opinion. Ferguson (1992) believes that such an approach, which focuses on the latter factors, is totally irrelevant; he argues that it is part of the mythology about globalization to consider cultural globalization as the forging of a single world with one particular culture within the structure of international society, conceived as a single monolithic entity.

In the arena of politics, globalization does not mean that the nation-states will inevitably be replaced by a world-state. The notion of 'world-government' run by a single power is again part of the mythology of globalization.

In economic terms a single economic global system is not an unavoidable consequence of globalization. Globalization is not meant to imply that any particular economic, fiscal, or commercial process necessarily encompasses the whole globe. But such processes may circulate through relatively narrow channels of the globe.

Finally, some use globalization to mean much the same thing as 'internationalization'. Although there is similarity in some aspects and functions between the two processes, it is more appropriate in analysing the current situation to define them in analytically distinct terms. Internationalization should be understood as the process of deepening mutual relations among nations, thus upholding in fact the distinct nations within their boundaries, while globalization is of a fundamentally different order, in that it often

---

(...continued)
       services may indicate a pattern of homogeneity, for example, the universal consumption of Western products, edibles such as Coca-Cola, Pepsi and pizza, and non-edibles such as television programmes.

violates or transcends formal boundaries between nations, and calls into question the very validity of the concept of a national boundary (Nobutaka, 1997: 83).

However, Waters (1995: 3), in response to the question about what the fully globalized world is, stated that: 'In a globalized world there will be a single society and culture occupying the planet. This society and culture will probably not be harmoniously integrated although it might conceivably be. Rather, it will probably tend towards high levels of differentiation, multicentricity and chaos.'

Finally, let us note that what is common between and supported by all these definitions, is that communication technology – from transportation, telecommunication, mass media, global TV and radio, to cinema, internet and newspaper and news agencies, in addition to the development of international affairs – have linked the cultural relations of all societies, and in effect created what McLuhan called the 'Global Village' (Gary, 1999). If, in the past, neighbourhood meant being in the same avenue or even small town, today the notion of 'neighbourhood' has a much wider social scope. Instantaneous communication has become available to everybody, from one side of the world to the other. This has enabled and vastly expanded social, economical, as well as cultural, contact between institutions and individuals at the local, regional and global level. It is the concomitants and ramifications of this process of expansion that one intends to look at here.

Avoiding any kind of dogmatic, predetermined conception of where globalization is heading, the starting point is the essentially cultural dimension of the process of globalization. The technological, economic and political aspects of the material, formal processes of globalization are viewed from this perspective as secondary and derivative. That is, they derive their significance from the impact they make on the cultural sphere, and from the role they play within the domain of the dissemination, propagation and ideologization of cultures, in particular, local ones extending in a global direction, as well as those with already established global outreach. Moreover, it is not simply a question of a major, global culture – that of the West – dominating and extinguishing, one by one, all other local cultures. What is observed is rather more complex and nuanced. One sees a process of mutual interpenetration, whereby local, particular cultures (whether defined ideologically, religiously, ethnically, or in civic, communitarian, sectarian, or any other terms) interact with, are affected by and, in turn, impact upon the major producers of 'global' culture in the West.

The lines of influence are thus two-way; they are complex and their consequences cannot be predicted in any precise fashion. Rather, one needs to examine particular contexts, asking precise questions, in relation to specific themes that can be empirically investigated. Conceptual analysis will then be based upon concrete findings rather than on theoretical generalizations, despite the fact that the analyst cannot escape entirely from the effects of primary assumptions, those which enter into the very definition of the situation being examined, the choice of methodology and the nature of the questions asked. But an effort is at least made in the direction of eliminating as far as possible any theoretical prejudices that will determine in advance the nature of the research. This having been said, let us briefly note the following three aspects of the cultural dimension of globalization which, following observation and reflection, appear to be of a fundamental nature, form the conceptual basis of the framing of this research:

Diversity of choice. Both within the local and from the local to the global level, the choices available to individuals, groups, and communities have been expanded, and are continuing to expand, exponentially. These choices are, at the most obvious level, within the sphere of consumption: goods and services, which were barely conceivable a generation ago, are now both available and instantly accessible. At a more subtle level, the choices extend into lifestyles, ideologies and cultural attitudes. Not only do the goods available carry loaded cultural messages, but, more directly, cultural forms, icons, ideas, discourses and propaganda are also being disseminated on a global scale and with an intensity and variety that have immeasurably diversified cultural choice for individuals and groups around the world.

This trend has also *intertwined cultures* of different local and region all over the world, such that not only have already cosmopolitan cities become more overtly multicultural, but also all over the world, cities, towns and villages have been drawn into this ever-expanding web of interconnected cultural relations (Burayidi, 1997; Kisbui, 1997 and Smith, 1997). This global multiculturalism does not only solely mean that different nationalities live together in a society that promotes cultural pluralism and tolerates ethnic diversity. This newer form of multiculturalism entails also the less tangible, less formal or empirical, processes by which different cultures interpenetrate on the plane of ideas, attitudes and ideologies; this interpenetration is made possible by the new global technologies. It is no longer necessary to live in a physical context composed of diverse cultures in order to participate in multiculturalism: in the global era; the instruments of communication bring multiculturalism into one's own home, wherever one may be living. Cyberspace is the territory where multiculturalism takes root; virtual reality not only makes accessible a multitude of cultures, an infinitely expandable set of cultures: it even creates its own cultures and subcultures – here, in the presence of a multiculturalism that knows no boundaries.

The unprecedented interaction between local and global cultures has produced a set of conditions in which the precise outcome cannot be defined in exclusively local or exclusively global terms. The mutual influence between the two sources of cultural production, local and global, results in a *reproduction* both of culture and identity fashioned in accordance with that culture; this new type of culture has been given the appropriate name, 'glocal', following on from those intertwined processes that Robertson terms 'glocalization'. Neither local nor global forces, considered separately, can reveal the dynamics operating in the production of culture. The culture that shall be focused on in this study is that culture out of which British Muslim identity arises; and it is this notion of 'glocal' culture that forms one of the key conceptual orientations guiding this research.

A few of the central conceptual aspects of globalization have been touched upon in this introduction. The following two chapters will elaborate upon these concepts, before discussion turns in Chapter 3 to an historical analysis of Muslim identity; and this in turn will serve as the background for the exploration, in Part II, of the empirical findings of this research.

ONE

Globalization: Characteristics, Realms and Cultural Theories

There is intense and wide-ranging debate about theories of globalization. These theories have been debated and elaborated in the social sciences, as well as other areas of human knowledge. Today a vast amount of research is focusing on this subject: academic conferences and even political and social campaigns are, to one degree or another, becoming embroiled in globalization, a term that seems to be widely used yet differently understood (Held *et al.*, 1999 and Tomlinson, 1999). Therefore it is awkward and problematic to review theories of globalization, unless we confine this multifaceted phenomenon within a particular field of study. In this research, the main subject of study will be cultural globalization.

First, a distinctive picture of what has been termed 'instantaneous globalization' as applied to the contemporary context needs to be outlined, contrasted with the classical concept of globalization, which formed part of the 'utopian concept' of the ancient Greek philosophers. Secondly, three major domains of globalization will be elaborated – economics, politics and culture – before we examine closer the relevant theories of cultural globalization. Thirdly, there will be an evaluation of the characteristics of what we call 'globalization' today. In brief, one of the main contentions here is that globalization cannot be segregated from Americanization and Westernization, if what is meant by cultural globalization is one dominant cultural trend exerting its influence over other less powerful cultures. In other words, the focus here is on the homogenization of culture. In the final section of this chapter the consequences of cultural globalization will be addressed in the area of religious identity in general, and Muslim identity in particular, evaluating the way in which the core elements of this identity have been affected by, and have responded to, the phenomenon of cultural globalization.

1.1. *Characteristics of Globalization Processing*

It is difficult to characterize globalization precisely, as it is a problematic and debatable concept, but the more we explore different aspects of globalization the more capable we are of examining the consequences of this phenomenon. Therefore, in this section an attempt has been made to clarify these aspects.

1.1.1. *Globalization: Space and Time*

Why is globalization considered to be a new phenomenon? There have always been global networks of power and imperialist empires, often accompanied by fierce local resistance from the colonized entities. Globalization is new in terms of the speed at which it occurs and the involvement of communication technology, which appears to shrink geographical distance and time (Cvetkovic & Kellner, 1997). Communication occurs beyond time and space. The message arrives at the destination a thousand times more quickly than if the sender of the message delivered it personally.

Instantaneous communication through a variety of media has changed our experiences of time and space. They have become distantiated – we experience distant events unfolding instantaneously on the screen in our homes – or 'compressed'; spatial and temporal differences are radically undermined (Gillespie, 1995: 3). Gillespie suggested that this speeding up, or growing intensity, of time–space compression, has created significant effects on social, economic and cultural processes. Society has been subjected to a constantly accelerating pace of change.

According to Falk (1999: 139), the fundamental aspect of globalization is the pervasive compression of time and space. This affects the way we think, feel and act, introducing speed and proximity as defining and inherent characteristics of our daily human experience. For instance, the visual presentation of world news, including even wars, in real time is abolishing our sense of distance, compacting space while intermingling virtuality with reality.

Morley & Robins (1995: 75) suggest that new information and communication technologies have played a powerful role in the emergence of new spatial structures, relations and orientations. Corporate communications networks have also produced a global space of electronic information flows. The new media conglomerates have created a global image space. What is particularly significant is the transformed relationship between boundary and space that this entails. Things are no longer defined and distinguished in the ways that they once were by their boundaries, borders or frontiers.

The cultural and cognitive consequences of this new relationship between time and space in the age of instantaneous communication are of critical concern for the present research. The concept of 'time' and 'space', being 'far' or 'near', 'in here' or 'out there', 'alien' and 'compatriot'; the meaning of 'citizenship' and 'diaspora', and finally the concept of 'society' and 'community' have been partially changed. This has changed our social understanding of our sense of belonging and therefore our identity. For instance, the concept of citizenship does not necessarily mean the sense of belonging to the country of which one is a citizen. People may live and be citizens in a particular country and yet not have any patriotic feeling towards it. That is why the concept of diaspora, which originated with the Jewish displacement, has extended today to any type of homelessness 'at home'. The concept of nostalgia 'at home' reflects the same meaning.

1.1.2. Instantaneous Communication

In the age of globalization, for the first time ever, instantaneous communication has become possible from one side of the world to the other. Growth of other types of electronic communication, many integrated with satellite transmission, has also accelerated over the past few years. No dedicated trans-Atlantic or trans-Pacific cables existed at all until the late 1950s. The first to be built held fewer than 100 voice paths. Those of today carry more than a million. Today many countries have stopped using Morse Code[1], which was invented 150 years ago, and have replaced it with satellite technology. Instantaneous electronic communication is not just a way in which news or information is conveyed more quickly. Its existence has altered the very texture of our lives, rich and poor alike. When the image of Nelson Mandela may be more familiar to us than the face of our next door neighbour, something has changed in the nature of our everyday experience (Giddens, 1999). Gillespie (1995: 3) suggested that instantaneous communication through a variety of media has fostered intense relations between the 'absent other' (Giddens, 1990: 18–21).

Instantaneous communication technology has provided for an extensive body of shared knowledge and information, held by many people simultaneously. This is what gives a global orientation to all the economic, cultural and political productions in the world system. This gradually generates a

---

1. Morse code or telegraph was invented in 1843 by Samuel F. B. Morse. This was a means of communication by which the letters of the alphabet were converted into electrical equivalents that could be either recorded on paper tape or transcribed by trained operators. Since the code was transmitted over wires at almost the speed of light, it soon became the quickest means of point-to-point communication (Abramson, 1998).

pellucid picture of global culture and produces an increasingly homogenous global consciousness. This global instantaneous reflection of production is one of the main elements of globalization processing, which has offered the import of the current pattern of globalization, differentiating it radically from the previous one, in that a globalized awareness – in subjective terms – has now emerged out of a process in which material or objective production and distribution is becoming ever more globalized.

1.1.3. Speed of Change

Rapid change is a feature of a globalizing society, which we have never experienced in the past. This speed is a consequence of today's communication technology. The power of this technology makes very rapid communication possible over almost unlimited space. Moreover, these media exist nearly everywhere on earth, along with the will and ability to use them. It raises the probability of perceived alienation of anomie at the personal and group level when too much change occurs over too short a period of time. On a deeper and more important level, however, speed is less at issue than the direction of change and who controls the change. In broad terms, the problem is one of power, not just meaning (Beyer, 1994).

The accelerated rate of change that society is undergoing is essentially due to environmental factors. Television, radio, the huge, well-organized and professional film-making industries, advertising and the appearance of various models of thinking are coming into contact with a variety of cultures through diverse media and publications. These all increase the speed of change. What has been created is a huge 'networking society' (Castells, 2000). An inherent part of this process is its ability to 'change' fundamentally the concepts and realities of entertainment, fashion and beauty. The speed of change within its cultural and artistic domains leaves 'little time for thinking and reflection'. The rapid pace of change inherent in the process of globalization leaves little time for individuals to assimilate changes within any stable framework of culture or selfhood, or for identity to assert itself in a continuous predictable fashion. In a constantly changing environment, it is very difficult to shape one's identity is a self-conscious way; identity is increasingly being defined by the complex, rapidly changing configurations of environmental forces.

1.1.4. Globalization: Universalistic and Particularistic Processing

Globalization has two circles of influences, which Roberston (1992a: 97) called 'universalization of particularism and the particularization of universalism'. Universalistically it covers all aspects of life – one may call this the umbrella function of globalization. The normative function of globalization is the particularistic effects it has across the globe. This is the concept that Mann (1996: 24) explained as 'global networks coverage'. He gave an example of the feminist movement, which spread through almost all countries, but usually only among rather particular, small groups. Another example is the Muslim fundamentalist movement, which has some presence in all continents but only has quite a narrow base across Europe or the United States, while having a much broader influence throughout the Muslim world. Capitalism may also be considered as a universal global network, which diffuses through economic and social life just about everywhere.

1.1.5. Expansion of Cultural and Religious Diversity – Multiculturalism

One consequence of changes caused by globalization is that more and more people are now involved with more than one culture, thus increasing the practical problems of intercultural communication (*Featherstone*, 1990: 8). Cultural diversity is a reflection of people's connection to their local environment, to the living world. Centuries of Western conquest, colonialism and development have already eroded much of the world's cultural diversity. However, it has also created a new type of American and European diversity – economic globalization is rapidly accelerating the process. Along with multilane highways and concrete cities, globalization is bringing to every corner of the planet a cultural landscape dominated by fast-food restaurants, Hollywood films, cellular phones, designer jeans, Barbi dolls and Marlboro cigarettes.

Madsen (1997: 494) argued that: 'With the collapse of state socialism, human discourse throughout the world is dominated by a "monoculture" – a common linguistic framework for defining human aspirations for freedom, rationality, and justice.' But freedom and the technology of globalization have also brought in their wake a need for cultural and ethnic self-identification, as people become uncomfortable with the borderless global community and feel a loss of control. From this perspective polyethnicity appears to be the wave of the future (Burayidi, 1997).

Although human societies have always been faced with the issue of alien cultures and foreign intervention, globalization produces a completely new level of multiculturalism and cultural diversity. Cultural diversity offers a choice of fashions in all areas. Social values, religious affiliation, religious belief and practice are not exempt from this. Therefore it becomes increasingly difficult to maintain religious traditions as sources of unchanging truth. Instead, the dynamics of consumer preference is introduced into the religious sphere. Religion itself becomes, to some extent, pluralistic and subject to 'choice preference'.

1.1.6. Non-Cognitive Change

Turner (1994) posed the question: What is the main reason for religious change in response to the impact of globalization? Are the changes cognitive and/or ideological? He believes that specific types of cognitive change, i.e. those within the structure and style of globalization, which tend to commodify everyday life, do not undermine religion. He suggests that the main threat to the Islamic character of knowledge is not cognitive. The main threat to religious faith, he argues, is in fact the commodification of everyday life. People do not adopt or reject belief systems simply on the rationalistic grounds that they are not intellectually coherent. Beliefs are adopted or rejected because they are relevant or not relevant to everyday needs and concerns. For Turner, what makes religious faith or religious commitment problematic in a globalized postmodern society is that everyday life has become part of a global system of exchange of commodities, not easily influenced by political, intellectual or religious leaders (Turner, 1994: 9–11).

In such terms the 'corruption of the pristine faith is going to be brought about by Tina Turner (head of CNN) and Coca-Cola and not by rational arguments and the rational inspection of presuppositions that are the basis of Western secularism' (Turner, 1994: 10). For Turner, 'This is what is wrong fundamentally with Ernest Gellner's book *Postmodernism, Reason and Religion* (1992) and Akbar Ahmed's book *'Postmodernity and Islam'* (1992). They are both talking about intellectual cognitive problems of religious leaders and intellectuals, not the problems of everyday life. What they both fail to emphasize is that the Ford motor car did more damage to Christianity than any type of argumentation (Turner, 1994: 10). In other words, people do not stop believing in God merely as a consequence of rational criticism; rather they stop believing in God when religious belief is eroded by transformations of everyday life, which makes belief either irrelevant or impossible.

According to Turner, then, globalization has driven the effect of religion out of the social domain into a personal environment, consequently changing human societies' way of thinking. Of course, what has been said should not be taken to mean a general decline in religion tendencies. It means that there is a reduction within the sphere of religious influence. For example, a brief look at society's collective conscience would show that there is no decline in the belief in God within Western societies, especially that of North American societies; on the contrary, there is a marked increase in religious belief. There is, however, a marked decline in the belief that religion is an ideology with its own way of thinking, social structure and system of education. The change within religious motivation does not stem from changes within deep-rooted ideological perceptions, like dialectical materialism replacing metaphysics. Rather, there has been a profound shift in people's disposition towards the day-to-day realities of mankind. The change is primarily due to people being preoccupied or dazzled by colourful pictures of daily living and the range of attractions they generate.

1.1.7. Homelessness and Rootlessness: Alienation and Nostalgia

The phenomenon of nostalgia and self-alienation is an important aspect of modernization as well as globalization milieu. For Baudrillard (1983) and Robertson (1992a), alienation and nostalgia are major problems that religious identity has to face in the present time. These phenomena turn into a kind of disease and widespread sickness that lead to breakdown and decay within the notion of religious identity.

According to Baudrillard (1983: 12), 'When the real is no longer what it used to be, nostalgia assumes its full meaning.' Baudrillard has claimed that postmodern culture distinguishes neither between reality and unreality, nor between true or false representation. For Robertson (1992a: 159), in the late 20th-century nostalgia is intimately bound up with the globalization body, which is embodied in consumerism. He describes the almost globally institutionalized nostalgia that is a product of contemporary processes (Robertson, 1990: 55).

Regarding the relationship between globalization and locality, Robertson (1995: 33) stated that: 'Globalizing trends are regarded as in tension with "local" assertions of identity and culture.' Thus ideas such as the global versus the local, the global versus the 'tribal', the international versus the national, and the universal versus the particular, are widely promoted.

Robertson suggested a new concept: the 'ideology of home', partly in response to the constant repetition and global diffusion of the claim that we now live in a condition of homelessness or rootlessness; as if in prior periods of history the vast majority of people lived in 'secure' and homogenized locales. Robertson has pointed out two important things: First, the formation of globalization has involved a considerable emphasis, at least until now, on the cultural homogenization of nationally constituted societies; but, on the other hand, prior to that emphasis, which began to develop at the end of the 18th century, what McNeill (1985) calls polyethnicity was normal. Secondly, from the phenomenological point of view, generalized homelessness of modern man and woman has developed as if 'the same people are behaving and interpreting at the same time in the same broad social process' (Meyer, 1992: 11); whereas there is in fact much to suggest that it is increasingly global expectations concerning the relationship between individual and society that have produced both 'routinized' and 'existential' selves. On top of that, the very ability to identify 'home' directly or indirectly is contingent upon the (contested) construction organization of interlaced categories of space and time (cited by Robertson, 1995: 35).

According to Baudrillard (1993), this depthless and shallow culture is reflected in the floating signs and images in which 'TV is the world', and all that can be done is to watch the endless flow of images with an aestheticized fascination and without possible recourse to moral judgements. Some of the postmodernists have discussed that evidence of these shallow cultures is to be found within everyday life and modes of signification – in the sign-play of youth cultures, the styles and fashions of the *flaneurs* who move through the new postmodern urban spaces, and in the particular fusions of art and rock, which produced contemporary popular music (Chambers, 1987; Frith and Horn, 1987; Harvey, 1989).

1.2. The Realm of Globalization

Globalization is clearly not only a political and economical affair. It concerns every aspect of life, as Robertson underlines it, at the level of 'national societies', individuals or selves, relationships between national societies or the world system of societies and humankind (Robertson, 1992a: 25).

Several theories have addressed this process from different angles. Some of them are politically orientated, others focus on economics or culture; and there are also many lively debates taking place in the arenas of industry, information technology, mathematics, ecology (Dyer, 1993), and so on. Therefore, globalization is a polyvalent concept. This is a natural reflection, on the theoretical plane, of the complex nature of globalization as an empirical phenomenon. Globalization is the end-product of a vast range of elements and tendencies expressing in different ways the intertwined technical, social, political and cultural structures of today's global reality, a product which is itself producing dynamic change almost everywhere and heavily influencing the world order.

The globalization debate began to make a serious impression as a sociological concept from the mid-1980s. Waters (1995) and Robertson (1992) have commented that this had a profound effect on the development of social–cultural debate. Since the 1980s the concept of globalization as a social, economic, political and cultural phenomenon has come to be extensively debated in sociology, anthropology, economics, politics and international relations.

The globalization of economics, politics and culture is currently taking place and this unforeseen consequence of technological development has resulted in a rethink amongst sociologists who, despite their differing views, premises and outlooks, did not envisage such a scenario. Sociologists have suggested different sources for this phenomenon. Some believe economic and others believe political factors to be the main causes.

Cultural sociologists on the other hand claim that all contributory factors, be they economic or political, take shape in the cultural domain (Waters, 1995). They claim that a political power cannot become a world or global power if there is no cultural acceptance of such power within the prevailing environment. Even an economic product, before it can be consumed, has to pass through the filter of cultural acceptance and demand. Everything must pass through the cultural context. Now that democratization of social life has been taking place in earnest, the issue of cultural roots for different matters has taken on a more serious and profound meaning.

In this equation, one can observe a marked shift from power and its centrality (military or otherwise) towards the dominance of social perception and public opinion. This indicates that the role of culture has increased within the modern society. Globalization, in other words, intensifies the importance of culture – thus self-perception and identity – in the newly emerging interdependent postmodern society (Shiller, 1976).

As Giddens (1999) says, the resources of globalization are not just cultural, political, or economic. Globalization is the fusing of all of these factors. Therefore we have looked at it here as a complex issue, which includes politics, economics and particularly culture. It is the cultural aspect that is more relevant to the theme of this research, as it feeds into the whole domain of individual and collective identity.

1.3. Cultural Globalization

Without denying the important and significant position of economics and politics within the structure of the world system, it should be stressed that culture penetrates the whole body of society. Politics and economics can be seen as subsumed within culture. They cannot exist within society uninfluenced by culture. Baudrillard (1993) argued that culture has gained a more significant role within social life and that today everything is cultural. In effect, cultures are now beyond the social norms and have been released from the traditional controls exerted by economics, social class, gender, ethnicity and geography.

That is why questions of identity – whether collective or individual – and cultural expression of the temporally compressed global social context receive the most attention from those who discuss cultural globalization.

Waters (1995: 9–10) sees cultural globalization as an umbrella for other areas of globalization – politics and economics. The theorem that guides his argument in the book *Globalization* is that 'Material exchanges localize; political exchanges internationalize; and symbolic exchanges globalize.' It follows that the globalization of human society is contingent on the extent to which cultural arrangements are effective relative to economic and political arrangements. One can expect the economy and the polity to be globalized to the extent that they are culturalized, i.e. to the extent that the exchanges that take place within them are accomplished symbolically. He concludes that we would expect that the degree of globalization to be greater in the cultural arena than either of the other two, i.e. symbolic meaning is globalized, goods and services are not accepted only on their own level; they are assimilated as symbols of a way of life, a cultural orientation.

Friedman (1994: 80) argues that: 'The notion of cultural globalization is itself a product of the global system.' Dyer (1993: 493) says global culture is 'the organization of diversity rather than the replication of uniformity'. Nak-chung (1998) has examined 'literature' as an important element of culture at the national and global level. Mignolo (1998) has looked at globalization in terms of the process of Western civilization and the centrality of some of the European languages and, in particular, the English language, which have taken centre-stage at the global level. Jameson (1998: 58) sees globalization more as a means for exchange of culture. He also argues that 'national culture' is being weakened by cultures that are imported through the channels of cultural globalization. Hetata (1998) also examined the role of cultural features such as films, radio, advertisements, newspapers and even novels, music, and poetry in the processing of globalization. He points out that television has been the subject of numerous studies in France: 'Such studies have shown that before the age of twelve a child will have been exposed to an average of 100,000 TV advertisements. Through these TV advertisements, the young boy or girl will have assimilated a whole set of values and behavioural patterns' (Hetata, 1998: 278).

Here the key question is: 'What does cultural globalization mean?' To help us answer this question, we can briefly assess some theories on cultural globalization. However, one point that should be stressed immediately is that cultural forces now operate outside and beyond the confines of the nation-state as a discrete entity. This means that central governments no longer have the same degree of control over cultural production and that the domain of culture now transcends the frontiers that divide the nation-states from each other (see Cvetkouic & Kellner, 1997: 7).

1.4. Principal Theories on the Globalization of Culture

One of the main sociologists contributing to the debates on modernization and globalization is Giddens. He has discussed globalization in several books (Giddens, 1989, 1991, 1994, 1998, 1999). In his latest book *Runaway World: How Globalization is Reshaping Our Lives,* Giddens (1999: 7) says, 'Different thinkers have taken almost completely opposite views about globalization.' Giddens split them into two groups – 'sceptics' and 'radicals'. According to him, sceptics are those who say, 'All the talk about globalization is only talk. Whatever its benefits, its trials and tribulations, the global economy isn't especially different from that which existed at previous periods' (Giddens, 1999: 8). Giddens identifies sceptics with the political left especially the old left. Leftists still insist on the power of governments, which can intervene in economic life and enable the welfare state to remain intact. According to the sceptic, globalization is only a smoke-screen, a concept rooted in the ideology of free-marketers who wish to dismantle welfare systems and cut back state expenditure.

In contrast to the sceptics, the radicals believe 'that not only is globalization very real, but that its consequences can be felt everywhere' (Giddens, 1999: 8). In economic terms, they argue that the global marketplace is much more developed than even two or three decades ago, and is indifferent to national borders. For them 'Nations have lost most of the sovereignty they once had, and politicians have lost most of their capability to influence events.'

In terms of economic global trends, Giddens thinks that the 'radicals' are right. From an economic perspective, the level of world trade has become higher than it ever was before and includes a much wider range of goods and services. He states that: 'The biggest difference is in the level of finance and capital flows ... In the new global electronic economy, fund managers, banks, corporations, as well as millions of individual investors, can transfer vast amounts of capital from one side of the world to another at the click of a mouse' (Giddens, 1999: 9).

However, Giddens believes that both the sceptics and the radicals do not understand what globalization is or what its implications are for today's society. He poses that: 'Both groups see the phenomenon almost solely in economic terms. This is a mistake. Globalization is political, technological and cultural, as well as economic' (Giddens, 1999: 10).

Although Giddens has rightly discussed globalization as a complex phenomenon with many parts, he does not consider the cultural aspect of globalization to any great degree. He focuses more on the economic aspects of globalization without any recognition of its more subtle cultural concomitants. Culture is important not just from a cultural viewpoint. It clearly conveys deep levels of meaning, and penetrates all aspects of everyday life. Therefore, economics, politics and even science is related closely to the cultural sphere and, as Baudrillard (1993) argues, today everything is cultural. Giddens' classification is also questionable. What he calls 'radical' and 'sceptic' are two extremes. This type of dichotomy does not take into consideration theories propounded by reproductionists, post-structralists, relativists and trans-formationalists.

According to our study, six different groups of theories have addressed globalization insofar as its impact upon culture is concerned. These are now discussed.

1.4.1. *The Hyperglobalizers*

One group of sociologists insists that the phenomenon of *a global culture* is an inevitable consequence of the process of globalization; this viewpoint is held by the *hyperglobalizers* (Held and et al., 1999). For hyperglobalizers, such as Ohmae (1995) and Wriston (1992), contemporary globalization has defined a new era in which peoples everywhere are increasingly subject to the disciplines of the global marketplace. They predicted the 'homogenization of the world under the auspices of American popular culture or Western consumerism in general' (Held and et al., 1999: 327).

Hyperglobalizers point out that economic globalization has brought about a 'denationalization' of economies through the establishment of transnational networks of production, trade and finance. For them, the rise of the global economy, the emergence of institutions of global governance, and the global diffusion and hybridization of cultures are evidence of a radically new world order, an order that prefigures the demise of the nation-state (Ohmae, 1995 and Albrow, 1996). Hyperglobalizers believe that American and Western culture will remain the main role model and reference culture for people all over the world.

Those who subscribe to the totalist viewpoint believe that world society is increasingly oriented toward a 'monoculture' society. This entails two images of culture at the same time (Featherstone, 1995: 6):
1. The extension outwards of a particular culture to its limit, in this case, the globe. This means that heterogeneous cultures become incorporated and integrated into a dominant culture that eventually covers the whole world. This image suggests a process of conquest and unification of the global space – the world becomes a singular domesticated space, a place where everyone becomes assimilated into a common culture.

2. The second feature suggests, on the other hand, the compression and intermixing of different cultures, which means that things formerly kept apart are now brought into contact and are in contrast with each other. A global composite culture, one made up of heterogeneous cultural forces, is thus envisaged.

As Featherstone (1990) pointed out, there are various problems with this concept: if what is meant by a 'global culture' is something similar to the culture of the nation-state, a culture that expresses the tendencies within the whole, just as tendencies within a nation-state have been given expression in its particular culture, then one cannot accept such a concept. This is because it would be impossible to identify an integrated global culture without the formation of a world-state, and the formation of such a state is a highly unlikely prospect. He also asserts that if we move away from the idea of the integration of particular cultures within a totalist structure, we observe two fundamentally opposed tendencies: not just processes of cultural integration, but also disintegration processes, are at work, and these processes operate both on an intrastate level and in ways which transcend the state-society unit and can therefore operate on a transnational or trans-societal level.

In contrast to the 'sceptics', the 'hyperglobalizers' have suggested that a particular global culture, world economic and global power will dominate the whole world. 'Hyperglobalizers' predict that American popular culture will be the 'central culture' and the rest of the world 'periphery' will be culturalized and socialized by 'the American way of life'. Other national, cultural and, in particular, religious identities, which have been considered as peripheral, will assimilate themselves according to American culture. One must admit that the increasing trend of cultural, religious and economic diversity, which has been rapidly developed all over the world, is a sufficient reason to reject 'the single cultural and religious identity' or 'monoculturalism.' We are observing the fragmentation of religious identities into diverse and sometimes contradictory identities. Resistance identity has emerged in the age of globalization as a phenomenal reality, which is the outcome of the Americanization process and could be considered as anti-Americanization.

One can argue that, even if we imagine domination of a 'world-state' and 'world-culture', the response of the consumers is unlikely to be the same. According to forces such as historical background, native culture, ethnicity, environment etc., they reproduce a new culture, which could be called 'glocal culture'. It is neither local nor global.

1.4.2. The Sceptics – World System Theory

In contrast to the totalists, those who are referred to as 'sceptics', such as Hirst and Thompson (1996) and McMichael (1996), believe that globalization is just a myth. In arguing that globalization is a myth, Held argues that: 'Hyperglobalizers are matched by sceptics who point to the thinness and ersatz quality of global cultures by comparison with national cultures and to the persistent, indeed increasing, importance of cultural differences and conflicts along the geopolitical faultlines of the world's major civilizations' (Held *et al.*, 1999: 327).

World-system theorists argue that the relative prosperity of the few is dependent on the destitution of the many – world politics occurs within a world-system dominated by the logic of global capitalism (Hobden & Wyn Jones, 1997). The world-system theory is mainly founded on the views of Marx and his followers. One of the eminent scholars in this area is Immanuel Wallerstein. He stresses that: 'The appropriate unit of analysis for the study of social or societal behaviour is a world-system' (Wallerstein,1991a: 267). For Wallerstein a system has two defining characteristics. First, all the elements within a system are interlinked. Second, they exist in a dynamic relationship with each other and, if one is to understand the attributes, the functions or the behaviour of one element, one must understand its position within the whole. Accordingly, Wallerstein argues that attempts to distinguish and differentiate between, for example, economic phenomena and political and sociocultural phenomena are misleading. Nothing in the system can be understood in isolation: a holistic approach is the only valid one. For him, the only kind of social system is a world-system, which King (1991: 10) defines as a unit with a single division of labour and multiple cultural systems.

Perhaps it would appear that the 'worldist' theorizers echo the views of the 'sceptics'. The worldists, chief among them being Wallerstein, refuse to accept the idea of a global culture, i.e. a single culture that would dominate the world. They believe that every single phenomenon should be analysed within the framework of a 'world-system', hence the term *worldism*. But this does not mean that the world is integrated within a single domain of culture.

The concept of global culture is discussed by Wallerstein (1991b) in terms of a 'gigantic paradox', its monumental proportions stemming from the fact that there are two paradoxes to consider simultaneously – a logical paradox, and an historical paradox. As regards the latter, for thousands of years now, some people at least have put forward ideas that they have asserted to be universal values or truths. Furthermore, for some 200 years now, and even more intensively for the last 50 years, many national governments as well as world institutions have asserted the validity and even the enforceability of such values or truths. One example of this can be found in the discussion about human rights concerning which the United Nations proclaimed, in 1948, in a Universal Declaration. Wallerstein mentioned two controversial ways of explaining global culture: 'One is the thesis of the linear tendency towards one world. Originally, it is argued, the globe contained a very large number of distinct and distinctive groups. Over time, little by little, the scope of activity has expanded, the groups have merged, and bit by bit, with the aid of science and technology, we are arriving at one world – one political world, one economic world, one cultural world. We are not yet there, but the future looms clearly before us' (Wallerstein, 1991b: 93).

The second thesis suggests a rather different course but the outcome predicted is more or less the same. There it is suggested that the historical and cultural differences of all groups have always been superficial. Wallerstein pointed out that: 'There have no doubt been several different such structures, but they make up a patterned sequence ... since, in this mode of theorizing, all societies go through parallel stages, we end up with the same result as in the theory of a secular tendency towards one world. We end up with a single human society and therefore necessarily with a world culture' (Wallerstein, 1991b: 91).

Wallerstein rejects both theories – the secular tendency towards one world culture and the stage theory of human development. For him, 'Culture is the set of values or practices of some part smaller than some whole' (Wallerstein, 1991b: 91).

As regards the relationship between 'part' and 'whole', he accepts that the process of cultural globalization – homogenization of the world culture, which is the result of the cultural diffusion of a particular culture – is proceeding, the different parts becoming more and more similar. 'Over time, the particular nation-states have come to resemble each other more and more in their cultural forms. Which state today does not have certain standard political forms: a legislature, a constitution, a bureaucracy, trade unions, a national currency, and a school system?' (Wallerstein, 1991b: 93). Finally, he addresses a very serious question, the answer to which is problematic: 'Culture is a collective expression that is combative, that requires an "other". In this putative libertarian-egalitarian world, does "culture" exist?' (Wallerstein, 1991b: 104).

Robertson (1985) has challenged Wallerstein for treating culture, and especially religion, as being epiphenomenal to the onward march of economic forces. He criticizes world-system theory for ignoring the quasireligious ideologies accompanying economic doctrines such as economic socialism, utopian socialism and traditionalistic communalism. Although he praises Wallerstein for methodologically refocusing social scientific analysis on a global level, he rejects the primary, indeed absolute, significance accorded to capitalist development .

1.4.3. The Relativist Theory

The third group is represented by Robertson (1990, 1991, 1992b, 1995) and a group of scholars in one way or another associated with the journal, *Theory, Culture & Society*, such as Featherstone (1990) Turner (1994) and Beyer (1990, 1994, 1998). These writers accept the notion of a *global culture*, but not in an exclusive or exhaustive fashion. They claim that no phenomenon can become totally and wholly global without even slight intrinsic change. Variety and expanding pluralism are unique characteristics of this theory. Proponents of this theory reject the proposition of a single and unified culture for the world. Reproductionalists (to be addressed below, 1.4.4) also reject the view, proposed by the hyperglobalizers, that the capitalist system with its relevant culture can be the only outcome of the trend towards globalization. They do not accept the sceptics' view that the world is nothing but a superficial and short-lived phenomenon. The esteem given to secular sciences as well as respect for rationalism and rationality, and the shared desire for Western culture, particularly amongst the vast majority of young people, point to a trend leading towards singularity and globalization.

For them, global culture is a reality defined within certain social strata and in relation to cultural phenomena within society, hence the term *relativism*. They believe that the cultural boundaries, which separate one nation from another, are no longer as real as they once were. They are merely convenient and conventional demarcations of ethnic, linguistic and cultural entities, which are no longer so distinct and separate as they were in the past.

However, there is no *total* homogenization of cultures, nor does it appear likely that there will be any time soon from this point of view. Rather, the world has become one vast network of interconnected social relationships, and between its different regions there is a flow and an exchange of cultural meanings as well as of people and goods.

Featherstone (1995: 13) points out that: 'Rather than the emergence of a unified global culture there is a strong tendency for the process of globalization to provide a stage for global differences not only to open up "world showcase cultures" in which the examples of the distant and the exotic are brought directly into the home, but to provide a field for a more discordant clashing of cultures.' Culture on the global level, according to him, is becoming increasingly pluralistic, or polytheistic, whilst at the same time cultural integration processes are taking place at the global level. He also believes that it is no longer as easy for Western nations to maintain the superiority of adopting a 'civilizational mission' towards the rest of the world, in which other nations are depicted as occupying the lower rungs of a symbolic hierarchy, which they are gradually being educated to climb up, in order to follow their betters. From this perspective the process of globalization does not turn the world into a domain of 'cultural uniformity'.

1.4.4. The Reproductionalists

The Reproductionalists' view is that the present trend towards globalization entails the fusing of old and modern identities and culture. The manner in which culture is being 'centred' is, according to this view, evolving and changing. Although this theory does not deal with the full extent of globalization, it does not conflict with the relativists' theory, since its main focus is on the mechanisms of the changes that are taking place.

Featherstone (1995), despite being referred to as a 'relativist' above, is also seen as a representative of the reproductionalists to the notion of the 'reproduction' of culture, a process that induces the dislocation of culture. He argues that the 'reproduction' of culture induces dislocation caused by globalization. He suggests that: 'In effect, culture is now beyond the social and has become released from its traditional determinisms in economic life, social class, gender, ethnicity and region … in effect culture has not been decentred, it has become recentred' (Featherstone, 1995: 2–3). Having said that, Featherstone has not taken the new culture as merely entailing a tragic loss, but as allowing new forms in which identity can develop amongst previously excluded outsider groups at the global level.

Featherstone suggests (1990) that it is possible to point to trans-societal cultural processes, which take a multiplicity of forms and some of which have preceded the interstate relations within which nation-states can now be regarded as embedded. He also points to processes that sustain the exchange and flow of goods, people, information, knowledge and images giving rise to communication processes, which gain some autonomy on a global level. He believes that a series of autonomous cultures are in the process of being formed on the global level; these he names *third cultures*.

For him, third cultures are transnational in nature, since they are orientated beyond national boundaries. These third cultures are conduits for all sorts of diverse cultural flows, which cannot be understood merely as the product of bilateral exchanges between nation-states. It is therefore misleading to conceive of a global culture as necessarily entailing a weakening of the sovereignty of nation-states, which, under the impetus of some form of theological evolutionism or other overarching logic, will necessarily become absorbed into larger units and, eventually, a world-state, which produces cultural homogeneity and integration. Featherstone also believes it is misleading to regard the emergence of third cultures as embodying a logic, which leads inexorably to homogenization. He argues that postmodernism as an intellectual construct or paradigm is both a symptom and a powerful cultural image of the swing away from the conceptualization of global culture in terms of unification and homogenization. It is a swing towards a concept which, on the contrary, is defined more in terms of the diversity, variety and richness of popular and local discourses, codes and practices, which both resist and respond to systemic trends, thereby feeding into and contributing to a system that is in the process of being formed out of heterogeneous elements.

1.4.5. The Post-structuralists

The fifth group of theories, which views globalization as a vehicle for the hegemonization of a particular culture, is referred to by Cvetkvich & Kellner (1997) and Mazrui (1998) as *post-structuralist*. Post-structuralists critically analyse the process of globalization, asserting that instead of fostering the tendencies towards a monolithic dominant culture, one should instead encourage the exchange of information and deepen dialogical interaction between cultures and civilizations. They claim that parallel to the globalization process, which is establishing the domination of Western culture, a 'reverse globalization' is also taking shape. This reverse process, they claim, will eventually lead to the cultural empowerment of the East. The reassertion of oriental cultural identity or identities, in relation to the West, and also the rest of the world, is the outcome of this reverse flow through the channels of globalization. From this point of view, it is not just Western culture that is being globalized, but also eastern cultures, in all their variety, that are spreading and increasingly establishing themselves within the global arena.

This theory does indeed seem to reflect the actual state of affairs as regards globalization trends. The increasing taste for eastern music, fashions and food within the West, the expanding appeal of eastern philosophical thought amongst not just the public but even amongst the philosophers in the West, and the attraction of ordinary people toward eastern mysticism and its relevant literature[1] as well as global Islamic revivalist movements – all of these are indications of the validity of this theory.

Structuralists have stressed the importance of fundamental and enduring economic, political, and cultural structures and institutions that organize contemporary life. They present cultural imperialism, Americanization and

---

1. Witness in this regard the extraordinary popularity of the poems of Jalal al-Din Rumi in America.

mass consumer culture as a proto-universal culture riding on the back of Western economic and political domination.

In contrast, post-structuralists point to the increasing sensitivity to the particularities of Western modernity, together with a discernible 'exhaustion' of the paradigm underlying the modern Western mentality, within a global framework in which other cultural and civilizational traditions have became impossible to ignore. Such factors have led some to argue that sociology's basic teaching programme should shift from revolving around local societies to focus on internationalization and global issues (Tiryakian, 1986).

Post-structuralists, such as Arjun Appadurai (1990), have been characterizing global culture as a series of 'flows'. He writes that it is possible to conceive of five dimensions along which global culture flows, doing so in non-isomorphic paths.

1. There are 'ethnoscape flows' produced by the flows of peoples: tourists, immigrants, refugees, exiles and guestworkers.
2. There are 'technoscape flows', comprising machinery and plant flows, which have been produced by multinational and national corporations and government agencies.
3. There are 'finance-scape flows', which have been set in motion by the rapid flows of money in the currency markets and stock exchanges.
4. The fourth mainstream flow is made up of 'mediascapes': the repertoires of images and information, the flows that are produced and distributed by newspapers, magazines, television and films.
5. There are also 'ideoscapes', which are linked to flows of images, associated with state or counter-state ideologies, which consist essentially of elements of the Western Enlightenment world-view – images of democracy, freedom, welfare rights etc.

His model questions those constructs of the global system that ascribe fundamental significance to the economy. Even those models, such as Fredric Jameson's, which focus on the 'cultural logic' of late capitalism, are criticized. From this perspective, discourses of transnationalism and globalization emerge from a tradition rooted in evaluations of capitalism; in contrast, certain forms of post-structuralism reject macro-theory and attack the premises of previous discourses, arguing that new economic, cultural, and political groups have developed, which have collectively undermined the assumptions of the older paradigms. Interest in globalization and its real significance has been generated not only by describing new developments in the history of capitalism, of charting the economic underpinnings of the current geopolitical map, but also by the sense that, in addition to the decline of the power of the nation-state, nationalism for many is no longer a viable political ideal (see Cvetkvich & Kellner, 1997: 16).

The discourse on the cultural hegemony of the West entered the mainstream of Western theory and criticism only 50 years ago. Whereas the economic theory of Imperialism was a logical extension of Marxist perspectives on capitalism, the cultural ramifications of this theory, i.e. the manifestations of cultural imperialism (Lee, 1980) and the critique of the West, which focuses on the forms of imperialism perpetrated throughout the world by means of the media and other cultural channels, has been introduced by Shiller (1976), and developed by others, such as Boyd-Barret (1977), Tunstall (1977), Lee (1980), Said (1981, 1983), Tomlinson (1991) and Fox (1992).

The arguments relating to the globalization of Islam in terms of 'reverse globalization' can be better appreciated in the light of the post-structuralist paradigm. Those who subscribe to this paradigm adopt a radical critique of the hegemony and spread of American culture(see Mazrui, 1998). They believe in a cultural balance of power, in mutuality and reciprocity in the exchange of information, equality in the dialogical encounters in the domains of knowledge, media, art, religion and culture.

1.4.6. The Transformationalists

The *transformationalists* such as Beck (1992, 1997) and Giddens (1999) propose that we are living in an entirely radicalized and transformed social reality. Since the intensification of the modernization process has accelerated to such an extent as to create fundamentally new social conditions, there is a corresponding need to develop new theories for a meaningful analysis of these conditions. The transformationalist' thesis suggests that globalization has been a central driving force behind the rapid social, political and economic changes that have reshaped modern societies and world order. For them globalization is associated with new patterns of global stratification in which some states, societies and communities are becoming increasingly enmeshed in the global order, while others are becoming increasingly marginalized. They describe the intermingling of cultures and peoples as generating cultural hybrids and new global cultural networks (Held *et al.* 1999: 327).

Held and his colleagues suggest (1999: 8) that: 'At the core of the transformationalist theory is a belief that contemporary globalization has reconstituted or "re-engineered" the power, functions and authority of national governments.' For them world divisions – North and South, First World and Third World – are no longer realistic phenomena; for 'developed' and 'undeveloped' or 'developing' populations are found intermingled within all the world's major cities. Rather than the traditional pyramid analogy of the world's social structure, with a tiny top echelon and spreading mass base, the global social structure that they have envisaged is that of a three-tier arrangement of concentric circles, each cutting across national boundaries, representing respectively the elites, the contented and the marginalized.

The transformationalists have not made any claims about the future trajectory of globalization; nor do they seek to evaluate the present in relation to some single, fixed ideal-type 'globalized world', whether this be in terms of a global market or a global civilization. Rather, transformationalist accounts have emphasized globalization as a long-term historical process, which is replete with contradictions and which is significantly shaped by conjunctural factors.

In arguing that globalization is transforming or reconstituting the bases of political power, national government and popular cultures, the transformationalists reject both the hyperglobalist rhetoric concerning the 'end of the sovereign nation-state' and the claim of the sceptics that nothing much has changed. Instead they emphasize the point made by the reproductionalists, namely, that national powers and local cultures are reproducing a new type of sovereignty, which is a by-product of the interplay between local and global factors. Therefore, the power of national governments is not necessarily diminished by globalization but on the contrary is being restructured in response to the growing complexity of the needs, modes and processes of governance in today's ever-increasingly interconnected world (Held *et al.*, 1999).

The transformationalist theory does not contradict the theories of the relativists, reproductionalists and post-structuralists. The relativists will concede that the world has experienced revolutionary change and is still witnessing ongoing changes. But they argue that these changes do not have a fixed and absolute orientation. All social, cultural and political phenomena are relative in this sense. For them, these changes do not have any absolute and integrated global identity. Identities, cultures, values and norms have diversified and assumed different forms in relation to a number of discrete issues. Reproductionalists have also observed these changes, which amount to a cultural transformation and which call forth a corresponding deep shift in modes of analytic discourse. For them, the mechanism whereby these changes are brought about is reproductional. This means that the output of these changes will be a combination of old and new identities.

Post-structuralists likewise have stressed the impact wrought by social, cultural and political transformations, but they disagree with the imposition of a particular culture upon the rest of the world. Having said that, it would appear that the transformationalist theory might be regarded as an umbrella theory, one which encompasses the other three theories; that is to say, these three 'subtheories' illustrate and articulate particular aspects of a perspective that is integrally addressed by the transformationalists. The transformationalist theory is comprehensive in terms of its ability to explain the multifaceted dimensions of social reality, as it possesses the analytic flexibility required by the ever-increasing complexity of global conditions.

In this chapter, we have given an overview of some of the theoretically posited characteristics of globalization of culture in general terms. The next chapter focuses on more particular aspect of this process, looking specifically at homogenizing and heterogenizing tendencies, in order to complete the conceptual background necessary for putting in proper perspective our empirical research.

TWO

Globalization: the Processes of Homogenization and Heterogenization

In this chapter some of the applications of the process of globalization that have an impact upon religious identity will be discussed. As we have mentioned in the introduction, globalization has proceeded through two interconnected processes – homogenization and heterogenization. This chapter will concentrate on the theoretical aspects of these two paradoxical phenomena in connection with the determination and formation of religious identities.

The tension between cultural homogenization and cultural heterogenization is considered as a central problem in contemporary global interactions (Appadurai, 1990: 295). McGrew (1992) has suggested that several mutually opposed and simultaneous tendencies are at play in the globalization era: universalization versus particularization; homogenization versus differentiation; integration versus fragmentation; centralization versus decentralization, and juxtaposition versus syncretization. Among them the dichotomy of 'homogenization/heterogenization' is the key concept in the evaluation of the process of globalization in general and in regards to the impact of globalization on religious identity in particular.

It is appropriate to begin the analysis in this chapter with a statement of the highly influential perspective of Emile Durkheim. According to his point of view, one can explain the process of globalization in relation to 'religious identity,' 'social solidarity' and 'common consciousness' at the local and global level. Durkheim's theories are applicable to homogenization as global solidarity and global collective consciousness, which may be defined here as a *'globalization of a particular type of a culture or an identity'*, and heterogenization as a process that has scattered and differentiated religious identities into several types of identity. One of the consequences of these processes is the *'fragmentation of Muslim identity'* into different types of identity.

Durkheim is known as a functionalist who looked at how the structural components of society function to provide order and solidarity. He was especially concerned with the need for moral solidarity in the midst of dramatic social change at the end of the 19th century: the shift from communal *Gemeinschaft* to industrial, impersonal *Gesellschaft*.

Durkheim was troubled by the declining strength of common morality that bound individuals together and provided for social order, as society evolved from organic bonds of solidarity to mechanical ties of association. He theorized that premodern social order was characterized by similarity of social function, and morality was upheld by common beliefs – what Durkheim called the 'collective conscience', or the intersection of culture, normative systems and values.

In modernity, Durkheim (1984: 122) said that we see a shift from solidarity based on common belief to one rooted in interdependence of function: the highly developed division of labour of modern capitalism. As society becomes more and more pluralistic, the moral glue that maintains social order beyond interdependence itself becomes progressively weaker.

With regard to the homogenization of followers of a particular religion, Durkheim believes, religion is the functional content of the collective conscience that binds individuals together in society through a common system of belief. He states (1984: 119): 'Indeed it is invariably the fact that when a somewhat strong conviction is shared by a single community of people it inevitably assumes a religious character. It inspires in the individual consciousness the same reverential respect as religious beliefs proper. Thus is it extremely probable ... that likewise religion corresponds to a very central domain of the common consciousness.'

Durkheim equivocated early in his career on the effectiveness of the religion of the individual in secular modernity. But at the end, he returned to the binding moral forces of religious expression, reiterating the importance of religion for social order. He wrote in 1886 that: 'As long as there are men who live together there will be some *common faith* between them. The only thing we cannot foresee and that the future alone will decide is the particular form in which that faith will be symbolized' (in Bellah, 1973: XXII).

In 1905, he said in the conclusion of his book, *Elementary Forms of the Religious Life*, 'Thus there is something eternal in religion which is destined to survive all the particular symbols in which religious thought has successively enveloped itself. There can be no society which does not feel the need of upholding and reaffirming at regular intervals the collective sentiments and the collective ideas which make its unity and its personality' (Durkheim, 1965: 474–5). Accordingly, Mol (1976) also mentioned that religion always appears to modify or stabilize the differentiations that it has been unable to prevent.

On the other hand, fragmentation of religious identity into several types of identity is a process of global cultural diversity, which is the result of extensive processes of social and cultural differentiation. Before societies were more local, today societies are more global; individuals and communities have more access to other cultures, values and arts. This gives rise to huge cultural diversity and establishes a sort of multicultural society. Although social division of labour in industrial life has created diversity in terms of occupation and specialization, globalization has also brought optional and diversified types of life models in the area of culture and economy.

Robertson, as a prominent and partially Durkheimian sociologist, sees globalization as a process by which the world has become a single place where political, economic and cultural spheres of life are interdependent. It also involves the process by which institutions have become globalized, i.e. having global significance or acting globally. However, the world is not a harmonious, integrated system in Robertson's view. The historical process making the world 'one' has been rife with conflict and reactionary movements, and has been a multidimensional process, not reducible to monocausal forces like capitalist development (Robertson & Lechner, 1985).

In the following section the implications of homogenization and heterogenization on the formation and deformation of religious identity will be elaborated.

2.1. The Process of Homogenization

In this section, both the processes of Westernization or Americanization alongside the process of reverse globalization, namely globalization of Islam and the strength of resistance against the dominant trends of globalization, can be understood in terms provided by the Frankfurt School[1] in its cultural studies. In 1947 two eloquent Frankfurtian scholars, Theodor Adorno and Max Hokheimer, coined the term 'culture industry' to designate the products and processes of mass culture. The products of the culture industry, they claim, are marked by two features: cultural homogeneity and cultural predictability (Adorno, 1977: 120–5).

---

1. The Frankfurt School is the name given to a group of German intellectuals associated with the Institute for Social Research at the University of Frankfurt. The institute was established in 1923. Following the coming to power of Nazism in Germany in 1933, the Institute moved to New York, becoming a temporary part of the University of Columbia until 1949 (see Jay, 1996 and Wiggershaus 1995).

2.1.1. The Process of Homogenization and the Frankfurt School

The Frankfurt School sees the culture industry as a source of standardization, conservatism, and mendacity, whereby consumer goods are manipulated in such a way as to depoliticize the working class (Lowenthal, 1961: 11). Lowenthal explains that: 'Whenever revolutionary tendencies show a timid head, they are mitigated and cut short by false fulfilment of wish-dreams, like wealth, adventure, passionate love, power and sensationalism in general' (Lowenthal, 1961: 11).

From this perspective, the culture industry has created a global ground for those who are involved with cultural consumption – film production, the broadcasting market or press business. In such terms, both the extent to which Hollywoodization or Americanization of the world is actually taking place and the extent to which the Islamic movement acquires a homogenous character through mass industry, giving it a global outreach, can be empirically tested and gauged.

The focus in the next section is, first, on the homogenizing impact of American culture and secondly on the expansion of Islamic movement all over the world, two paradoxical processes as they emerge out of globalization.

2.1.2. Globalization – Westernization and Americanization

For many sociologists globalization can be understood simply as the global diffusion of Western modernity, that is, Westernization. World-system theory, for instance, has equated globalization with the spread of Western capitalism and Western institutions [Cvetkovich & Kellner, 1998; Beyer, 1994, 1998; Featherstone, 1995; Mazrui, 1998). By contrast, others draw a distinction between Westernization and globalization and reject the idea that globalization is synonymous with Westernization (Giddens, 1990).

Sociologists like Water (1995), Beyer (1994, 1998), and Featherstone (1995) have defined globalization as global Westernization, irrespective of whether this definition holds true in all cases or not. This means that the globalized world offers the same Western education to all its children, speaks the same language, consumes the same media images, holds the same values and even thinks the same thoughts. In effect, globalization means the destruction of cultural diversity. It means monoculture and manipulation of a particular culture – American hegemony.

For Beyer (1994: 7-8) globalization theories suggested that modernization in the West has directly resulted in the spread of certain vital institutions of Western modernization to the rest of the globe. This is especially true with the modern capitalist economy, the nation-state, and scientific rationality in the form of modern technology. This global spread has resulted in a new social unit, which is, much more than a simple expansion of Western modernity. This assertion of both identity and difference between modernization and globalization brings us back to the central issue of relativization or fluidity of identity.

Beyer (1998: 82) suggested that 'globalization is a Western imposition on the non-West; meaning that the West is more global and the non-West more local.' In this sense, globalization is Western imperialism, whether economic, political, technological, or broadly cultural. However, Beyer suggested that globalization theories cannot describe contemporary global society as simply the extension of a particular society and its culture (i.e. as one part becoming the whole), because the cultures they extend into also change dramatically in the process.

Globalization might serve as a substitute term for modernization and thus continue as a legitimating ideology for the Westernization of the world, obscuring cultural differences and struggles. For Cvetkovich & Kellner (1998) globalization is a continuation of imperialism, which displaces focus on the domination of developing countries by the overdeveloped ones or national and local economics by transnational corporations.

It has been argued that Westernization 'gathers in a number of fairly discrete discourses of domination: of America over Europe, of the West over the rest of the world, of the core over the periphery, of the modern world over the fast-disappearing traditional one, of capitalism over more or less everything and everyone' (Tomlinson, 1999: 80). But in general, Westernization is a process, which includes worldwide domination of European culture alongside the American model of life over the rest of the world.

Many of the post-structuralists see the domination of the West over the rest as a conception stemming from an inherently Eurocentric perspective. Therefore to understand the process of Westernization, we need to elaborate more upon the notion of Eurocentrism.

i. Eurocentrism
Eurocentrism is considered as an implicit conceptual resource of European and American hegemonic sovereignty. Globalization as a means of global communication creates a fertile ground for global Westernization processes based on Eurocentric premises, which facilitate the expansion of the American and European spheres of influence. Eurocentrism has formed the basis for a school of thought that believes that human civilization is fundamentally built on the civilizational bases of Rome, Paris and Athens, and that the development of human society is indebted only to European thought.

Many important sociologists and leftists have discussed the issue of Eurocentrism and Westernization processing as a means of facilitating the development of the Western Empire (see Amin, 1989; Lowy, 1995; Sayyid, 1997; Stam, 1997; Dussel, 1998 and Mazrui, 1998). For them, Eurocentrism is a very important factor in bringing these standards to the forefront of European cultural and political policy. Historically, this has led to the compilation and writing of the history of civilization and science based predominantly on the work of Western scientists (and Western cultural heritage), without any acknowledgement of the contributions made by philosophers and scientists from civilizations in other parts of the world.

Lowy (1995: 714) identifies Eurocentrism as a process through which Europe and European values became a foundational source of meaning through which individuals, groups, and nations from the continent could develop attitudes based on emerging ideologies of racial, religious, cultural or ethnic supremacy over the various indigenous peoples that they encountered during the period from about 1450.

Amin (1989) proposed that Eurocentrism refers to an essential dimension of the capitalist ideology, whose manifestations would be characteristic of the dominant attitudes of all of the societies in the developed capitalist world, the centre of the world capitalist system. Amin charges Eurocentrism with a lack of ability to see anything other than the lives of those who are comfortably installed in the modern world.

According to Amin, Eurocentrism can be retrospectively viewed in the context of the Renaissance and the forces and processes that produced what we now call the modern world: 'With the Renaissance begins the two-fold radical transformation that shapes the modern world: the crystallization of capitalist society in Europe and the European conquest of the world. These are two dimensions of the same development, and theories that separate them in order to privilege one over the other are not only insufficient and distorting but also frankly unscientific' (Amin, 1989: 71). He proceeds to argue that the New World is freed from 'the domination of metaphysics' even while the material foundations for capitalist society are laid. Thus,

> The cultural revolution in the modern world opens the way for an explosion of scientific progress and its systematic use in the service of the development of the forces of production, and for the formation of a secularized society that can successfully carry the democratic aspiration to its conclusion. Simultaneously, Europe becomes conscious of the universal scope of its civilization, henceforth capable of conquering the world.
>
> (Amin, 1989: 71)

According to Sayyid (1997: 127):

Amin's theoretical practice is based on historical materialism, a number of difficulties arise from his insistence that Eurocentrism is primarily a culturalist phenomenon. The most significant of these is the way in which he reduces the cultural to a superstructural moment, as a consequence of which Eurocentrism emerges as the superstructural adjunct to capitalism. By conceptualizing centrism in such a manner, Amin is able to suggest that socialism is a solution to both the iniquities of capitalism and Eurocentrism.

Sayyid's view of Eurocentrism differs from Amin's, in that Sayyid locates it in the context of the decentring of the West, while Amin's notion remains within the discourse of modernity. Like Amin, however, Sayyid maintains that the logic of Eurocentrism is currently hegemonic – reflecting the preponderant influence of the West over others. Sayyid has suggested that: 'the emergence of Islamism is based on the erosion of Eurocentrism' (Sayyid, 1997: 155). He believes that after two world wars and the process of decolonization, the notion of Western superiority is no longer so straightforward. The balance between the superiority of the west and inferiority of Islam is no longer weighted against Islam. Sayyid has also mentioned that: 'one effect of this global process of the provincialization of Europe was that the choice between Islam and the West was no longer the choice between the centre and periphery; the playing-field had been levelled out a little' (Sayyid, 1997: 155).

Halliday (1999: 892–902) disagrees with Sayyid. He argues that: 'The fight against fundamentalism has not been between the West and the Muslim world, but within the Muslim world itself: the briefest acquaintance with the recent history of Iran, Afghanistan, Pakistan, Egypt or Algeria would bear this out.'

For Stam (1997) Eurocentrism is the discursive residue or precipitate of colonialism, the process by which the European powers reached positions of economic, military, political and cultural hegemony in much of Asia, Africa and the Americas. In this framework, 'Eurocentrism is ethnocentrism gone global.' Stam argued that Eurocentrism as an ideological substratum common to colonialist, imperialist and racist discourse, is a form of vestigial thinking that permeates and structures contemporary practices and representations, even after the formal end of colonialism. Stam has also attempted to place polycentric multiculturalism in place of Eurocentrism. For him the notion of polycentrism involves globalized multiculturalism. Within a polycentric vision, the world has many dynamic cultural locations, many possible vantage points. From his point of view, 'The emphasis on "polycentrism" is not on spatial relations or points of origin but on fields of power, energy and struggle. The "poly" does not refer to a finite list of centres of power but rather introduces a systematic principle of differentiation, relationality, and linkage' (Stam, 1995:

102). From this perspective, there is no epistemologically privileged single community or part of the world, whatever its economic or political power.

According to Dussel (1998), Weber situates the 'problem of universal history' with the question: 'To what combination of circumstances should the fact be attributed that in Western civilization, and in Western civilization only, cultural phenomena have appeared which lie in a line of development having universal significance and value?' This means that Europe possessed exceptional internal characteristics that allowed it to supersede, through its rationality, all other cultures. Hegel clearly described it as a German hegemony – 'the German spirit is the spirit of the New World.' For Hegel, the spirit of Europe (the German spirit) is the absolute truth that determines or realizes itself through itself without owing anything to anyone. According to Dussel, Eurocentrism imposed two paradigms. First, it imposed itself on the entire intellectual realm of the world periphery. Eurocentrism suggests that from the Italy of the Renaissance, through the Germany of the Reformation and the Enlightenment, to the France of the French Revolution; Europe is central and the rest of the world peripheral (Dussel, 1998: 4). Secondly, Eurocentrism embodied 'the culture of the centre of the world system, of the first world-system, through the incorporation of Amerindia, and as a result of the management of this centrality.'

Eurocentrism is a cultural phenomenon in the sense that it assumes the existence of an irreducibly distinct cultural variant that shapes the historical paths of different peoples. Although Eurocentrism is a force of global hegemony, it is also an anti-universalistic phenomenon, since it is not interested in seeking possible general laws of social evolution. But it does present itself as universalist, for it claims that imitation of the Western model by all peoples is the only solution to the challenges of our time.

For Dussel (1998) the 'pseudo-scientific' division of history into Antiquity (as the antecedent epoch), the Medieval Age (preparatory epoch), and the Modern Age (contemporary Europe) is part of an ideological and deforming organization of history, which aims to impose European centrality. He argued that: 'The human experience of 4,500 years of political, economic, technological, and cultural relations of the interregional system will now be hegemonized by a Europe which had never been the 'Centre,' and which, during its best times, became only a 'periphery' (Dussel, 1998: 5).'

This view sees all the creations, phenomena, innovations and 'general thinking' theories in all the sciences as being European. In such an atmosphere, the great human civilizations, which have ancient historical track records, are neglected and forgotten.

Mazrui (1998: 10–11) suggested several fundamental factors related to the contradiction between the Eurocentric world and Muslim identity. He explained that two-thirds of the Muslim world: from Kano to Karachi, Cairo to Kuala Lumpur, and Dakar to Jakarta, was colonized by the West in the first half of the 20th century. In this period the Muslim world became more fragmented than ever and even more receptive to Western cultural penetration. This type of Western domination may be categorized as preglobalization processing. It occurred before the appearance of communication technology, the growing impact of Western media upon the distribution of news, information and entertainment, and ranging from magazines, cinema, television and video to the New World of computers.

For Mazrui (1998) the omnipresent technology of the West is a force that carries with it not only new skills but also new values. Here the net result is a form of globalization of aspects of culture. Eurocentric and Americocentric brands of globalization masquerade as universally true and so other cultures eventually embrace one aspect or another of Western culture. He gave two examples, which reflect the influences of the European culture – the Christian calendar and the day of rest:

> Many African and Asian countries have adopted the Western Christian calendar as their own. They celebrate their Independence Day according to the Christian calendar and write their history according to Gregorian years, using such distinctions as BC (Before Christ) or AD (*anno domini* [in the year of our Lord]). Some Muslim countries recognize Sunday as the day of rest instead of Friday, and others have reperiodicized all of Islamic historiography according to the Christian calendar.
>
> (Mazrui, 1998: 10–11)

Many other theories have discussed the Eurocentric way of Western domination, such as the one-way flow of Information (Tunstall, 1977 and Varis, 1985); media and cultural imperialism (Boyd-Barrett, 1977, Lee, 1980 and Tomlinson, 1999); and cultural dependency (Fox, 1992). Schiller (1976) stresses the standardization of the political, cultural, social and economic structure of society based on the Western paradigm. The monopolization of academic and informational services can also be regarded as aspects of Eurocentric influence, which have induced resistance, crisis or transformation of identities, including Muslim identity.

ii. Americanization

According to Cvetkovich & Kellner (1998) most of the new global popular culture that produces resources for identity-formation comes from North American media industries. From this perspective, globalization becomes a form of Americanization, which imposes on the world such figures as Rambo,

Madonna, Beavis and Butt-Head, gangster, rappers, and other figures from American culture. These figures produce seductive models for new identities that find their adherents all over the world.

Many European and even some American thinkers examining the rise of the United States in recent years and its global cultural impact, even in Europe, have stated that: 'The American empire is the only one in the world. It is absolutely supreme, and it is the first time in human history that this curious phenomenon has survived. The United States is a unique empire: it is a major producer of all sorts of goods as well as an avid consumer. Its history from the very beginning is marked by an extreme tendency toward expansion' (Abu-Rabi, 1998: 27). This is the theme of many theories that define globalization as an Americanization or Westernization of the world. According to Abu Rabi, many Third World intellectuals see globalization as the triumph of Americanization, which has advocated a new kind of cultural and economic model. For them, besides being an economic system, globalization is an ideology that serves this system. From this point of view Americanization and globalization are tightly intertwined. Globalization is already leading to a new form of colonization and imperialism, which is more subtle and destructive than the classical one.

From this perspective, the asymmetries in the availability of, and access to, production equipment, distribution networks, venues etc., leads to a structural bias that favours some producers at the expense of others. This bias brings to mind a system of colonialism, and notions of cultural colonialism (Shiller 1976). These global pessimists see the cultural domination of the United States overriding the sundry national cultures. For this school of thought, the Canadian example is the most illustrative. Because of Canada's geographic and cultural proximity to the United States, it has the longest experience in fighting the forces of 'globalizing' culture. The results have been catastrophic for the Canadian cultural industry: In Canada, about 96% of the films in movie theatres are foreign, most of these American. US television dominates Canadian television; seven American firms control the distribution of sound recordings in Canada; three-quarters of the music on Canadian radio is not Canadian; 89% of magazines on newsstands are non-Canadian; and six in every ten books are foreign, mainly American (Cvetkovitch & Kellner 1997: 11; *The Economist*, Sept. 12, 1998).

Jameson (1998) suggested that for those people around the world who watch exported North American television[1] programs, it is enough to realize that this cultural intervention is deeper than anything known in earlier forms of

---

1. Boddy (1998: 23) said that the flood of exported American television begun in the 1950s provided models of programme styles and popular taste for producers around the world.

colonization or imperialism, or simple tourism. At the same time many Western sociologists raise the same idea of hegemonization of American culture via globalization. Anthony Giddens (1990) argues that the consequences of modernity are becoming global in scope, that what used to characterize a few Western societies, with the United States as a frontrunner, is becoming a global characteristic.

Trent (1998) has focused on the use of video and films as a means of community organization and as a tool for social change in the process of cultural globalization. As a member of the Frankfurt School, she examined the impact of Hollywood on the productions of indigenous film-makers in the context of 'culture industry'. She argues that: 'The highest award-winning film-makers in Mexico, those who have won awards in Mexico that are similar or identical to the Academy Awards in the United States, cannot find theatres in Mexico to release their films' (Trent, 1998: 230). While Spanish films do not require subtitles – they cannot find theatres. At the same time Hollywood's English films that require Spanish subtitles have been victorious throughout the cinema theatres of the world.

Featherstone (1995) considered the 'cultural message' of issues like McDonaldization. He believes McDonaldization or Coca-Cola-ization does not only entail economic (in the form of time/money) efficiency gains through standardization of the product. They also represent a cultural message, which means, for instance, that the burger is not only consumed physically as material substance, but is also consumed culturally as an image and an icon of a particular way of life. Along with the Marlboro Man, Coca-Cola, Hollywood, Sesame Street, rock music and American football insignia, McDonald's is one more icon of the American way of life. It is important that American goods have become associated with transposable themes, which are central to consumer culture, such as youth, fitness, beauty, luxury and romantic freedom. American dreams have become intertwined with those of the good life. This is not only because of the flow of consumer goods and finance in which Japan as well as America is involved. It is also because American goods flow along with evocative images and information (Featherstone, 1995: 8–9).

On the other hand, some cultural relativists working in the discipline of modern ethnography have argued against these kinds of universalistic tendencies by pointing to the variety of cultures in terms of authentic, self-contained wholes. Samuel Huntington (1996) claims, in the context of his widely discussed and much criticized theories about the 'clash of civilizations', that the main axis of international conflict on a world scale will be the difference of cultures rather than of nations and between political and economic systems or standards of development. He stated that: 'For the relevant future, there will be no universal civilization, but instead a world of different civilizations, each of which will have to learn to coexist with the others' (Huntington, 1996: 23).

One thing that Featherstone (1995) suggests is that from the point of view of postmodernism, there is a strong sense that modernity will not be universalized. 'This is because modernity is seen as both a Western project and as the West's projection of its values on to the world. In effect modernity has allowed Europeans to project their civilization, history and knowledge as civilization and also history and knowledge in general' (Featherstone, 1995: 10).

According to Turner (1994) it is problematic to make the attempt to embrace Western technology without Western values. Sociology has suggested that you cannot have modernization, technology, urbanization and bureaucratization without the cultural baggage that goes with it, and this baggage is essentially a post-Enlightenment system of thought. One can suggest that modernization does not have the same meaning for all nations and cultures. Different historical backgrounds can affect the perceptions and implications of modern technology in the everyday life of individuals and societies. For example, while the process of modernization in Turkey has resulted in deep and extensive secularization, the same cannot be said of Saudi Arabia, where outwardly it is not inherently secular but secular tendencies may manifest themselves within the inner structure of society.

One of the important couriers of culture is language. The English language adds additional force and intensity to American culture as a global force of power, not in a cultural form, but as a means of economic transaction and academic exchange of knowledge and experience. This is the concept, which is elaborated by Jameson (1998): 'For most people in the world English itself is not exactly a culture language: it is the lingua franca of money and power, which you have to learn and use for practical but scarcely for aesthetic purposes. But the very connotation of power then tends in the eyes of foreign speakers to reduce the value of all forms of English-language high culture' (Jameson, 1998: 59). For Jameson, this dissymmetry between the United States and other cultures will impose American culture on the world. Alongside the free market as an ideology, the consumption of the Hollywood film markets an apprenticeship to a specific culture, to an everyday life as a cultural practice: a practice of which commodified narratives are the aesthetic expression, so that the populations in question learn both the aesthetic and ideology at the same time.

Today, humanity is closer to having world languages. The English language functions in more than ten countries as a national language, is spoken as a major language on at least two continents (homogenization), and is widely used all over the world as an international language for business and political as well as academic purposes (hegemonization). Arabic is asserting a strong claim as a world language, but this is based partly on the globalization of Islam and the role of Arabic as Islam's religious and ritual language (Mazrui, 1998).

English has emerged as a global language but few other European languages have enjoyed similar popularity. Mignolo (1998: 37) argued that the period of globalization that we are witnessing is a radical transformation, which is characterized and shaped by a particular articulation of languages (English, French, German, Italian), literatures of these languages (with their legacy in Greek and Latin), and cultures of scholarship (mainly in English, French and German). Mingolo suggests that at least 95% of all scholars and all scholarship from the period of 1850–1914, and probably even to 1945, originates in five countries: France, Great Britain, Germany, Italy and the United States.

iii. Liberalization and Democratization of the World

The core content and precise social, cultural and political embodiment of modernization – Westernization of the world or what is viewed as a 'new age' – is liberalization and democratization of the world. The process of globalization has played a significant role in accelerating and expanding the process of liberalization and democratization of the world. Democracy as well as cultural and political liberalism is a significant part of the Western legacy, which has spread all over the world. Therefore we should not segregate Westernization or Americanization from the process of liberalization alongside democratization.

Democracy has been defined as a system that has involved effective competition between political parties for positions of power. In democratic systems, there have been regular and fair elections, in which all members of the population may take part. This right of democratic participation goes along with civil liberties – freedom of expression and discussion – together with the freedom to join political groups or associations (Giddens, 1999: 68–9).

One of the manifestations of the globalization of politics is the emerging dominance of a particular political system – the democratization of the world. Giddens (1999) suggested that, during the last two decades, the number of countries that accepted democracy had significantly increased. Muqtedar Khan (1998: 97) mentioned that:

'The total number of Muslims living in democratic societies exceeds 600 million, yet we continue to question the Muslims' ability to adapt to democratic practices. Amazingly, Muslim states have even elected women as heads of state: Tansu Ciller in Turkey, Khalida Zia in Bangladesh, and Benazir Bhutto in Pakistan – an achievement that America has yet to duplicate.'

Morley & Robins (1995: 71) point out that one of the important consequences of globalization is that 'positive national identities are being replaced by a global non-identity'. Political globalization is intertwined with economic as well as cultural globalization processing. It means the 'capitalist system' is institutionalized in the 'democratic system' with the 'cultural hegemony' of the Western Empire.

Giddens (1999: 80) argues that democracy might be fostered above the level of the nation-state. For him the transnational organizations have the same level of influence as the international ones. However he believes that for example the United Nations, for the moment at least, rarely challenges the sovereignty of nations, and indeed its charter asserts that it should not do so. But he sees it as forging a way that could, and very likely will, be followed in other regions too.

Some of the theorizers of liberalism have agreed that liberalism is to be traced to the aftermath of the Reformation. Freedom of conscience in religious matters came first, and was then extended to other areas of opinion. So, tolerance of different opinions about religion lies at the very foundations of political liberalism, and religious pluralism may be viewed as a very late arrival, which seeks to provide a theological basis for this tolerance. Characteristic of political liberalism is a sharp division between the public and private, and the assertion that individuals enjoy a number of rights that safeguard the private realm from interference by the state. Secularism is the first product of the liberal separation of the private from the public. Foremost among the individual rights protecting the private realm is freedom of opinion, especially religious opinion, which gradually has been transformed into the notion of freedom of expression (see Berlin, 1969; Habermas, 1975; Dworking, 1981; Rorty, 1988).

2.1.3. Post-structuralists: Reverse Globalization

The process of 'reverse globalization' reflects the post-structuralist's approach as well as those theories that focus on the resistance against Westernization of the world. At the same time it portrays homogenization of culture, religion and civilization at the global level.

From this perspective, it is not just American culture, which works as a homogenizing force – other specific identities and cultures could also become globalized. Similar cultures and identities formerly held apart are now brought into contact and juxtaposition. Some of the cultures or religious identities pile on top of each other in heaps without obvious organizing principles. Others may get together based on very solid organizational co-operation and communication. Examples of this include 'The Khojah World Federation' in the Shia community and Ismailis' in the Muslim world. American culture may be considered as the dominant world culture today, but it is not the only global

---

1. See Lapidus (1998).

culture circulating in the world. That is why we raise the idea of homogenization in the religious belief and social behaviour amongst the masses as globalization of Islam become more prevalent. Responses to the Rushdie affair would be a good example where expressions of global solidarity and social mobilization of Muslim identity in our contemporary world have taken place.

Robertson's views reflect a very important contribution in the post-structuralist theory. Robertson (1991) has continuously defined globalization as the process by which the world becomes a 'single place', where events in one part of the world have significant consequences for action in another part of the world. He is not promoting, however, an image of an harmonious, integrated system. There are conflicting definitions of how that 'single place' should look. He argues that culture and religion are significant forces in the several-hundred year process. 'Certainly it is clear that religion has ... made crucial contributions to globalization, but the explicit historical study of that phenomenon is only (in) its early stages' (Robertson & Garrett, 1991: 220).

In developing the concept of globalization, especially in earlier work, Robertson and Lechner (1985) advise against reducing the global system to social or other large-scale actors, or collapsing global culture into macro-political or economic forces. This last point Robertson has made quite forcefully over the last ten years, establishing his opposition to Immanuel Wallerstein and what he calls World System implicit adherence to a strong version of the secularization thesis. Although Robertson (1987) has praised Wallerstein for methodologically refocusing social scientific analysis to the global level, he rejects the absolute and primary *significance of capitalist development*. Robertson has challenged Wallerstein for treating culture and specifically religion as being epiphenomenal to the onward march of economic forces. He also criticizes the 'world system' theory for ignoring the quasi-religious ideologies accompanying economic explanations such as economic socialism, utopian socialism and traditionalistic communalism (Robertson & Lechner, 1985). For Robertson and Lechner the problem of globality has involved economic relationships, but also cultural, religious and political forces; in other words, globality is multidimensional. Robertson & Lechner (1985: 109) concede that Wallerstein mentions the 'metaphysical presuppositions' that played an important part in the development of the West, but concludes that: 'Wallerstein's own interest in culture is skewed in an atypically Marxist direction.'

Robertson (1992a) has opposed the general direction of secularization arguments in the sociology of religion. This approach makes Robertson closer to the post-structuralists. He has hinted that globalization might involve the resacralization of the world (world in the sense of that which is secular or profane). In order to make sense of our lives in this new, global context, many groups are re-enchanting the world using old or new religious symbols. Robertson says he would be surprised if there was not a resurgence of religion in response to globalization.

His point is that the sociology of religion has primarily focused on religious symbolism at the level of national societies, or the state. Robertson pointed out that the state has subsumed interest in what Parsons called 'telic matters', which deal with the 'ends of man,' such as issues of birth, death, old age, sexuality, human rights, etc. (Robertson & Garrett, 1991). Therefore, he has refocused from national society to the global human condition. He even seems to pose the problem in terms of secularization versus globalization.

Finally, Robertson suggested that: 'The depoliticization of religion has been a central myth of the project of social modernization' (Robertson & Garrett, 1991: 288). Religion has become repoliticized, but in such a way that it stretches beyond the bounds of the nation-state. In the following section, we will elaborate the concept of religious resistance and globalization of Islam, which mirror the embodiment of Robertson's theory on repoliticization of religion – resistance identity and globalization of Islam.

i. Resistance Identity

From the post-structuralists' point of view, 'resistance' identity is a significant phenomenon, which has crystallized more as a social phenomenon in response to the preponderant influence of globalization. Nationalists, environmentalists, Sufists, traditionalists, culturalists and Islamists have all tried to retain their own identity against the general impact of globalization. Today, 'dissident culture' as a reverse process against dominant culture within the European society is significantly increasing. Resistance against processes of globalization/Westernization and the struggle for being globalized are interlinked through the process of globalization.

Resistance is the result of the process of 'push' and 'pull', as well as 'challenge and annoyance'. When individuals or people feel intensively that their religion, historical and national heritage, or any other loves and beliefs, are subject to challenge and attack, then they attempt to resist it. Many sociologists have discussed the meaning of 'resistance identity' (Robertson, 1985; Turner, 1994; Wallerstein, 1991b; Castells, 1997 and Falk, 1999).

For Robertson, the process of globalization is not without 'resistance.' However, resistance may take the form of opposition to the world as a single whole (which Robertson calls antimodernity), or opposition to the conception of the world as a series of equivalent, relativized, ways of life (which he calls anti-postmodernity). He says, 'It is around the universalism–particularism axis of globalization that the discontents of globality manifest themselves in reference to new, globalized variations on the oldish themes of Gesellschaft and Gemeinschaft' (Robertson, 1991: 77).

Robertson has devoted a great deal of work to the resulting tensions between church and state (or religion and politics, religion and government, etc.) at the global level. This is because states, although secular as a global pattern, often use religiocultural symbols to crystallize their identity and legitimize their authority. Paradoxically, religious movements are increasingly challenging the authority of the secular state, in response to the encroachment of the state into previously 'religious affairs.' This occurs in tandem with the growing strength of the modern state, itself a product of globalization. Robertson points out: 'I agree ... that the problem of global order and the crystallization of conflicts in defining the global-human situation are the main factors involved in solving the analytical puzzle as to why we are witnessing ... a near-global proliferation of church–state tension' (Robbins & Robertson, 1987: 46). Examples of this conflict include: Iran and Islamic movements, the Liberation Church in Central and South America, Jewish fundamentalism in Israel, the Catholic Church in Poland, the Chinese in Nepal and Tibet, and Coptic Christians in Egypt.

Religion supposedly became marginalized in the private sphere. This is the concept that has been advanced by many of the contemporary sociologists of religion, and is tied to secularization theories. Robertson is critical of this view, because modernity is rife with battles between religion and state power, as well as religious movements fostering collective activity at global levels beyond the authority of the nation-state.

Turner (1994) suggested that such minority groups, which have been isolated, often remain frozen in traditional patterns, beliefs and rituals, avoiding the secularization and modernization experienced by the host community. Within Turner's framework, Islamic fundamentalism is seen as a reaction and resistance against cultural and social differentiation and fragmentation. More specifically fundamentalism is an attempt at dedifferentiation. For him, in order to understand the recent political and cultural history of Islamic societies, two related arguments must be considered:

> The first argument attempts to recognize the profound problems of having, within a world cultural system, competing world religions which claim exclusive and largely absolutist truths or values ... The second argument is concerned with the problem of the relationship between the cultural, aesthetic, and stylistic pluralism of postmodernity and the fundamentalist commitment to the coherent and unified world organized around values, styles and beliefs which are held to be incontrovertibly true. The problem

of meaningfulness arises from consumer culture or appears as a set of commodities for sale on a world cultural market.

(Turner, 1994: 77, 78)

Turner (1994: 78) suggests that:

> Against Weber and his followers, Islam was perfectly compatible with the modernization project involving, as it did, a high degree of secularization of traditional religious cultures, but Islam cannot deal satisfactorily with postmodernity which threatens to deconstruct religious messages in mere fairy tales to destroy the everyday world by the challenge of cultural diversity. The problem of cultural perspectivism is an effect of the pluralization of life-worlds brought about by the spread of a diversified, global system of consumption.

Therefore, fundamentalism is the cultural defence of modernity against postmodernity.

For Turner, fundamentalism might also be treated as forms of collective nostalgia that seek to restructure the world in terms of more simple entities and communal cultural relations. In political terms, fundamentalism has attempted to create a set of boundaries that will contain political pluralism and the abstract generalization of the citizen on a global scale, but in terms of some notion of community or household. In the cultural arena, fundamentalism is an attempt to impose certain boundaries on modernization, and more particularly on postmodernism and postmodernity. It has also attempted to reverse the historical process towards a hypersecular consumerism and pluralism by providing, paradoxically, a traditional defence of modernity (Turner, 1994: 84).

Wallerstein has seen cultural resistance as an eternal theme. Wallerstein argues that popular culture has long been relatively stable. Popular culture has asserted its values and forms against elite cultures. Wallerstein believes that the only differences between cultural resistance today and in the past refer to the level of organization system. For him, 'Cultural resistance today is very often organized resistance – not spontaneous resistance or eternal resistance, but planned resistance' (Wallerstein1991b: 100).

Wallerstein has also suggested that cultural resistance is like planning political resistance: its efficacy is also its fatal flaw. He noticed that cultural resistance is part and parcel of political resistance. He emphasized that when an antisystemic movement organizes to depose or replace existing authorities in a state, it provides itself with a very strong political weapon designed to change the world in specific ways. For Wallerstein, the same thing is considered to be true of cultural resistance. If they deliberately assert (or reassert) particular cultural values that have been neglected or disparaged in order to protest against the imposition of the cultural values of the strong upon the weaker, they are strengthening the weaker in their political struggles, within a given state, within the world-system as a whole.

Considering the Wallersteinean approach, *religious resistance* today may be defined as planned resistance, which is a patchwork of politics, culture and within cultural resistance, religious fundamentalism or traditionalism. However, it seems to me that Wallerstein avoids discussing issues of social demonstration of religion as a very serious resistance phenomenon. This may refer to his socialist advocacy and also to his universal humanistic theory – the world has been moving towards a world consciousness, a consciousness of a universal persona beyond even that of the so-called world religions. He discusses the social values, but he does not mention where these values originated nor how these social values were constructed.

For Castells (1997: 65), religious fundamentalism, cultural nationalism, territorial communes, which are aspects of resistance identity, are, by and large, defensive reactions. For him three fundamental threats, perceived in all societies, by the majority of humankind, at the end of second millennium have generated a defensive reaction. The first threat is globalization, which dissolves the autonomy of institutions, organizations and communication systems where people live. The second reaction is against networking and flexibility, which blur the boundaries of membership and involvement, individualize social relationships of production and induce the structural instability of work, space and time. The third reaction is against the crisis of the patriarchal family, at the roots of the transformation of mechanisms of security-building, socialization, sexuality and, therefore, of personality systems.

The logic behind these reactions is that:

> When the world becomes too large to be controlled, social actors aim at shrinking it back to their size and reach. When networks dissolve time and space, people anchor themselves in places, and recall their historic memory. When the patriarchal sustainment of personality breaks down, people affirm the transcendent value of family and community, as God's will.
>
> (Castells, 1997: 66)

For Castells (1997: 66), the defensive reactions or resistance identity can form and become sources of meaning and identity by constructing new cultural codes out of historical materials. The reason is, in information flows, the building of autonomy has to rely on reverse information flows.

God, nation, family and community will provide unbreakable, eternal codes, around which a counter-offensive will be mounted against the culture of real virtuality. Eternal truth cannot be virtualized. It is embodied in us. Thus, against the informationalization of culture, bodies are informationalized, i.e. individuals bear their Gods in their heart. They do not reason, they believe. They cannot be dissolved, lost in the whirlwind of information flows and cross-organizational networks.

Castells (1997: 19) stated that: 'The construction of contemporary Islamic identity proceeds as a reaction against unreachable modernization (be it capitalist or socialist), the evil consequences of globalization, and the collapse of the postcolonial nationalist project.'

Falk (1999) sees religion as the most vibrant source of resistance to reductive views of human nature, especially those associated with materialism. For him, religion is the centre for a spiritual view of human nature and of the meaning of life. From this perspective, in response to the dominant motifs of globalization, either religion will disappear owing to the challenge or it will re-emerge as a force for renewal that offers resistance to globalization and provides an alternative reading of reality.

Ahmed and Donnan (1994: 6) point to Bosnia as an example, which has created a sharp awareness of Muslims as a world community, both in the West and among Muslims, themselves. Bosnia has become a rallying point for Muslims throughout the Muslim world, much in the manner of the Palestinians. The case of Bosnia is even used in Khutbas (sermons) in a closed society like Saudi Arabia to attack the monarchy for not doing enough.

It seems to me that religion is not necessarily between two extremes, either disappearance or domination. Religious identity will be fragmented into several types of social and individual identity, that includes also resistance and secular identity.

ii. Universalization of Islam

Islam and Muslim identity can be viewed as one of the global forces. Since the beginning of Islam, one of the most important missions of the Prophet of Islam was *the universalization of Islam*. The call to Islam – *Da'wah* – was considered a central part of the responsibility of every Muslim, and the importance that this idea has had for Muslims throughout their history has been reflected in the spread of Islam all round the world. Muhammad has established a new local polity, founded on his prophetic vision. However, almost immediately, that polity had taken on far-reaching international dimensions. Very soon Islam was contesting power within Arabia not only with the Quraysh but also with both the Byzantine and the Sasanian empires

(Hodgson, 1974, vol. 1: 187). Islam became within almost a century (622–732 AD) a dominant religion over the whole of the Arab Middle East, along the shores of North Africa, across the Sahara in northern West Africa, through much of the East Africa down to Kenya, through Iran, Afghanistan, and what is now Soviet Central Asia. It continued to make substantial gains in North and North-east India, in Malaysia and Indonesia, in Turkey and a part of the Balkans. It advanced into Europe and became established in Spain and Portugal (Ezzati, 1978; Lapidus, 1988; Razwy, 1997 and Smart, 1998).

Within decades history witnessed a significant transformation of all those cultures that came into contact with Islam including Arabs, Turks, Asian, African and even Andalusian. Each of these societies had their own specific beliefs, cultures and ways of life, which combined with *Qu'ranic education* as the main resource for the formation of Muslim identity.

In the premodern period, world religious systems had little opportunity to realize themselves globally, because the systems of communication and transport were wholly underdeveloped or non-existent. Prior to the emergence of modern communication systems, the world religions have operated on a largely localized basis with tenuous linkages to their cultural centres and articulated at a global level by an underdeveloped and fragile system of trading relationships (Mann, 1986).

In the modern period, the opportunity to achieve global religious systems has been facilitated by the emergence of modern forms of transport, communication and integration. In the era of globalization, the globalization of Islam and other religions has also been facilitated by the development of technology of global communication systems, launching several global satellites and advancing the global network society through the internet communication system, which makes possible for the first time a globalization of Islam – this in fact is the Islamization of cultures through the norms and practices of Islamic movements. While Islam had always claimed a universalistic status, it has, prior to the emergence of contemporary global communication systems, actually been unable to impose this type of uniformity and universalism.

To understand the globalization of Islam through Islamic movements, Weber's theory of rationalization has provided a basis in sociological theory for an analysis of contemporary movements in cultures, which are either Islamist or traditionalist, and which attempt to restore moral coherence as the basis of modern religious and social practices. On the one hand, Weber has recognized a profound process of rationalization and modernization in society leading to the differentiation of religious, scientific and moral realms, and a profound secularization of values. On the other hand, Weber has recognized, following Nietzsche, that the project of reason always discovers its own unreasonableness by exposing the arbitrary character of all forms of rationalization. While rationality may select appropriate means for action, it cannot provide a rational ground for ends (Turner, 1994: 84).

For Turner (1994: 77) there have been two separate but related processes in modern Islamic culture. 'The first is the emergence of a global Islamic political system and the second is the cultural reaction of Islamic fundamentalism against Westernism and consumerism'. In this framework, Islamic fundamentalism is seen as a reaction against cultural and social differentiation and fragmentation. More specifically fundamentalism is an attempt at dedifferentiation. In theological terms, Islam has been based on an idealistic construction of the *umma* (community), which Islam has never completely institutionalized. The idealistic concept has involved an integration of politicoreligious authority, a terrain or household in which Islamic practice is uniformly followed, and an outward religious thrust or *jihad* involving a struggle against unbelief. However, it is important to avoid a sociological orientation, which considers Islam in isolation from other world religions, because all the major religions are necessarily involved in global processes.

In the premodern period, the world religious systems had little opportunity to become global, because the systems of communication and transport were wholly underdeveloped or non-existent. In the modern period, the possibility of achieving global religious systems has been facilitated by the emergence of modern forms of transport, communication and integration (Turner, 1994: 83). Turner also emphasizes the point that:

> The availability in modern times of effective global communication systems makes possible, for the first time, a globalization of Islam, which in fact is the Islamization of cultures, through the norms and practices of Islamic fundamentalism ...The paradox of modern systems of communication is that it makes Islam simultaneously exposed to Western consumerism and, at the same time, provides the mechanism for the distribution of a global Islamic message.
>
> (Turner, 1994: 86)

2.2. The Process of Heterogenization

Many sociologists such as Beyer (1990, 1994, 1998), Robertson (1985, 1987, 1991), Turner (1994) and Featherstone (1995) have discussed the heterogeneity of identities as well as the impact of globalization on religious values, religious organizations and, very rarely, religious identities. These viewpoints have been revealed in four interconnected theories, which will be discussed in the following sections.

2.2.1. The Transformationalists – Global Force and Fragility of Identities

The transformation theory has suggested that a new force, which we have called the *third force* – or *global force* – has been added to the forces involved in the construction of religious identity – *local force* and *force of history*. Returning to globalization and its effect on religious identities, especially that of Muslim identity, one must admit that according to the transformationalists, the process of globalization has created a slippery surface for those actively and dynamically intent on conforming to and having a religious identity.

Giddens(1991: 32) said that 'Transformations in self-identity and globalization are the two poises of the dialectic of the local and the global in conditions of high modernity.' Giddens(1998: 33) in his recent theories in the arena of politics – the 'third way' – has suggested that: 'Globalization is changing every day life, particularly in the developed countries, at the same time as it is creating new *transnational systems* and *forces*. It is more than just the backdrop to contemporary policies: taken as a whole, globalization is transforming the institutions of the societies in which we live.'

According to the global conditions, one of the central theses that Beyer (1994: 3) defends is that the *global system* corrodes inherited or constructed cultural and personal identities; yet it also encourages the creation and revitalization of particular identities as a way of gaining control over systemic power. It is in the context of this last feature that religion plays one of its significant roles in the development, elaboration and problematization of the global system.

Kellner (1995) has postulated the dangers of globalization in relation to identity. Kellner (1995: 233) has argued that as the pace, extension and complexity of modern societies accelerate, identity becomes more and more unstable, and more and more fragile. Within this situation, the discourses of postmodernity problematize the very notion of identity, claiming that it is a myth and an illusion. Postmodernists have claimed that fragmentation of religious identities implode into masses. Baudrillard (1983) suggests that a fragmented, disjointed and discontinuous mode of experience is a fundamental characteristic of postmodern culture, of both its subjective experiences and texts. Many of the postmodern theorizers have considered media culture as a site of the implosion of identity and fragmentation of the society, yet there have been few in-depth studies of media texts and their effect from this perspective (Kellner, 1995: 234).

2.2.2. The Relativists – End of Fixity and Certainty

One can also argue that in the globalization age, ethical and religious values have lost their absoluteness and have been turned into relative concepts. This in turn has led to the adaptation of pluralistic attitude(s) towards religion as well as the generation of extreme conflicts between religion and other by-products of cultural globalization.

Robertson (1991, 1992b) as one of the leading contributors to a growing sociological discussion of globalization and religion has explained religious identity from the relativist point of view. Featherstone (1990, 1995), Beyer (1994) and Eade (1997) have also made important contributions in this regard.

Robertson (1992) in his representation of 'the model: the global field', has emphasized a number of processes of relativization. Relativization is meant to indicate the ways in which, as globalization proceeds, challenges are increasingly presented to the stability of particular perspectives on, and collective and individual participation in, the overall process of globalization. As Robertson highlights, this picture of the global field indicates overall processes of differentiation of the main spheres of globality, which have increased over time. He points out that: 'Thus differentiation between the spheres was much lower in earlier phases of globalization; while the effects of such differentiation have been encountered unevenly and with different responses in different parts of the world (Robertson, 1991: 29).' For him, an important aspect of the process of differentiation is depended on the ways in which school, college and/or 'multicultural' lines have been interacted.

Robertson's most pervasive theme clusters around issues of identity-formation or reformation. This is the process by which, because of the compression of the world into such a small place, many groups and individuals are forced to interact at new levels of intensity. Hence they reformulate their identity with respect to one another. This involves the alteration, retrenchment or invention of new social identities and transformation of symbolic boundaries.

Robertson (1992b) explains reformation of identity in relation to the dialogical process between local and global – universal and particular. The most important aspect of Robertson's work on globalization relates to dichotomies of universalism-particularism, or globlism-localism. These tensions have become part of the global-human condition, and have constituted a global-cultural form, a major axis of the construction of the world as a whole (King 1991). Robertson does not see them as states of being, but as a process. Actors negotiate and reformulate their identity as part of the process of managing the tensions between the universal and the particular. In this dialectical tension, universal processes impact particular identities such as Muslim identity, and particular identities promote universalization. Robertson (1992b) has named this process: 'the universalism of particularism' and 'the particularization of universalism.' In the first case, particularistic identities (national, ethnic, religious, etc.) are reinforced by universalizing processes which relativize any one given identity. The second process involves giving sociopolitical concreteness to universal symbols, processes, or meanings.

Featherstone (1990: 8) points out that the closeness and proximity of cultures and religious thinking have made the process of decision-making more difficult. Intercultural communication is one of the globalization phenomena that makes people more and more involved with a variety of cultures, which alter the *fixed culture* to the *relative culture* – an absolutism to a relativism.

On the other hand, Featherstone (1995: 72–85) has looked at relativism from the postmodern perspective. He suggests that consumer culture and postmodernism are both taken as signs for dramatic changes that are altering the nature of the social fabric as a result of a double relativization – of both tradition, and the tradition of the new (modernism). The latter results in a questioning of all modes of fundamental values – a transvaluation of values has not only moved humankind beyond the possibility of constructing a moral consensus and the good society, but has also caused some to see the only solution as being the rejection of all forms of subjective identity construction in favour of immersion in the various sensual flows of the body without organs (Featherstone, 1995: 86).

Beyer (1994: 4) has explained the relativist point of view from a different perspective: the 'Rushdie affair exemplifies the point that globalization brings with it the relativization of particularistic identities along with the relativization and marginalization of religion as a mode of social commun-ication.' On the other hand, Beyer has pointed out that globalization has also created a situation in which the revitalization of religion is a way of asserting a particular identity, which in turn has been a prime method of competing for power and influence in the global system. But this is to a large extent according to the fact that religion has an affinity for particularistic identities and because it, like so many groups in our world, has become somewhat marginalized as a consequence of globalization.

Eade (1997b: 2) indicated that: 'The multiplication of social and cultural worlds encourages an increase in individualism and the relativization of Identity'. Eade has suggested that multiculturalization of the world has been erected by the global mass communication network. Multiculturalization has encouraged and increased the processes of the relativization of identity. Plurality within the domain of culture, religious thinking and beliefs has been a further by-product of relativism that globalization has generated. This mode of thinking totally rejects absoluteness of any values and questions the monopoly of truth being in any one particular kind of thinking.

2.2.3. Reproductionalists: Reformation of Religious Identity

The reproductionalists, while agreeing with the relativists on few matters, nevertheless also foresee the *reformation* of religious identities under the auspices of globalization of culture – American culture or Western consumerism in general. Beyer (1990, 1994. 1998), Featherstone (1990, 1995) and Cvetkoich & Kellner (1998) are four sociologists who have discussed the process of religious reproduction in response to the impact of globalization.

Beyer has emphasized that in the reproductional process of globalization, religion will lose some of its powers and social influences but it will remain as the main plank in the identity structure. Beyer (1990: 373–5) has written a book and several articles in relation to globalization and religion. He started with the discussion on Luhmann's views on the process of secularization. For him globalization has two paradoxical and simultaneous functions. First, globalization has articulated the process of secularization. Beyer has clearly suggested that: 'We cannot separate the secularization of modern society from its globalization' (Beyer, 1990: 380). Secondly, globalization has also provided fertile ground for the renewed public influence of religion. By public influence, he means that: 'One or more religions can become the source of collective obligation, such that deviation from specific religious norms will bring in its wake negative consequences for adherents and non-adherents alike; and collective action in the name of these norms becomes legitimate' (Beyer, 1990: 373). Beyer points out that the public influence of religion in the age of globalization breaks into three interconnected arguments:

1. If religion is to be influential publicly, it is not enough for there to be a high level of individual religiosity or a religious organization, leaders and professionals; although this could be considered as a prerequisite for religion as such. For religion to possess public influence and significance, it is necessary that religious leaders have control over a service, which is seen as indispensable in today's world as do, for instance, health professionals, political leaders, scientific or business experts.

2. The process of globalization of society has significantly altered the ways that religion can attain such public influence. In a global society, no one considered as an 'outsider' can serve as the social representative of any institutional force, religion included. The official representatives of religion need, therefore, to be regarded as 'within' global society if they are to regain widespread influence.

3. Therefore Beyer believes that the public face of religion will have a very difficult time in gaining public influence at the level of global society as a whole. But, he argues that, if religious leaders apply traditional religious modalities for the purpose of mobilizing subsocietal, political responses to the globalization of society, such an influence at the global level will be easier to attain.

Beyer (1994: 67) in response to the question of 'How does religion fit into the global picture?' has suggested that, historically, there was a close relation between 'group culture' and 'religion.' He got the idea from Wilson (1976) when he claimed that the basic function, operation and existence of religion is located in the 'community.' From this perspective, religion has been a mode of relating to the world that thrives in traditional, especially segmented, societies, and not in modern, instrumentally-dominated society. Therefore, since the previous cultures expressing those communitarian structures of the past have changed, so religion is subject to significant change. Beyer argues that, although there is a close relationship between group culture and religion, religion is and has been more than ecology of themes for social communication. It is also a specific way of communicating: religion is not just cultural, it is also potentially political, economical, artistic and involved with many other ways of communication.

Beyer points out that: 'Specifically, under modern, global conditions, to the degree that a religious tradition is seen as part and parcel of a particular group culture, to that degree religion will bear a relation to exclusive identities and the different types of social system similar to that borne by group cultures' (Beyer 1994: 67).

In his latest article, Beyer has differentiated between an 'instrumental system', and 'cultural model' to identify both the basic structures of global society and how the various polarities, such as religions, nations, cultures and, in a less clear sense, worldviews and genders, while appearing as oppositions, are actually better seen as mutually conditioning ways of constructing difference and identity in global society (Beyer, 1998: 79–94). As examples, Beyer discusses the concept of nation and religion. For him the examples of the relation of nations/states and religions/religion could illustrate what one might call the dialogical nature of globalization. From this perspective, the globalization of Islam could be discussed: 'What may form certain perspectives appear as resistance to, or the opposite of, globalization is actually seen as an integral aspect of the development' (Beyer, 1998: 91).

Featherstone suggests that culture has reformed and 'recentred.' He (1995) highlights the current sense of cultural fragmentation and dislocation. He questions the assumption that culture has become decentred, that there is an absence of coherence and unity; that culture can no longer provide an adequate account of the world with which to construct or order our lives. He argues that culture has gained a more significant role within social life and that today everything is cultural.

For Featherstone, culture is now beyond the social and has become released from its traditional determinisms in economic life, social class, gender, ethnicity and religion. In terms of his reference to the decentring of culture, this could be taken to be a counter-argument: in effect culture has not been decentred, rather, it has become recentred. Featherstone brought in an example to show how culture has recentred and has been moved from the periphery of the social science field towards the centre. His book *Consumer Culture and Postmodernism* (Featherstone, 1991) was reviewed by the *British Journal of Industrial Relations* in the early 1990s. For a book on culture and theory to be reviewed by an industrial relations journal would hardly have seemed possible in the 1970s.

Cvetkoich & Kellner (1998: 10) also see globalization as a process of reconstruction of identity in terms of relationships between local traditions and global forces. The confluence of global culture with local and national cultural is appraised quite differently. For some, a global media culture provides new sources for pleasures and identities that redefine gender, new role models and fantasies, and new cultural experiences. The global media culture has also led to the fragmentation of old identities and subjectivities, and constructions of new identities out of the multifarious and sometimes conflicting configurations of traditional, local, national, and now global, forces of the present time. From this perspective, the intersection of the global and the local is producing new matrixes to legitimize the production of hybrid identities, thus expanding the realm of self-definition. Thus, although global forces can be oppressive and erode cultural traditions and identities, they also provide new material to rework one's identity and can empower people to revolt against traditional forms and styles to create new, more emancipatory ones.

In this chapter we have discussed the paradoxical impact of globalization as a process of homogenization and heterogenization in relation to the construction and deconstruction of religious identity. According to the framework of this research, homogenization and heterogenization are the result of communication and tension between local and global forces as well as force of history. In the next chapter I shall focus more on periodization of history of the Muslim societies in order to understand important changes in terms of Muslim identity formation.

THREE

Historical Analysis of Muslim Identity

In the previous discussion we have discussed theoretical aspects of globalization and religious identity. Here we will offer an overview of the construction of Muslim identity throughout the history of Islam. Different aspects of Muslim identity in relation to the social structure within traditional and modern society will set the scene for an exploration of Muslim identity in the era of globalization.

Religious identity is the by-product of the multiple interactions between religion, society and the individual. It is through these interactions that the fundamental principles of any religious ethos become manifest in different forms of action.

Religious identity can be seen to comprise two basic dimensions: on the one hand an 'inward orientation' or 'subjective assimilation' of a sense of identity; and on the other hand an 'outward expression' or 'objective manifestation' of that sense of identity. As regards the outward expression of identity, this can be gauged in relation to the symbols, forms and indicators of identity that are fused together; it is most often the case that individuals use these indicators to measure the strength of their religious identity. The subjective and the objective dimensions intersect at this point and from this intersection the social analyst is able to evaluate the social manifestation of identity, at the same time as make an effort at exploring the inner dynamics of individual identity.

Religious identity, then, is the output of the interaction between overt social structures and the latent understanding of the religion. In respect of our case-study, the meaning, nature and impact of both 'social structures' and 'understanding of religion' have drastically changed in recent times. Without a clear understanding of what these factors meant in the past, one cannot understand the impact of the transformation wrought by globalization on Muslim identity in the present. History – and also current interpretations of history – enter crucially into any analysis of contemporary Muslim identity. Therefore, if Muslim identity should be evaluated according to the determinative factors involved in the construction of 'identity', and if these factors have themselves been subject to radical transformation in historical terms, it then becomes necessary for the analyst to present a historical overview of these factors. Turning first to address the sociological dimension of identity, we might posit two major turning-points in human society: from Traditional Society to Modern Society; and then from Modern to Postmodern Society – the 'Globalization Era'.

Within these three social structures, it might be said that Muslims have experienced six distinct periods. The major factors that have entailed a shift from one period to the other were mainly related to the changes in the understanding of religion, economic affiliation or structure, as well as political and social factors. In the following section we will discuss first the difficulties of periodization of the history of Islam in general. Then each of the social structures and the relevant periods that have impacted Muslim identity in the Muslim world will be elaborated.

What we are about to present is not intended to be an exhaustive periodization of Islamic history; rather, we wish to provide a general overview of this history from a purely sociological and, in certain respects, a psychological vantage point. This is because our principal purpose is to focus on this history insofar as it is relevant to the analysis of Muslim identity.

It is a very complicated task to attempt to formulate a general *periodization* of the history of Islam in terms of the formative and determinative elements of Muslim identity that encompass the entire Muslim world. Two main factors making for this complication present themselves immediately. Firstly, Islam has developed in many places and thus a whole host of diverse indigenous cultural, political and economic forces, not to mention geographical and racial factors, have been involved in the construction of the social and individual identity of Muslims. Therefore Muslims identify themselves in widely different ways, with divergent accentuations on different elements, such that there is not necessarily a unilateral or monolithic identity.

Secondly, Muslims have nearly always been divided into many sects, based on different perspectives on Islamic doctrines and practices, the essential elements of which were established by the Prophet of Islam, then developed by his companions, and which were thereafter elaborated in heterogeneous forms and dimensions by later generations of scholars; it is around these scholars that a multitude of groups with divergent perspectives crystallized.

Despite these differences, it is possible to identify a type of pattern or overarching schema within which the identity of Muslims throughout their history can be assessed. Accordingly, we may bring attention to bear upon the fundamental factors, both intrinsic and extrinsic, that have had a major role in the construction of Muslim identity. To do this, it is better to avoid any attempt at defining Muslim identity in narrow, exclusive or specific terms. In the introduction to this dissertation we made mention of the fundamental impetus for the original 'Muslim identity', that is the world view defined by the twin sources of the Islamic Revelation, the *Qur'an* and the *Sunnah* of the Prophet Muhammad. This constitutes the first period of our schema below. Following on from this period, which, alone, can be identified in terms of relative simplicity, we enter into the domain of greater complexity, the simple elements of this original identity entering into a more composite form of identity. Hence, we refer to a framework for assessing the capacity of the different 'forces' that have caused progressive transformations in the nature, forms and modalities of Muslim identity.

3.1. Muslim Identity in Traditional Society[1] (7th–17th Century AD)

In traditional societies, identity is not a new issue; rather it is something that is, practically speaking, taken for granted. Therein, man's existence and destiny are, to a large extent, stable and predictable. An individual's identity comes from an authoritative system of unquestioned 'guiding traditions', relatively unchanging rituals and perpetually renewed mythological beliefs. Man occupies a predetermined place in a symbolic system that not only is immediate, intimate and familiar, but also bestows ultimate meaning upon life, shedding light on the significance of all actions, showing the value of life both within the individual and in the cosmos around. An individual is born as a member of a certain family, clan and tribal system, belonging to a circle of social life that is confined within a clearly demarcated and stable social and cultural setting, and is largely unable – should it be so wished – to escape from one's allotted destiny, status or situation. In such societies, individuals are not able to transform their identity in a fundamental way and, therefore, it is meaningless to speak of the notion of identity crisis in such societies. In such a society 'an

---

1. We distinguish traditional society from modern society according to the periodization of Hodgson (1974, vol. I: 110); he differentiates between the 'Agrarian Age' and the 'Technical Age'. For him the 'Agrarian society' is a 'period when agrarianate society was historically dominant, within the range of the Oikoumene the "Agrarian Age" (lasting from the time of Sumer down to the seventeenth and eighteenth centuries), in contrast to the Modern "Technical Age' since the eighteenth century.' From his perspective, agrarianate society or culture refers not only to the agrarian sector and the agrarian institutions, but to the degree of cultural complexity by which agrarian relations were characterized (Hodgson, 1974, vol. I: 107). What Hodgson explores is the dynamics of traditional society, which was obviously not completely devoid of change, but in which the rate of change, in comparison with that which is taking place in a globalizing world, was of a radically different order.

individual is either a hunter or a member of the tribe, that is all' (Kellner, 1995: 141).

From a sociological point of view, the identity of man in a traditional society is easily discerned since it is based on past history (Giddens, 1990). It is the 'past' that rules over the present and it is through the logical and comprehensible continuation of the 'past' that the 'present' and the 'future' come into being. In fact, the concept of identity takes shape independently of conscious choice – individual or collective.

In traditional societies, because of limited social intercourse, exclusively internal cultural relations, the absence of advanced means of transportation and the lack of technologically sophisticated media of communication, any change in social or religious identity would take place very slowly, if not imperceptibly, and with extremely limited effect. As a result, society was inherently conservative, undergoing change very gradually, if at all. Owing to the slowness in the effects of change on a traditional society, national and religious traditions and the social norms and mores did not fundamentally alter over long periods of time. Social stratification, cultural roles, psychological motives, rewards and incentives remained consistent.

The most important of the numerous roots and factors involved in this subject is that of society's tight restrictions in the social relationships and the 'limitations in the mind's ability to conceptualize.' Social relationships in societies were restricted to the association of individuals within the boundaries of the village and/or one's own city. However, by paying attention to the lack of means to create social communications and lack of mechanical modes of transport, the possibility for social contact is the place of worship, home and locations, such as the bazaar. The slowness of the changes within traditional society has created an appearance of permanence with regard to religious identity, whereupon this identity was passed from one generation to another with hardly any change taking place between each generation. A very strong and powerful religious norm was in control of all the religious activities that took place within a society. Any attempt to change within the domain of religious thinking or action would have faced strong social resistance.

Based on the above factors, one could safely assume that 'integration', 'continuity' and 'solidity' were part of the religious characteristic of a traditional society. According to this framework, five periods can be distinguished in traditional society:

3.1.1. The Prophetic Period (613–632)

If we were to search for the beginning' of the formation of 'Muslim identity', we would have to look for it at the inception of Islam in Mecca in the early seventh century.

The foundation of Islamic belief and practice is the *Qur'an* and teachings of the Prophet Muhammad (Esposito, 1994). At the beginning (Figure 3.1), Muslim identity was built on Muhammad's personality – his traditional (*Sunnah*) career and the revelation of the *Qur'an* (Hodgson, 1974, vol. 1). There arose the great edifice of a new faith, which in turn helped to define a new civilization (Smart, 1998: 285–306).

Figure 3.1: Resources of Muslim Identity in the 'Age of Globalization'

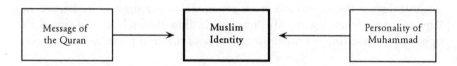

Muslims rejected Arab associationism (i.e. setting up deities to share the power with God), destroyed the idols of the *Kabah* and dedicated the *Kabah* to the One and only God. Therefore, since the dawn of Islam, the 'other' has played an instrumental role in the formation of Muslim identity, both in theological and in communitarian terms. What must be stressed, however, is that in both respects Islamic identity was constructed on the basis of a veritable triumph over the 'other'. That is, there was no hint of doubt amongst the first Muslims that their theological conceptions, based on the *Qur'an*, were correct and that the ideology that they were confronted by and which they overcame, was in error. Likewise, the community of Muslims, led by the Prophet, triumphed in outward, tangible form over those who opposed the religion.

Another important point to take into account is the way in which the tribalism of the pre-Islamic era was overcome by what might be called 'the social ethics of monotheism': that is to say, just as on the plane of theology the concept of one God replaced that of competing deities, so on the plane of

---

1. The first Muslim year began on July 16, 622 AD, when the founder of the Muslim community, Muhammad, emigrated from his native town of Mecca to the nearby *Yathrib* (later to be known as *Medina*). But the first revelation started in 610 AD (Ahmed, 1988).

society, fidelity to the unified *umma* replaced competing allegiances to multiple tribes. The specifics of tribal identity gave way, in principle at least, if not always in practice, to the universality of the community of believers.

Muslims in this nascent phase of Islam, then, were motivated by a sense of identity that was based not just on an uncompromising opposition to idolatry, a rejection of Arabian hedonism as a celebration of vanity and purposelessness, but also on a quasi-unconditional victory over the social groups and the ideological forces that articulated the pre-existing identity.

Finally, one cannot overlook the importance of the model of resistance that preceded the victorious affirmation of the new identity, i.e. at the onset of his mission, when the Prophet began to oppose the old cults, most of his tribe and community in Mecca naturally ridiculed and opposed him (Hodgson, 1974, vol.1: 167). For some thirteen years, then, the small, embattled group of Muslims around the Prophet held on heroically to their faith in the face of bitter persecution; this aspect of the original 'Muslim' identity must not be forgotten, given the importance it has as a model or paradigm of 'resistance' in later centuries when, again, Muslims would find themselves confronted by opponents possessing overwhelmingly superior material power and resources.

3.1.2. Period of the 'Rightly-Guided' Caliphate (632–661)

The period of the first Caliphs who are known as the orthodox (al-Rashidun) began with the election of Abu Bakr, the first Caliph, in 632, and comes to an end with the assassination of Ali, the Prophet's son-in-law and fourth successor, in 661 (Nicholson, 1930: 181).

Historians are agreed, in large part, that the rule of the third Caliph, Uthman, saw the return of a form of 'tribalism', not in principle and explicitly, but in practice, and still functioning in the name of the supratribal ethic of the *umma*. This modified form of tribalism emerged on the basis of a key administrative and financial principle established by the second Caliph, Umar. It was under his rule that the key distinction was made between those Arab Muslims who entered Islam before the conquest of Mecca and those who only entered after the conquest. This distinction was then the basis on which the new waves of converts to Islam were given a second-class status, as 'clients' or Mawali (Lapidus, 1988: 63–4; see also Grunebaum, 1970).

Figure 3.2: Major Resources of Muslim Identity During the Caliphate

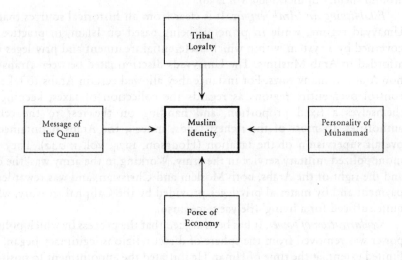

In this way, tribal loyalty and economic factors came together again to forge a new form of tribalism even within the Islamic context. This new form of tribalism could not, however, dislodge or supersede the principle of Umar; it was forced to operate on a *de facto*, not a *de jure* basis, and the principle of the universal brotherhood of believers was always in the background, actualized in the consciousness of Muslims to different degrees: witness the return to the 'ethics of monotheism', as we termed it above, effected by the Caliph Umar II.

3.1.3. The Umayyad Caliphate (661–750)

The Umayyad state has been considered a turning-point in Muslim political history. At the time of the Umayyad Caliphates, three important factors came into play which significantly affected Muslim societies throughout the territories of the newly established empire, and which should be considered as important forces in the evolving articulation of Muslim identity (Figure 3.3).

Revitalization of the old tribal aristocracy. The aristocracy that had prevailed in the pre-Islamic tribal order was revitalized at the time of Uthman (644–656). But, 'in the Umayyad state, this mundane aristocracy won the upper hand' (Spuler, 1969: 35). Spuler pointed out that: 'The nobility in Madinah, who had lost almost all political influence when the seat of government was removed to Damascus, began to lead an elegant epicurean life, graced with poets and singing-girls, which gave great offence to the sincerely religious groups dwelling around them.' (Spuler, 1969, vol.1: 38).

Establishing an 'Arab' empire. It is clear from all historical sources that the Umayyad regime, while in principle being based on Islam, in practice was governed by a system within which preferential treatment and privileges were afforded to Arab Muslims. The Umayyads discriminated between Arabs and non-Arabs in many ways. For instance they allowed certain Arabs to take full control over entire regions as regards the collection of taxes, keeping for themselves a fixed proportion, and handing on the rest to the central authorities. In most of the richest lands, indeed, the Arabs maintained an overall supervision of the taxation (Hodgson, 1974, vol. 1: 242). They also monopolized military service in the army. Working in the army was 'the duty and the right of the Arabs, both Moslem and Christian, and was rewarded by payment and by material privileges provided by the Caliphal treasury, which quite sufficed for a living' (Belyaev, 1969: 159).

Secularization of power. It has been argued that the process by which political power was removed from the sphere of direct religious legitimacy began, to a limited extent, at the time of Umar. He initiated the appointment to positions of power and authority of former slaves who had been freed on account of their embracing of Islam, the term referring to them being the *Uttaqa* (Jafarian, 1994). The Uttaqa were not on the whole considered as real believers within the community of the faith. When some of the Companions of Muhammad complained about Umar's appointments, Umar responded that the companions of Muhammad were very holy and spiritual men, but they were not capable of being politicians. This indicated that either politics should be segregated from religion, or that politics should be managed by politicians, no matter whether they were practising Muslims or not. It was Mu'awiya, however, the founder of the Umayyad dynasty, who more fully and explicitly attempted to separate politics from religion. Religion was not his concern unless public opinion forced him to emphasize religious principles, as the historical sources indicate.

Figure 3.3: The Major Resources of Muslim Identity at the Time of the Umayyads

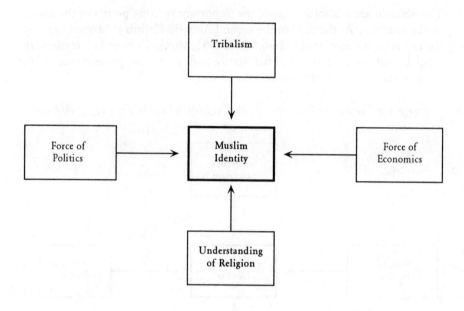

Shaban (1970) argues that Umayyad discrimination in favour of the Arabs and against the Mawali converts was the central factor responsible for the Abbasid Revolution. The rights of the dispossessed and those unfairly discriminated against was the moral basis on which Abbasid propaganda was erected; this moral and political rallying cry was complemented by the spiritual legitimacy they claimed as descendants of the Holy Prophet.

During the rule of the Umayyads, the role of economic and political factors assumed heightened importance amongst the Muslims to the point where it catalysed processes of segregation and fragmentation within Muslim society. The crucial change in this period was the crystallization of new types of Muslim tribalism, under the old tribal leadership. Religious teachings, which had formerly been based on the principles laid down by the Prophet and faithfully transmitted by his companions directly, were now being modified by different *understandings and interpretations of religion,* interpretations arrived at by individuals who had no direct contact with the Prophet. These modifications introduced features of new religious understanding that could relatively change Muslim identity.

3.1.4. The Abbasid Empire (661–1258)

The Abbasid age is another one of the important turning points of the history of the Muslims. At the time of the second Abbasid Caliph al-Mansur (754–75), the capital had transferred to Iraq, where al-Mansur built Baghdad, restored the Iraqi bureaucracy to its imperial status and gave new prominence to the Sasanian tradition of which it was the carrier.

Figure 3.4: The Major Resources of Muslim Identity at the Time of the Abbasids

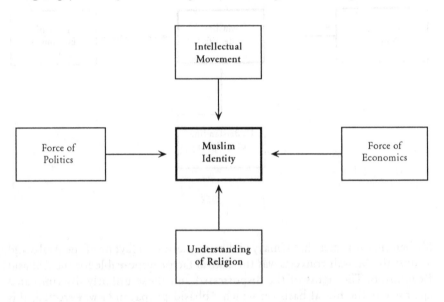

Hodgson (1974, vol.1: 280) has suggested that: 'From the viewpoint of the Piety-minded, the Abbasi regime represented at best a compromise with their pious ideals for Muslim society – and some aspects of Abbasid rule, notably its arbitrariness, presented extreme corruption of, or even a rude and alien intrusion into, the proper Islamic social order.' Spuler (1969: 48) argues that Abbasids focused on the 'Family of Prophet', who might be expected to carry out more thoroughly the Qu'ranic prescriptions on equal treatment for all Muslims.

Although the Abbasids continued the Umayyad administrative and governmental organization – they attempted to centralize political power in the hands of the Caliph and the ruling elite – under their rule several substantial changes occurred, which Shaban (1970, 1971) and Lapidus (1988) have rightly called 'the Abbasid Revolution'. These revolutionary factors have influentially changed aspects of Muslim identity:

Although the Abbasid dynasty was Arab, the Abbasids swept away Arab caste supremacy and accepted the universal equality of Muslims. No longer were there classifications such as Arab and non-Arab (Mawali). Lapidus argued that: 'Under the Abbasids the empire no longer belonged to the Arabs, though they had conquered its territories, but to all those peoples who would share in Islam and in the emerging networks of political, social, economic, and cultural loyalties which defined a new cosmopolitan Middle Eastern society' (Lapidus, 1988: 70–1). The Abbasids also abolished the military privileges of the Arabs and brought new forces into being, which though partly Arab in composition, were recruited and organized so that they would be loyal to the dynasty alone and not to tribal or caste interests. According to Shaban (1970: XV): 'Those who took part in this Revolution certainly had a more universal interpretation of Islam than the relatively limited Umayyad Arab view.' Therefore, Arab tribalism was gradually abrogated from the social and economic life of the Muslims.

The Abbasids established new administrative and bureaucratic systems. According to Lapidus (1988: 71): 'The openness of the Abbasid regime was particularly evident.' They involved Persians from Khurasan, who had begun to enter the central government under the late Umayyads. Nestorian Christians were powerfully represented, probably because they made up a large proportion of the population of Iraq. The minorities such as Jews were also active in tax and banking activities. At the time the government became more routine and three types of services or bureaux (*diwans*) developed. This system replaced the old tribal diwans principle. The first was the chancery, the *diwan al-rasa'il* – the records and correspondence office. The second was the bureaux for tax collection, such as the *diwan al-kharaj*. Thirdly, there were bureaux to pay the expenses of the Caliphs' armies, court and pensioners; the army bureau, *diwan al-jaysh*, was the most important of these (Lapidus, 1988: 72). The Caliphs also appointed *Qadis* or judges.

The first 'Intellectual Movement' for cultural and information exchange within the Muslim world and between it and Hellenistic cultures was established at the time of the Abbassid Caliphs. Lapidus (1988: 91–3) has pointed out that, in the reign of the Abbassid Caliphs, many scientific, political and cultural books were translated from the heritage of Persian literature and Greek into Arabic. At the time of the Caliph Hisham(724–743), the first translations of Persian political documents were made. Lapidus (1988: 93) suggested that: 'Through the movement of translations and fusion with Arabic, elements of Persian heritage became an integral part of Islamic civilization'. In relation to Hellenistic thought, theological questions first came to the attention of the Muslim elite. In the middle of the 9th century, the *Bayt al-Hikma* of Hunayn ibn Ishaq made an important contribution through the translation of the scientific works of Galen and the philosophic and metaphysical works of Aristotle and Plato. The translated works then created a forum for dialogue between Muslim and Christian scholars. For the first time in the history of Islam, theology and philosophy were established as Islamic disciplines. Consequently, two important schools of thought – Mutazilism and Asharism – were institutionalized. These two ways of thinking brought in different interpretations and understanding of the *Qur'an*, jurisprudence, ethics, theology and philosophy. This intellectual movement had a critical impact on Muslim identity in terms of the development of sectarian differentiation and religious identity.

Lapidus (1988: 121) has argued that: 'The proponents of Arabic and Persian identities fought for a century until Arabic triumphed as the primary language of the empire and Persian and Hellenistic literatures were absorbed into Arabic literary forms.' From Shaban's (1970: 168) point of view, the one important achievement of the Abbasid Revolution that did not suffer any diminution was the complete assimilation of all members of the Muslim community. This has gradually induced changes in the identity of Muslims and the formation of the rapid spread of Islam among the non-Arab subjects in the empire, especially in the east.

3.1.5. The Mongol, Ottoman, Safavid and Moghul Empires (1258–1922)

The establishment of the Mongol Empire ended the Caliphate political system and central government in the Muslim world (Nicholson, 1930). The Mongol Empire brought East Asia, the Middle East, and the East European steppes under their rule. Within a few decades the Mongols ruled all of Eurasia, from Central Europe to the Pacific. The Mongols dealt a devastating blow to Islamic civilization (Lapidus, 1988: 276). There was a range of new elements in the historical situation at this time. This was the first time that non-Muslim governors had dominated Muslims in such a pervasive and extensive manner.

Historians such as Hodgson (1974, vol. 2: 372), believe that the Mongol conquest brought in many cultural and economic developments, to the degree that the level of aesthetic and intellectual awareness may have risen in some of the Mediterranean Muslim lands. But in reality, Mongols destroyed the vestiges of the caliphal state and overwhelmed many Arab and Iranian cities and eliminated the Iranian cultural and intellectual heritage. The populations of many cities and towns in Iran were exterminated and depopulated by invading armies and by the influx of Turkish and Mongol nomads who drove the peasants from their land (Lapidus, 1988: 278).

Lapidus (1988: 279), argues that, eventually, 'Unlike the Arabs, who changed both the language and the religion of the region, the Mongols were absorbed by Islam and Persian culture. However, they brought a new phase of creativity to the culture.'

In respect of the essential elements that make an identifiably Muslim identity, the period immediately following the Mongol invasions of the central Muslim lands in the 13th century is extremely revealing. For, despite the near-destruction of so many of the key institutions of Muslim polity and society, Islamic identity not only persisted but, in fact, in conjunction with other factors, succeeded ultimately in assimilating within itself the Mongol overlords. Within a few generations, the Mongol rulers had themselves embraced Islam: Uljaytu the great grandson of Hulegu was one of the patrons of a flourishing Islamic culture, and the Timurids also contributed greatly to the arts, sciences, culture, philosophy, mysticism etc. of their times (Lapidus, 1988: 279). What this shows is the tenacity and deep-rooted nature of Islamic identity, which sustained itself despite overwhelming military and political defeat.

Hodgson explained that Mongols put Muslims in contact with the most distant and alien cultures such as China; and introduced new standards of politics, law and, above all, art. The Mongols presented a critical challenge to Islamic life even in areas where the Mongols never penetrated (Hodgson (1974, vol. 2). Therefore one can admit that Mongols had an important role in transnationalization of Muslim society.

Hodgson and others have drawn attention to the key elements responsible for maintaining the continuity of Islamic culture and identity in an environment characterized by weak or non-existent formal institutions. These key elements were Shari'ite legality complemented by Sufi spirituality, the formal, definitive Law, on the one hand, and the supraformal, interiorizing Spirit, on the other. It should also be noted that it was the Sufis who were the most successful missionaries for Islam, not just in the expansion of the religion throughout the world, but also in converting the Mongol rulers (Lewisohn, 1995). What this post-Mongol period reveals is that, in times of crisis and breakdown, the response of large sections of Muslim society is to withdraw inwards, to a mystical, spiritual concentration on the essential elements of the religion, whilst simultaneously maintaining the formal aspects of the religion, albeit only to the extent that alien rule implied; i.e. the nature of the political system, its values, functions and its leadership could not be determined by Islamic norms, but this did not prevent a basic minimal Muslim life from being led by the majority. It is important to note that it is from this time onwards that the great Sufi orders[1] became formalized, institutionalized and increasingly prevalent throughout the Muslim world.

Alongside the Mongol Empire, the Ottoman Empire was one of the largest and longest-lived dynasties the world has experienced (1280–1922). During the rule of the Ottomans, they stretched from Budapest to Yemen, from Baghdad to Algeria, and in 1529 Sulayman even came close to taking Vienna (Ahmed, 1988: 65; Lapidus, 1988: 306). One can consider that during the Ottoman Empire, there was a line of reforming administrators who attempted to revitalize the imperial structures. Some of the most famous of those reformers came from the Koprulu family. The first Koprulu to become grand vizier, the chief Ottoman administrator, was Mehmet Pasha, who assumed that position in 1656. The 18th century reforming viziers increasingly came to accept the idea that adoption of specific European techniques might aid the empire. Such an approach was reflected in the policies of grand viziers like Husayn Koprulu (1644–1702), Damad Ibrahim (1781–1730) and Mehmet Ragib in the mid-century (Voll, 1982: 40).

The Ottoman period will be discussed more in the next section – the Modernization era – which will elaborate the reform movement and secularization of society that emerged in Turkey and Egypt as a result of the process of *Tanzimat* or the reorganization period.

The third important change was the establishment of the Safavid Shia State in Iran. In 1501 Shah Ismail I came to power. The most important decision of the Shah was to declare that the official religion of the state would be *Twelver – ithna ashari –* Shi'ism, and to eliminate their own Sufi followers as well as the Sunni ulama (Lapidus, 1988: 302). This decision brought in extraordinary changes in terms of religious identity and in the relation between state and religion in Iran. Lapidus (1988: 302) pointed out that at the reign of Safavids, 'Iran was virtually unique among Muslim societies in the degree to which the state controlled the religious establishment and in the extent to which it absorbed all religious tendencies found within the Muslim spectrum.'

The Moghul Empire manifests a remarkable and long-lived synthesis between Islamic faith and Hindu civilizational norms; the clearest example of this synthesis being the Taj Mahal, at once an Islamic mausoleum and an unmistakeably Indic monument. Although there were many tensions between those Indian Muslims who looked to Persia and Arabia for their religious

---

1. See Arnold (1935), The Preaching of Islam, where he argues that the chief agents of Islamic preaching and conversion were the Sufis and the traders – often the traders were also Sufis, especially once the Sufi *tariqas* were formally established from the 12th century onwards. Arnold shows that the subcontinent of India, southeast Asia, and much of sub-Saharan Africa were converted to Islam through Sufi missionary activities.

guidance and those who wished to assimilate more deeply those aspects of Indian culture that did not contradict the essential tenets of the Islamic faith, there was nonetheless a sense, shared by both groups, of belonging to a wider community of believers. This community, the global *umma*, may not have had any direct political or administrative expression, but it did, in differing ways, to different groups and with different degrees of salience, have an impact on the identity of the Indian Muslims (Razwy, 1997). Whereas in Ottoman Turkey and Safavid Persia there was no equivalent tension as regards 'local' and 'external' forms of Islam – the religious culture in both these empires being far more homogenous – in all three sociopolitical entities there was a sense on the part, again, of different groups, of belonging to a wider community, an *umma* which was administratively, linguistically, politically and culturally diverse, but which was still a single entity.

3.2. Shift from Traditional to Modern Society

As Giddens (1990) suggested, the trend towards modernization did not occur all at once. It was a process that began with the industrial revolution and developed as communication systems and technology advanced. The division of social work on a grand scale and the invention of new machinery and the application first of manufacturing, especially textiles, iron, steel and transport (roads, canals, railways and sea) demanded a new rationality with a greater division of social work (Durkheim, 1964).

One view that Marx, Durkheim and Weber all shared was that traditional religion was becoming more and more marginal to the modern world and that secularization was an inevitable process. Of the three, probably only Weber would have suspected that a traditional religious system like Islam could undergo a major revival, and become the basis of important political development in the late 20th century. Yet this is exactly what occurred in the 1980s in Iran (Giddens, 1989: 470–1).

Alongside the rise of modernization in the west, Muslim civilization from culminated points started to turn downwards. After the appearance of the industrial revolution in the 18th century with manufacture as its core (Giddens, 1989: 51), Western society began to be transformed in terms of social relations and production from a relatively single agrarian formation to a much more complex one. Scientific and technological superiority enabled Europe to establish its hegemony upon the modern world. A by-product of colonization was the introduction of modern industrial organization to the Muslim world.

3.2.1. *Western Empire: Process of Modernization*

The process by which the West gradually established its power over most of the Muslim world was complex and multifaceted. The detrimental impact on the identity of Muslims worldwide can hardly be overestimated. For the first time in its history there was no political expression of the *umma* in the form of a caliphate; the Muslim world was defeated not only militarily, politically and territorially but even in terms of morale. A loss of self-confidence set in, the consequences of which we see still today.

As regards the actual wars of conquest, economic and then political imperialism, and finally the ideological onslaughts that wreaked havoc within the Muslim world both materially and psychologically, the key point to make is that, unlike the Mongol destruction, which was relatively short-lived and could not dislodge basic Islamic cultural and religious norms, this victory by the West was to last for several generations and was to trigger shock waves that distorted self-identity in myriad ways. The ideological consequences of the emphatic defeat of the Muslims can be summarized as follows: *an apologetic modernism* meaning what was needed for the resurgence of Islam was total assimilation of modern norms, which in turn meant Westernization; *Islamic reform (salafism)*, which advocated a return to a predecadent form of Islam, that of the first generations, this return going hand in hand with a rejection of mysticism (see Khan, 1998).

It is important to note that most of the Muslim resistance movements in the face of encroaching Western imperialism were led and executed by Sufis. The most significant of such movements were those of (Johansen, 1995):

1. The Algerian people against France: Emir Abd al-Qadir held out with his forces for 20 years, establishing his own Islamic state (1830s);
2. Osman dan Fodio led the Nigerians against the combined imperialist forces in West Africa;
3. The Mahdi of Sudan versus the British in the 1860s;
4. Imam Shamil of Dagestan, with the Chechens, versus the Russians in the 1830s;
5. Morocco;
6. Umar Mukhtar led the Libyan resistance to the Italians in the 1930s.

This resurgence of Sufism in a political form demonstrates the importance of the relatively un-institutionalized, non-formal dimension of Islamic identity throughout history, a dimension of identity that rises to the surface with particular force in times of challenge and crisis, but one which is also a more or less permanent feature of Muslim societies, even if the particular name 'Sufi' is not present[1].

Lapidus (1988: 268) has explained the political and social circumstances of Muslim society in the 18th century: 'The worldwide system of Islamic societies had reached its apogee and begun its political decline. The Safavid state had been defeated by Afghan invaders and, deserted by its tribal vassals, disintegrated completely. The Ottoman Empire went through a period of decentralization, though the concept of an imperial state was unimpaired. The Mughal Empire disintegrated into numerous competing provincial and feudal regimes.'

The process of modernization has been relatively synchronized with the process of secularization in most Muslim regions. This is the result of the intervention of European and American enlightenment, and the establishment of colonial regimes.

Modern Islamic societies are basically the product of interaction of regional Islamic societies with Europe, which brought many changes in relation to Muslim identity. These changes include the creation of new patterns of economic production and exchange of new technologies. In turn the new state and economic structures were the bases for the rise of new Muslim elites. Political managers, technocrats, soldiers, intelligentsia, intellectuals, commercial farmers and industrial workers and specialists became important forces in Muslim societies. Furthermore, the European influence stimulated the acceptance of new value systems – an appreciation for national identity and political participation, economic engagement, moral activism and a new scientific worldview. The establishment of the modern school was another aspect of European influence in the Muslim world, which inculcated the values of European civilization, blended as best they could be with indigenous cultures. Therefore, the impact of Europe on Muslim identity is mediated by the collaboration or resistance of elites (Voll, 1982; Hodgson, vol. 3, 1974: 176–248; Lapidus, 1988: 551–70).

The formation of a new modern Muslim society was the direct result of state reform programmes, but the circumstances of their formation differed. By the beginning of the 19th century, the indigenous reformism began to be overshadowed by the modernizing reform programmes instituted by leaders in the major Islamic states, especially Mehmet Ali in Egypt and Mahmud II in Istanbul (Voll, 1982).

The Ottoman Empire became a frontier of many changes in relation to religion. A process of differentiation has induced gradual separation of the

---

1. See Nasr (1991, vol. II), which is the most comprehensive account of Sufi tariqas, region by region and order by order; and Trimingham (1998)

sphere of religion from politics, and the leadership of the political elite began to look askance at the Islamic component of Ottoman culture. However, the Muslim lower classes did not follow the rulers in this secular stance, and the cleavage between the governing elite and the governed, which had always existed, became starker and now refocused on a religious axis. However, gradually, the programme of modernization of the Ottoman institutions caused many changes and reactions in terms of the identity of Muslims in Turkey (Mardin, 1989: 103–47).

Unlike the Safavid Empire, the Ottoman State emphasized more the military aspect of reform. Mardin (1989: 106–7) pointed out that the Ottoman reform movement which preceded the *Tanzimat*[1] began by establishing a new army and by trying to cover new sources of taxation to support the creation of a standing army. It was extended after 1839 with the creation of a new administrative, judicial and educational network. The reform movement originated in the higher ranks of the officials trained in the Palace School and had a much more secular cast that the body of ulema trained in medreses. The secularizing policies of the political system gradually deprived the higher ulema of their share in the preparation, elaboration and execution of state policy. Religion was gradually segregated from judicial and administrative affairs, and educational institutions were secularized.

The process of secularization, which started with officials wresting a number of institutions away from the *ulema* in the 1840s, was developed by the secularization of the education system. With the establishment of an education system of 11 years duration, with subparts fitted into one another and making up a whole, a secular student body different from the body of religious students was now a reality, and secular student identity followed (Mardin, 1989).

In Egypt, Muhammad Ali's reform programme (1805–1848) was unusual in the degree to which the state attempted to control the Egyptian economy. Egypt was one of the provinces of the Ottoman Empire, but the increasing forces of decentralization provided opportunities for virtually autonomous rule by the politicomilitary elite (Voll, 1982).

---

1.   Ottoman attempts at industrialization in the 1840s and 1850s failed. Reformers of the so-called *Tanzimat* era accordingly decided to streamline military training. They attempted to establish a transformation of education, reform administration, secularize courts of justice and modernize communications, hoping that these changes could eventually win them a place among the advanced industrial countries. The Tanzimat or reorganization period lasting from 1839 to 1876 (Lapidus, 1988: 598; Mardin, 1989: 9).

Although the dissolution of the Ottoman empire was one of the more complex cases, one could say that the dismemberment of the Ottoman empire culminated at the end of World War I in the creation of a plethora of new states in Turkey and a new system of Middle Eastern National states (Lapidus, 1988: 592: 590–615).

In the beginning of the 20th century, Kemal established an independent Turkish nationality first in a limited area and developed, by economic investments, to make Turkey a Western nation (Hodgson, 1974, vol. 3). He pursued his idea through the Republican People's Party. Hodgson describe the Party's principles, which were ultimately embodied in the constitution of the Republic and were summed up as:

> Republicanism, the principle of an elective, constitutional government; nationalism, basing that government on cultivation of a specifically national culture and loyalty; populism, recognition of the dignity and needs of the common people as its first concern; etatism, the responsibility of the state to establish and maintain economic prosperity; laicism, rejection of any communal religious privilege; and finally revolutionism (or reformism), the continuing adoption of the new and better at the expense of the merely traditional.
>
> (Hodgson, 1974, vol. 3: 263)

For Hodgson (1974, vol. 3), etatism was adopted through the Turkish businessman, which has an important role on the subsequent process of secularization.

According to the views of Ataturk style modernizers, religion should be Westernized like any other aspect of social life. Therefore, religion should be privatized from social life and remain a private matter for the individual conscience. As a result of these changes Muslim identity has been markedly changed by the process of modernization, but not necessarily in the manner that the modernizers anticipated. Much reactionary resistance has emerged through Muslims, including Sunnis, Shi'is and Sufis, against the process of secularization.

In other Muslim regions similar intelligentsias came into being without the mediation of the old-regime state elites and internal programs of reform, but as a result of direct European rule, the displacement of former political elites from their governing positions, and their subordination to colonial administrators. In India, British control deprived the Muslim elites of political power. They generated economic changes that weakened the grip of Muslim landlords on rural revenues, and threatened to undermine Muslim culture. In Indonesia, Dutch rule similarly transformed the historic ruling classes, the priyayi, into subordinate functionaries of Dutch administration. The Dutch themselves provided the former elites with a Western professional education in order to generate the Indonesian cadres who were needed to maintain Dutch administration (Lapidus (1988:551–90).

Lapidus (1988:560–1) argued that, in almost all Muslim countries, politicians, professionals, technicians, social scientists and intellectuals, trained in Western techniques, sought to define new political ideologies for the development of their societies. The doctrine of Muslim political elites and intelligentsia was Islamic modernism, which should be distinguished from Islamic reformism – a doctrine of the *ulama* such as Jamal al-Din (1839–1897) and Abduh (1849–1905).

The prominent characteristics of the modernization era, which have been involved in the formation of Muslim identity in the Muslim territories, can be summed up under three headings:

1. The *process of modernization* has assimilated many Muslim countries to Western culture and secularized major social institutions from Islamic principles and marginalized religion into private life. The result of this impact is not the same in Muslim society.
2. *Homogenization of learning systems*, based on secular sciences alongside the assimilation of social works according to the industrial structure of the modern society, has brought Muslim society closer to Western culture. This process has been fostered by many features of Western culture such as music, cinema, fashion, art and fiction.
3. *Nationalism* is another feature of both Westernization and the decentralization of the Muslim world, which originated in the establishment of many nation-states and resistance against alien cultures. For almost thirteen centuries Muslims established central states and empires, which ruled over vast territories of the world without having to appeal to anything which even vaguely resembled modern nationalism.

Religious resistance in the forms of Sufism, traditionalism, nationalism and even reformist movements are part of the reaction to Western domination. This will be further elaborated in later chapters.

3.3. Construction of Muslim Identity in the Age of Globalization

From the time globalization set in as a social force, religious identity has gone through unique changes. The most important change was that religious society found itself facing, in addition to its religious bases, other institutions totally detached from religious belief that offered new sciences devoid of all religious inclinations. To understand the depth of this change, one needs to understand the meaning of secularization, a multifaceted process of social change through which religious thinking, practice and institutions lose their social significance. Secularization in general has come to be interpreted as a multifaceted rather than a unitary phenomenon, like religion itself (Harding & Phillips, 1986: 31–3).

The process of secularization that has transformed modern civilization began with the Enlightenment in the West. It originated in an age still intensely religious when societies were still profoundly under the sway of religious forms of moral authority. Yet it became a strong counterforce to the moral dominance of religious orientations, delimiting them profoundly where it did not challenge or undermine them. The vitality of the Enlightenment derived above all from the moral principles and ideals that it came to pronounce. The concepts of reason, natural law, progress, humanity, freedom, universal rights and so forth captured the moral imagination of the age. They gained sufficient control over moral consciences to bring about a certain constriction in the scope of the moral authority of religious orientations.

However, one could say that secularization was the main reason for the decline of religious belief (Glasner, 1977; Lidz, 1979: 191–217).

One of the consequences of processing secularization alongside globalization has been reflected in the fragmentation of religious identity. Understanding of religion, religious belief, traditional moral values and being involved in practising religious values have been subject to great change. Global interactions between individuals and different cultures, civilizations and religions have significantly contributed to the processes of identity-change.

Since globalization has been involved in the construction of social structures, secularization has accelerated profoundly. Turner (1994) suggested that the process of globalization is in many respects a process of secularization, because it is difficult for religions to protect themselves from the critique of postmodern culture, which regards all religious accounts of the world as merely 'grand narratives' (Turner, 1994: 185). We will elaborate upon the changes due to the process of secularization in Chapter 5.

Many social scientists[1] have suggested that fragmentation of religious identities, relativization of religious belief and pluralization of religious understanding are only a few distinct characteristics of the globalization era. It is within such a cultural environment, particularly from the 1960s onwards, that one sees postulates being presented to the effect that religion should be looked at as a private affair, and the effect of religion to be diminishing daily. Those who propose such postulates as well as those advocating them are

---

1. See Turner, 1994; Featherstone, 1995; Castells, 1997; Cohen & Kennedy, 2000; Ameli, 2000.

primarily looking at the Christian world or/and socialist societies. Their conclusion is drawn from events taking place in these societies.

In more specific terms while globalization has fragmented religious identity, and to some extent reduced religious knowledge and practice, it has also created a wider ground for religion. If we look at the works of three eminent sociologists who have researched the issue of the role of religion in society – Durkheim, Marx and Weber – we would find that all of them are of the opinion that religion has a decreasing role to play and will be marginalized even further. However out of the three aforementioned sociologists, only Weber considered Islam to be an exception to this general rule. Weber believes that, owing to the inherent social potential that exists in Islam, it would remain an effective and a potent force within society (cited by Giddens, 1989: 470–72).

Giddens (1989: 471) supports Weber and claims that at this time and age when other religions are seen to be totally irrelevant to the development of societies, the appearance of a religious revolution in Iran would lead us to accept that even in our times religion as a social phenomenon has a very important role to play.

What has been cited so far would lead us to conclude that the issue of identity and globalization are among two of the most important cultural crises of the second millennium. The environment created by globalization differs totally from our entire past history. The new cultural environment, as Waters (1995) puts it, has created a geopolitical earthquake under different societies and has influenced the entire social structures.

Muslim responses to the pressure generated by the globalization of culture are not the same, from one society to another. One cannot witness a uniform approach or response in this matter. There is a structural difference between the old generation's response, and that of the new generation. The fundamental difference between men's and women's reaction to the phenomenon of the latter part of the second millennium is very significant.

In this chapter we have concentrated on the development of Muslim identity throughout the history of Islam. The challenges posed to this historical development by the forces of globalization surveyed in the previous two chapters provide the immediate backdrop against which our research into the current nature of Muslim identity in Britain was conducted. Before proceeding to the discussion of methodology, the essential points to be stressed from the observations of the present chapter are as follows.

First, religious identities as well as national identities are constructed out of diverse elements and not simple discursive notions. In this sense, such identities are not just the consequences of religious idealism, but are social, political, economic and cultural constructions and cannot be studied apart from the social changes that have taken place throughout the course of Islamic history. Therefore, the central argument arising out of the analysis and observations of this chapter is that Muslim identity is not an unchanging and pre-existent 'fixed identity', a possession of an absolute and exclusive form of collective self-identification as Muslims and nothing else; rather, Muslim identity is a constitutive description of the self in relation to religion and society, and thus undergoes continuous and unpredictable transformations in accordance with changing conditions in time and space, in relation to the dynamics of individual and collective life, and in evolving social and cultural contexts.

However, from another point of view, these very transformations of elements of identity within the Muslim world shows one of the enduring strengths of the clearly identifiable civilization of Islam: its ability to contain diversity within unity; to combine outwardly variegated cultural and social forms and identities with a unitive, essential defining element, that of the spirit of the religion itself and a certain minimal common ground in terms of legal forms. In other words, the *contexts* of Muslim identity vary enormously, but the *content* of this identity has retained a certain core discernible through all the varieties of widely different cultural contexts in which it is found.

The travels of such explorers as Ibn Battuta, and Ibn Jubayr show this in a remarkable way: travelling thousands of miles through different continents, cultures and societies, they described what was always an identifiably 'Islamic' people, i.e. a society whose essential element of identity was Islam. A certain relationship between the doctrine of *tawhid* and the actual formation of diverse Muslim societies in history is observable here: just as the principle of *tawhid* means, taking its literal denotation, 'making one', and not just 'unity', it is clear that Islam 'makes one' those societies that enter into the *umma*. They retain certain of their distinctive ethnic and cultural characteristics, while being integrated within the Islamic religion; one thus observes unity within diversity, and diversity within unity (see Nasr, 1987).

In the next chapter alongside discussion on research method, the field of study will be elaborated, together with the presentation of our hypothetical typology of Muslim identity, a typology that will be tested against the empirical findings of this research.

PART II

Empirical Findings

FOUR

Sample Group and Typological Analysis

This chapter will present an overall view of the Muslim arrival in Britain as well as a brief discussion on the Muslim population in the London borough of Brent, from which the sample group of this study was chosen. The main focus of this chapter is on the typology of British Muslims in the global age.

4.1. Muslims in Britain: Brief Background

In order to understand the attitude and behaviour patterns of British-born Muslims in Brent, we need to know more about the historical migration of Muslims to the British Iles as a starting point.

According to Nabil Matar: 'Throughout the period roughly extending from the accession of Queen Elizabeth in 1558 until the death of Charles II in 1685, Britons and other Europeans met Muslims from the Atlantic Ocean to the Mediterranean and Arabian Seas' (Matar, 1998: 2).

For Matar (1998: 8), 'the Turks and Moors' of North Africa had already infiltrated the English mainland causing mayhem from Minehead to Dartmouth, from Bristol to Portsmouth, and in the Thames where a Turkish ship was captured in 1617.

Apart from a few individuals, Muslims only began to settle in Britain in significant numbers largely as a result of British colonial rule in India. During the late 18th and early 19th centuries seamen recruited by the East India Company often found themselves laid off when their ships docked in London. However, it was only when ships started recruiting in Aden after the opening of the Suez Canal in 1869 that such settlements of seamen led to the founding of small Muslim communities in port cities such as Cardiff, South Shields, London and Liverpool (Nielsen, 1995: 69). The first group of Muslim immigrants were the Lascar-Indians originating from Bengal, Gujarat, the Punjab and Sind, the Arab sailors who were mainly Adenese and from the Yemen. Arab and Somali seamen seemed to have first settled in South Shields in the 1860s (Mumtaz Ali, 1996: 15; Wahhab, 1989: 6; Nielsen, 1988: 53). 'Another group came from the Yemen, particularly after the opening of the Suez canal in 1869 when increasing numbers were recruited into the merchant navy' (Lewis, 1994: 11).

Geaves sums up the presence of major Muslim communities from the subcontinent since the 1950s to Britain in the following terms: 'They came in response to the host nation's demand for cheap labour and to join their family members already here. They risked leaving their countries of origin to find work yielding greater rewards, often intending to return home eventually. Most, however, have remained in Britain and formed themselves into communities established around their religion, places of origin and kin networks' (Geaves 1996: 52).

Woking Mosque is the oldest mosque in Britain, established in 1889. For the last two decades hundreds of Mosques have been built all over Britain. Perhaps the most prestigious is the Central Mosque at Regent's Park (Lewis, 1996: 13). 'The majority of UK Muslims are now native to this country: community newspapers in English such as *Q-News*, thrive, while their Urdu or Turkish equivalents wither away' (Winter, 1999: 22). Diaspora culture based on original 'home culture' is also observable in the form of Pakistani, Bengali, Indian, Iranian and Arab restaurants, and grocery shops.

In terms of numbers, statistically the latest estimates on the size of the Muslim population in Britain are currently put at between 700,000 to 2 million (Lewis, 194: 13; Nielsen, 1995: 72). Apart from the Religious Census of 1851, no Census has ever asked for information on religion but only as to the place of ones birth'. Therefore presently there are no definite reliable data on the size of the Muslim population in Britain.

According to the *World Christian Encyclopaedia* (1983), over 80% of these Muslims were immigrants to Britain who had come since the 1950s from Pakistan and other British Commonwealth states with their dependants (Vertovec, 1996: 169).

A Policy Studies Institute survey in 1984 indicated that 46% of Asians living in Britain were Muslims. Most such accounts are based on the fact that around 11% of the population of India is Muslim, and this figure is taken to pertain here too (Iqbal, 1989: 7).

---

1. After long debates between the representatives of the different religious communities (in particular Muslim communities) and State, the Census 2001 considered the category of religion as a voluntary question on the census; this will provide more comprehensive information about the distribution of population according to religion in Britain.

4.2. British Muslims in the Borough of Brent

The London Borough of Brent was formed under the Local Government Act of 1963 and came into being in April 1965 with the merging of the two Borough Councils of Wembley and Willesden. The River Brent, which for centuries divided two areas, now acts as their common link.

The London Borough of Brent claims to be one of the most multicultural, multifaith and multiracial in Britain and contains the most ethnically diverse population in Europe (Figure 4.1). The visible minorities account for over 44% of the local population and almost one in ten residents are Irish. At least 11% of the population are Muslim (*BIF News*, 1994: 2).

Figure 4.1: Ethnic Group in Brent (Census 1991)

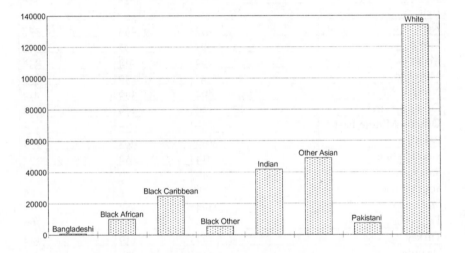

In total, the non-white population numbers 108,919 people or 44.8% of the Borough's population. 17.2% are Indian, 10.2% are Black Caribbean and 4.1% are Black African. In Outer London as a whole, 16.9% of the population are non-white, compared to 25.6% in Inner London.

Compared to the rest of London, Brent has the highest proportion of Indian and other Asian residents and the third highest proportion of Black Caribbean and Pakistani residents. Around 5% of all Indians, Black Caribbean and Black Africans in England and Wales live in Brent.

According to the *Brent Borough Population Profile* (1994: 27) Brent pupils have a wide range of religious affiliations. In 1992 just under half of the primary and the secondary school pupils were Christians, a quarter were Hindus and around 15% were Muslims.

Table 4.1: Muslim Population in Brent by Sex (1991)

Country	Total Population	Males	Females
Albania	1	1	–
Algeria	148	106	42
Bangladesh	445	253	192
Egypt	636	369	267
Gambia	54	30	24
Ghana	384	141	243
India	3085	1433	1652
Iran	1084	612	472
Iraq	–	–	–
Kenya	471	244	227
Libya	99	55	44
Malaysia	462	214	248
Morocco	45	30	17
Nigeria	802	390	412
Other – Africa	401	209	192
Other – Middle East	–	–	–
Pakistan	3616	1911	1705
Sierra Leone	114	52	62
Singapore	40	20	20
South Africa	6	2	4
Sri Lanka	1584	952	632
Tanzania	1590	824	766
Turkey	264	140	122
Uganda	247	134	113
Total Muslim population in Brent: 15568 Females: 7446 Males: 8122			

An accurate figure detailing the number of Muslims living in Brent has been difficult to quantify because cultural analysis tends to be based on race rather than religion. However, according to the 1991 Census, the Muslim population can be estimated at 15,568 in Brent.[1] The majority of them are Pakistani, Indian,

---

1. It is also estimated that there are between 30,000 to 35,000 Muslim in Brent. This
(continued...)

Tanzanian, Sri Lankan, Iranian and, recently, Arab. Its population seems to be ethnically diverse enough to represent the whole Muslim community in Britain.

In Table 4.1 the source of estimates of the Muslim population of the Borough of Brent is based on the percentages of the Muslim population by their countries of origin.[1]

Brent claims that its association with Islam and Muslims goes far beyond the late 1950s and early 1960s when the first wave of Muslims – mostly from the subcontinent – settled in the borough. In 1924 and 1925 Wembley hosted the British Empire Exhibition, which contained many exhibits from the Muslim world. The most spectacular of these was 'full sized models of the Taj Mahal reproducing the beauty of the original in Agra' (*BIF News*, 1994: 3).

The pattern of Muslim migration to Brent followed the pattern familiar in other parts of the country: once a family or group of people moved into the area, either close relatives or friends from the same region joined them. The Borough's 'Asian' profile was significantly increased following the large movement of Ugandan Asians in the early 1970s. Such a large concentration of people from the subcontinent saw the emergence of a vibrant and colourful mall on Ealing Road not far from the world famous Wembley Stadium. Over the years the market here gained a reputation because of the exotic shops and goods on sale, which included foodstuffs, clothes and gold products. The area is also famous for its substantial eating houses, which include many restaurants catering for specialized tastes from vegetarian to halal tandoori.

In the early 1980s and 1990s Brent became the home for a new influx of immigrants, most of whom were either Muslim refugees or political asylum seekers. As a result Brent is now host to a substantial number of people from Bosnia, Afghanistan, Algeria, Morocco, Somalia, Palestine, Iraq and Kurdistan among others. The effect of this is to make the local Muslim population, as we mentioned above, one of the most multilingual and multiracial in the country (*Brent and Harrow Refugee Survey*, 1995).

(...continued)
    figure is based on a survey conducted by Brent Council in 1987 (see *BIF News*, 1994: 2).

1.   Peach (1990) offers a calculation of the Muslim population based on two sources. One figure – a lower one – is arrived at by applying the proportion of Muslims present in the sending country, for example the percentage of the Muslims in Pakistan was the basis for the number of Muslims among the Pakistanis who currently live in Britain. The number of Muslims tabulated in Table 4.1 has been based on this lower estimate given by Peach. A higher estimate is produced by applying the findings on South Asian religious affiliation in England and Wales published in the *Policy Studies Institute Survey* carried out in 1982 and checking them against those of the earlier *Political and Economic Planning Survey*.

The new Muslim immigration into the borough has also dramatically changed the Muslim socioeconomic profile. Today, although Brent's Muslims are dispersed all over the Borough, the majority tend to live in enclaves mostly in relatively deprived areas like Kilburn, Willesden and Harlesden. Furthermore, the increased number of Muslims has also put considerable pressure on the community's under-resourced infrastructure. There are only five mosques in the borough, three Muslim schools and only three community centres to serve the whole Muslim population in Brent (An-Nisa's *Report on Brent's Muslim Community*, 2000: 1).

To the best of our knowledge no research has been undertaken to explain the reason why Brent has been so attractive to Muslims from different backgrounds. One possible explanation could be the fact that the Borough – owing mostly to accidental reasons – has developed some rudiments of a Muslim cultural 'infrastructure' – mosques, community centres, halal markets and educational establishments. Whatever the reason behind the strong numerical presence of Muslims in the borough, the development of Muslim organizations and institutions in Brent should be evaluated firmly within the context of the Muslim community's effort to live *as a Muslim community* and not just as Muslims in an alien environment.

Broadly speaking we can group Brent Muslim institutions[1] into five categories:
1. Those related to the field of education;
2. Those facilitating communal prayers and functions like Mosques or Centres;
3. Those that bring together people with shared experience like refugee groups and minority groups;
4. Those involved in social activism;
5. Those actively engaged in international concerns and issues.

The obsession with education among Brent Muslims is only natural for a community whose belief system puts much premium on the value of knowledge. Moreover, good education – particularly among people from the Third World – is seen as crucial to a successful life. Brent is home to Britain's most famous Muslim educational establishment – the Islamia School. Since its inception nearly two decades ago the school has attracted particular attention because of the profile and role of its founder and chairman, Mr Yusuf Islam, the former pop singer Cat Stevens. Other prominent schools include the al-Zahra (for girls) and al-Sadeq (for boys), which have been established and are run by the al-Khoei Foundation. There is also the al-Manar School, which is

---

1. See the list of Muslim organizations of Brent in *Brent Eid Festival*, 1997: 4.

run by a group of Libyans and which provides primary education. The Islamic College for Advanced Studies, recently established in Willesden Green, now provides an opportunity not only for secondary education but also graduate and postgraduate studies. In effect, then, Brent might be the only borough in the United Kingdom that can provide full-time education in the Islamic environment from primary to university level.

However, like most of the other parts of the country, the most important and widespread suppliers of Muslim education are the *madrassahs* or supplementary schools. Such institutions provide hundreds of children with their first and probably only Islamic education input. In Brent we have at least ten such schools.

In Brent there is only one custom-built mosque, and even that is still under construction. The Willesden Green Mosque is affiliated to the Pakistani Workers Union of Brent. It is a modest affair and not a multipurpose centre. Four of the other mosques-cum-community centres in the Borough are actually converted places of worship: the al-Khoei Shi'i complex was once a synagogue and the Islamic Centre of Brent in Chichele Road, the Dar al-Islam Centre and the Wembley Central Mosque in Ealing Road, all used to be churches. The latest and most modern centre in Brent, the Islamic Centre of England, based at the border between Kilburn and Maida Vale, is actually a former cinema/bingo hall.

Most of these centres have multipurpose programmes in their day-to-day activities but are not actually ideal centres that most community activists nowadays demand of Muslim centres. Part of the outcome of having such a diversified group of Muslims is the intense debate over the nature and essence of even such a basic Islamic institution like the mosque. Essentially the argument is that British Muslims, regardless of which part of the world they come from, have to come up with solutions to the issues they face within British society. Therefore, it is only logical that the process of formulating a British Muslim identity has not only to be critical of traditional cultural understanding of Islam and its institutions but also imaginative enough to come up with relevant answers posed by such a modern secular society as Britain in the 21st century.

A recent seminar[1] organized in Brent, for instance, tried to discuss the role of mosques and centres as potential points for providing health education. Interestingly, it was pointed out that one major role of a mosque in Britain

---

1. A seminar was organized by the Centre for Muslim Policy Research and Brent North Primary Care Groups on 27 February 2001 at the Brondesbury Park Hotel in Brent. The primary aim of the seminar was to develop effective partnerships and ways of working between the health authority and mosques and community centres.

today is to act as a venue for quality family time¹. Historically, this has never been a role of the mosque in almost any traditional societies.

An important development has been the formation of groups with either a shared experience or interest. Brent and the neighbouring Borough of Harrow have at least 21 refugee groups consisting mostly of people from the Muslim world. Primarily the aims of the groups are to meet and socialize, but also to get either advice or training on how to access existing welfare resources or job opportunities (see *Brent and Harrow Refugee Survey*, 1995). Not all such groupings are of refugees. Brent also has organizations catering for the cultural and spiritual needs of such established old communities like the Ghanaians, the Sri Lankans, Kashmiris, Kokni Muslims and so on.

It is argued by some that, from a sociological point of view, the most important groups in the Borough are those involved in social activism. Brent groups are on record for being among the pioneers in the struggle for the recognition of a Muslim identity in all questions relating to the social services. The An-Nisa Society, a female-led organization in the borough, has been in the forefront, since its formation in 1985, of the effort to obtain recognition for the Muslim community as a distinct faith-based community and not as a racial one. This struggle has been coupled with projects aimed at strengthening the family, particularly through the education of women and children. Part of the Muslim activists' task has been to ensure that Muslims get equal and fair access to welfare resources and to work with different agencies with the intention of making them more sensitive and relevant to Muslim needs and requirements. From its launch it has always been the aim of the An-Nisa Society to try and reflect and assimilate the global nature of Islam with their local environment. These has meant involvement in campaigns that, for instance, aim at ensuring that halal meals in hospital and schools does not mean only Indian or Pakistani curries; or in sponsoring and organizing cultural events that are reflective of the wider Muslim world (see Brent Eid Festival, 1997: 12; An-Nisa *Bulletin Election Supplement*, 1998; An-Nisa Society, 2000).

The last category of Muslim institutions in Brent, as enumerated above, belong to what one might call the 'globalists'. If anything, this group reflects the confidence and maturity of the local community and the global nature of the Muslim identity. Most of the institutions in this group represent the volatile mixture of being British and Muslim, local and global: hence the Islamic Human Rights Commission uses European and Western understanding of human rights to campaign for the rights of Muslims all over the world. The Islamic Human Rights Commission was set up in 1997, as an umbrella

---

1. This was the core of Fuad Nahdi's speech on 'the Mosque in Islam' in the Seminar on 'Mosque, Centres and Health Education', at the Brondesbury Park Hotel on 27 February 2001.

organization for a variety of projects relating to Muslims and their rights both on the local and global level (see www.ihrc.org). Similarly, such Muslim charities as Interpal, Muslim Hands, Islamic Relief and Muslim Aid use all the methodologies developed by British charity organizations to raise money to help Muslims throughout the globe.

Other institutions would be difficult to fit in any of the above categories because they can either fit in several of them or perform several of the functions simultaneously. A good example is *Q-News*, a monthly publication published in Brent for the last decade. While its primary aim is to both 'educate and entertain' it also plays a significant role in identity building through facilitating debate and discussion over the issue. The magazine has tried to project a British Muslim identity that draws upon the numerous Muslim cultural and ethnic groups, in a manner that conforms to the conditions of the British cultural climate, and which goes beyond such outward labels of identity as beards, headscarves and halal meat.[1]

Typical of other similar British publications, a regular feature of *Q-News* is its campaigning articles. There are many pieces discussing a wide variety of issues ranging from religious discrimination to domestic violence. Also, the publication – though very British in emphasis – seems intent on highlighting the global nature of Islam and the global challenges it represents. Issues covered include the global environmental crisis, the problems of usury and health concerns.

The findings of this survey show that the borough of Brent has a diverse field of Muslim activity, being concentrated in such areas of business, education and religion; this diversity makes the Muslim community in Brent a very useful one to study, lending the findings a greater scope and breadth, and enabling us to explore the relationship between the process of globalization and that of British Muslims generally and not just in the Borough of Brent.

4.3. Sample Group

I collected my data through a questionnaire on two levels. First, I tested my questionnaire on a pilot scale to find out whether the questionnaire covered the whole area of my study or not. Based on the feedback I received via the pilot, the questionnaire for the major survey was reconstructed. The pilot study involved 53 people who filled in the questionnaire forms. The final analysis was

---

1. See, for example, *Q-circle*: 'Nationality means nothing: Islam is transnational', August 1997; and 'Islam in England' written by T J Winter, 1999.

done using 37 questionnaires. The reason for the analysis of the lower number was that some respondents were not born in the UK, their stay was not sufficiently long for the respondents to be regarded as falling within the category of 'British Muslim', or they were not old enough for this study (14 was the minimum age). Therefore, sixteen forms were put aside.

In this research, the target group consists of British Muslims who were born in England and have culturally blended with English society in the Borough of Brent.[1] We will examine the response of British Muslims who have been born and have grown up in Britain, whose lives have been deeply influenced by this interaction with the wider society. We have chosen this group as representing the category of 'British Muslim' for the simple reason that the individuals in this group have grown up in London, a truly 'global' city. In fact, London could be considered as one of the central forces for the flow of information, culture, knowledge as well as 'religious thought' at the global level. This is primarily due to its advancement in communication and information technologies. We mentioned three major factors in the introduction that make London an ideal place for a study of the impact of globalization on British Muslim identity: its rank among the technologically advanced centres of global communication; its central role in diffusing or globalizing distinctive cultural attitudes; and its cosmopolitan character. In such a context, the link between Islamic culture and other global cultures and the degree of influence that globalization has had on Muslim identity can be studied.

The youth are the primary target of this study, because they are British born, have attended schools here and have been socialized within British culture; they have been influenced by their peers, the global mass media and the entertainment industry while remaining in contact with their home culture, which is highly involved with Islamic culture. They thus stand at the very interface between Islam, mediated principally through the home environment, and British culture, mediated through the multiple channels of the social environment.

The sample group of this research consisted of the following three subgroups:

1. Major survey (247 persons)

---

1. The *Brent Borough Profile* (1994) informs us that the London Borough of Brent was formed under the Local Government Act of 1963 and came into being in April 1965 with the merging of the two Borough Councils of Wembley and Willesden. Today, Brent covers an area of approximately 4421 hectares and stretches around 7 miles east to west at its widest point between Sudbury and Carlton. The total resident population of Brent in 1991 was 243,025 (1991 Census). Between 1981 and 1991 the size of the resident population in the Borough declined by about 3.3%. This compares with a 5% decline in greater London.

2. Questionnaire for citizenship and British Muslim (67 persons)
3. Interview (30 persons)

In the major survey we distributed about 550 questionnaires, to which 324 people responded. The final analysis was done using 247 questionnaires, 67 forms were put aside, for the same reason as in the pilot. The sample audience consisted of GCSE and A Level students, University students and a sample taken from the other British colleges and different individuals in ordinary public domains. As can be seen from Table 4.2, 31% of the male respondents were from Islamic schools and colleges, with the rest attending secular colleges. With regard to females, 57.8% of them were students of Islamic schools and colleges. The rest were individuals who were either in secular colleges or in the public domain. Therefore, although it can argued that the sample groups surveyed here are 'selective', coming from highly 'Islamized' educational backgrounds, this is compensated for by the fact that 55% of the respondents were chosen randomly and were from different Muslim backgrounds in Brent. This allows for statistical variation to determine average responses and attitudes among Muslims in the country at large. The findings are not just relevant to the minority of Muslims actually educated in formally Islamic environments. However, we do admit that the London Borough of Brent is itself not representative of all the areas in the country where Muslims live, there being a distinctive Islamic culture, owing largely to the high number of schools in the borough, and also to other factors that will be discussed below. The findings are therefore relevant to areas of Britain where Muslims comprise a significant minority, a minority which is asserting itself in the public space with increasing vigour. This fact alone makes the survey of dimensions and degrees of Muslim identity within the community of particular importance.

Table 4.2: Group Code of Respondents According to Major Survey and Gender

	Group code					Total
	Khoei School (%)	Islamia School (%)	Islamic College for Advanced Studies (%)	Students in different colleges (%)	Muslims in the public domain (%)	
Males	21 (17.6)	8 (6.7)	8 (6.7)	41 (34.5)	41 (34.5)	119 (48.2)
Females	23 (18)	46 (35.9)	5 (3.9)	25 (19.5)	29 (22.7)	128 (51.8)
Total	44 (17.8)	54 (21.9)	13 (5.3)	66 (26.7)	70 (28.3)	247 (100.0)

The age group distribution shows that the majority of the respondents are in the age group of 20–29 (71.2%). There is a good balance between numbers of males (48.2%) and females (51.8%). There were 23.8% who were employed; the rest were either students or unemployed. Among those who were working, 30% had professional jobs, 23.2% had managerial and technical positions, 29.8% were engaged in the skilled non-manual sector and the remainder worked in the unskilled sector.

Table 4.3: Ethnicity of Parents' Respondents (According to the Major Survey)

Country	Father's country of birth (%)	Mother's country of birth (%)	Country	Father's country of birth (%)	Mother's country of birth (%)
Albania	1 (0.4)	−	Kashmir	4 (1.6)	2 (0.8)
Algeria	4 (1.6)	2 (0.8)	Malawi	−	2 (0.8)
Afghanistan	6 (2.4)	5 (2)	Malaysia	−	1 (0.4)
Azerbaijan	1 (0.4)	2 (0.8)	Mauritius	1 (0.4)	1 (0.4)
Bahrain	−	1 (0.4)	Morocco	1 (0.4)	1 (0.4)
Bangladesh	22 (8.8)	23 (9.3)	Nigeria	3 (1.2)	3 (1.2)
Britain	13 (5.2)	18 (7.3)	Nairobi	2 (0.8)	1 (0.4)
Dominica	1 (0.4)	−	Other African Countries	3 (1.2)	3 (1.2)
Egypt	3 (1.2)	2 (0.8)	Pakistan	54 (21.6)	54 (21.6)

Country	Father's country of birth (%)	Mother's country of birth (%)	Country	Father's country of birth (%)	Mother's country of birth (%)
European Countries	6 (2.4)	5 (2)	Palestine	1 (0.4)	–
Guyana	3 (1.2)	1 (0.4)	Singapore	–	1 (0.4)
India	35 (14.0)	31 (14.5)	Somalia	2 (0.8)	3 (1.2)
Iran	29 (11.6)	31 (12.5)	South Africa	6 (2.4)	3 (1.2)
Iraq	53 (21.2)	48 (19.4)	Sudan	5 (2)	6 (2.4)
Kenya	3 (1.2)	4 (1.6)	Uganda	1 (0.4)	3 (1.2)
Lebanon	5 (2)	4 (1.6)	USA	2 (0.8)	1 (0.4)
Libya	2 (0.8)	2 (0.8)	Zambia	2 (0.8)	2 (0.8)

As can be seen from Table 4.3, the respondents' nationalities were very diverse. This should be taken into consideration in relation to this research, which aims to reflect in a comprehensive manner as many shades as possible of British Muslim culture that are present in the borough.

With the exception of the Iraqi community, which showed no representation in the 1991 Census carried out in Brent, the rest of the population mirrors the population distribution of Muslims in Brent. There has been considerable immigration of Iraqis to Britain over the last decade, and many of them have chosen to reside in the borough of Brent. This could be due to the fact that Brent has recently became an important borough for the Muslim community in London, possessing a high number of educational and religious institutions that have contributed to the establishment of an embryonic indigenous Muslim culture within the British social environment.

The second group of respondents who were questioned on the issue of citizenship and inclinations towards the British way of life were seen to be from 23 different countries. Table 4.4 shows the distribution of the respondents in the four different areas. This group was chosen from colleges in the Brent area and some individuals in the public domain: 37.3% of their parents were British and the rest were Asian (26.9%), Arab (31.3%) and African (4.5%) respectively.

Table 4.4: Gender and Parents' Country of Birth with Regard to the Respondents to the Questionnaire for British Muslim and Citizenship

Gender	Parents' country of birth				Total (%)
	British (%)	Asian (%)	Arab (%)	African (%)	
Males	13 (34.2)	10 (26.3)	12 (31.6)	3 (7.9)	38 (56.7)
Females	12 (41.4)	8 (27.6)	9 (31)	–	29 (43.3)
Total	25 (37.3)	18 (26.9)	21 (31.3)	3 (4.5)	67 (100.0)

The third group of interviewees included 30 British Muslims with a variety of backgrounds ranging from very religious traditional orientations to those with Sufi leanings and those with secular outlooks.

Table 4.5: Frequency of Respondents According to Gender and Ethnicity of Parents

Gender	Parents' ethnicity of interviewees							Total
	Pakistani	Indian	Iranian	Kenya	Bangladeshi	Iraqi	British	
Males	5	2	1	2	3	2	4	19
Females	2	1	1	1	2	2	2	11
Total	7 (23.3%)	3 (10%)	2 (6.7%)	3 (10%)	5 (16.7%)	4 (13.3)	6 (20)	30 (100.0)

The interviews were carried out using semistructured questionnaires in order to maintain consistency and accuracy of the data collected: 36.7% of them were females and the rest were males. While they were originally from seven different countries, nevertheless all of them had British nationality (see Table 4.5). However, their parents' country of birth was different. All of this group comprised either A level (20%) or degree students (80%).

4.4. Typology of British Muslims

Based on my initial study of British-born Muslims in Britain, I shall attempt to present and discuss a typology, which is concerned with *religious orientations*, examining not just *religious Muslim identity* but also *secular Muslim identity*. In this research I attempt to bring a somewhat more precise and nuanced light to bear upon the reality of Muslim identity such as it manifests itself in contemporary Britain. Before I explain my classification for this study, I review other typologies of Muslim society suggested by previous research.

William E. Shepard (1987) classified Muslims by ideological orientation into five main types:
1. Secularism
2. Islamic Modernism
3. Radical Islamism
4. Traditionalism
5. Neo-Traditionalism.

Then, he highlighted the differences between modernists and Islamic totalists. For him, the first three types are highly influenced by modernity, and avoid any type of absolute and monolithic interpretation of Islam. In contrast, those categories that he calls traditionalism and neo-traditionalism are more oriented towards Islamic totalism. For totalists, Islam is an all-encompassing religion, which has a solution for all problems and issues in human life.

For Shepard (1987: 308), 'modernity' as a label for Muslim groups means 'in the first place a tendency to place a high value upon modern material technology and the use of modern techniques of social organization and mobilization, but also a tendency to accept certain modern institutions such as parliaments and political parties, certain attitudes such as a positive orientation toward change, and certain ideas such as a belief in progress'. According to Cantwell Smith (1957: 47), 'The fundamental malaise of modern Islam is a sense that something has gone wrong with Islamic history. The fundamental problem of modern Muslims is how to rehabilitate that history, to set it going again in full vigour, so that Islamic society may once again flourish as a divinely-guided society should and must'.

Shepard (1987: 308) described Islamic totalism as an ideal group who 'view Islam not merely as a religion in the narrow sense of theological belief, private prayer and ritual worship, but also as a total way of life with guidance for political, economic, and social behaviour'. These types of Muslims are looking for an Islamic state, that is, a state in which all laws are based on the Sharia.

It seems that Shepard's definition of traditionalism in terms of 'Islamic totalism' is questionable. Although traditionalists have engaged in forceful resistance in the past and have emphasized the importance of religion as a total way of life, this does not mean that they are willing, ready and able to contemplate taking large risks or dangerous ventures for the sake of the collective or outward expression of their religious ideals. In other words, they are too conservative to push for *fundamental change*: those who do call for such *fundamental change* in the whole structure of society, leading to the formation of an Islamic state, are what Shepard calls 'totalists'. Hence, 'traditionalism' ought to be seen in contrast to 'totalism'.

Indeed, Shepard's typology of Muslim identity is not aligned to the current tendencies, forms and features of Muslim identity. This is due to the exclusively ideological orientation of his analysis; thus, this typology excludes, among other elements, hybrid forms of identity, nationalistic influences upon identity and 'legitimizing' types of identity. Muslim society is highly diversified and differentiated in terms of ethnicity, intellectuality, culture and environment. Furthermore, it is difficult to formulate any general typological schema, without refining it in relation to a particular culture, ethnic group or society. Also, needless to say, Muslims cannot be forced into a single typology, which can be indiscriminately generalized throughout the Muslim world.

Tariq Ramadan (1999), in the appendix of his recent book, *To be a European Muslim*, attempted to consider the reality of European Muslims. He attempts to present a typology in a more generalized way, corresponding to the dynamics of the Islamic world as a whole. The principles of his classification are based on his view that 'Islam is one'. Ramadan (1999: 239–47) identifies six types of identity within European Muslim society:

1. *Scholastic traditionalism*. The central characteristic of those within this group is their rigorous reference to the scriptural texts, the *Qur'an* and *Sunnah*. Their practice of Islam adheres completely to the juristic opinions established within the framework of their specific schools of thought. They insist on 'fundamental elements of worship, on dress code, on the rules for the application of Islam, and, in doing so, they depend on the opinion of the "ulama" as codified between the 8th and 11th centuries'. There are no elements of modernization of Islamic knowledge based on the needs and demands of the society for this type of Muslim.

2. *Salafi traditionalism*. Adherents of this perspective call themselves 'Salaf' because they consider themselves followers of the *salaf al-salih*, that is the 'pious forebears', the companions of the Prophet of Islam and the Muslims of the first three generations of Islam. The difference between this group and the first group is that this group has a 'literalist character', which means that, whilst they insist on referring to the holy scripture, they reject any interpretative reading of the texts. They are very close to the Ahl-al-Hadith among the Ahl al-Sunna and the Akhbaris among the Shias.

3. *Salafi Reformism*. Proponents of this type of reform are very close to the traditionalists except they insist on applying the concept of *ijtihad*[1], which makes them nearer in this respect to the Ahl al-Ra'y. They were born out of the influences generated by the reformist thinkers at the end of the 19th and

---

1. Literally 'striving'; inference of the divine rules pertaining to specific cases and situations that arise and lack an explicit rule from the more general and express principles of Islam based on the authentic sources of Islamic law or to formulate a specific legal opinion in the absence of texts of reference.

first half of the 20th centuries, who enjoyed a wide hearing in the Islamic world. The revivalists are those eminent thinkers such as Jamal al-Din al-Afghani, Muhammad Abduh, Rashid Rida, Muhammad Iqbal, Ibn Badis, Hassan al-Banna, al-Mawdudi, Sayyid Qutb and Ali Shariati.

4. *The political and literalist Salafiyya.* For Ramadan (1999: 243), this group is orientated in a radical fashion towards the establishment of an Islamic state and, ultimately, a Caliphate. As he explains, 'Their discourse is sharp, political, radical, and opposed to any and every notion of collaborative involvement in European societies, something that would appear more as treachery'. They call for *jihad* and opposition by every means against the West, conceived as the *Dar al-Harb* (the realm of war). The best example of this group is the Hizb at-Tahrir or the al-Muwwahidun. While these types represent a very small proportion of thinkers among Muslims in Europe, they have been able to secure a great deal of public attention.

5. *Liberal (or rationalist) Reformism.* This orientation is the outcome of the process of secularization, which has taken place in Europe. It was adopted in all its rigour by Ataturk in Turkey. The result was a definitive separation of the sphere of religious authority from the management of public and political life; it ushered in a thorough adaptation to the European way of life. These Muslims emphasize the spirituality of Islam, claiming it as an individual and inward dimension, while upholding an attachment to the culture of the land of one's birth.

6. *Sufism.* Ramadan stresses the importance of this group of Muslims in Europe. They are very diverse, belonging to the Naqshbandi, Qadiri, Shadhili and many other *turuq* (orders). They are spiritual and mystical in their origins. The *turuq* are circles requiring initiation and are more or less internally organized with a hierarchy which stretches from the initiate to the guide (shaykh).

This typology is not completely workable for British-born Muslims. First, this classification basically refers to the last generation of Muslims before the invention and institutionalization of 'instantaneous communication'. Secondly, it is clear that Islam is not a monolith; there are many 'Islams' – that of the Sufis differs from the Islam of the Salafis, which in turn is very different from the Islam of the Shi'a and even of the mainstream Sunni *madhhabs*, and so on. So any classification based on an exclusively religious orientation will bring us to a misleading conclusion. Thirdly, any classification based on religious affiliation or Islamic ideology limits research to the type of respondents who are involved with religious matters, rather than taking into account all Muslims. Therefore, secular Muslims, Westernized Muslims or those who have a type of hybrid identity would be excluded.

Therefore, the Muslim typology in this research is more focused on a sociological perspective. Here, we study Muslims as a social phenomenon, no matter which ideology or affiliation they belong to. Accordingly, two types of classification will be considered in this study. A general one, which basically refers to Castells' analysis of different types of identity in today's network society. This classification distinguishes fundamental boundaries and directions, but does not specifically illustrate the characteristics of Muslim identity. This classification may be considered as laying the foundation for further elaboration of a typology of British Muslim identity.

4.4.1. General Classification of Identity

Manuel Castells (1997) proposes the following distinction between three forms and origins of identity building:

i. Legitimizing Identity

Legitimizing identity is that which is introduced by the dominant institutions of society in order to extend and rationalize their domination vis à vis social actors, a theme that is at the heart of Sennett's theory of authority and domination, but that also fits with various theories of nationalism. Such identities are the result of conformity between selfhood and the social institutions of a society. In other words, this identity is the by-product of an acceptance of the institutionalized norms of a society.

The Muslim minorities that live in the West are surrounded by many social institutions secular in their nature and character. Across the entire political infrastructure and in all areas of education, entertainment and leisure (schools, television, radio, cinema, newspapers and other literature), the environment and general culture of the West are in large part considered alien to the Muslim mode of thinking. In such circumstances one needs to consider the extent to which legitimizing identity can be expected to emerge among Muslims in Britain, for it is logical to assert, as Castells (1997) does, that legitimizing identity can only take shape in a 'civil society', one in which identity is fashioned according to the general conditions, norms and the legal and social order of the society in question. Castells argues that legitimizing identity is the outcome of a 'network society'. For him, the rapid disintegration of civil society inherited from the industrial era, and the gradual fading away of the nation-state, have given rise to a fundamental crisis in respect of the main sources of legitimizing identity.

ii. Projective Identity

Projective identity is formed when social actors build a new identity that redefines their position in society and, by so doing, seek the transformation of the overall social structure, on the basis of whichever cultural materials are available to them. For Castells, this is the case, for instance, when feminism leaves the trenches of simple resistance in the name of women's identity and women's rights, to actually challenge the system of patriarchalism, thus the traditional family, along with the entire gender-discriminating structure of production, reproduction, sexuality and personality, on which societies have been historically based. Projective identity is the product of the attempt to 'project' a different life, perhaps on the basis of an oppressed identity, but expanding in the direction of a transformation of society (Castells, 1997: 8).

iii. Resistance Identity

Castells (1997) sees the dissolution of former legitimizing identities that used to constitute the civil society of the industrial era, as giving rise to resistance identities, which are pervasive in the network society.[1]

He stated that resistance identity has emerged as a product of the impact of globalization. Resistance identities have become entrenched in communal abstractions, and refuse to be flushed away by global flows and radical individualism. They build their communes around the traditional values of God, nation, and the family, and they secure their encampments with 'ethnic emblems' and 'territorial defences'. For Castells, those who are formed by this type of identity communicate amongst themselves within the network society, but they do not communicate with the state, except to struggle and negotiate in pursuit of their specific interests/values. 'Because the communal logic is the key to their survival, individual self-definitions are not welcome' (Castells, 1997: 356).

4.4.2. Typology of British Muslim Identity

While the above three *modes* of identity can be applied to British Muslim society, they may in fact be correlated to eight different *types* of identity. Each one of these types of identity can be seen to correspond to one of the modes of identity. The typology we proposed above, based on the influences of local,

---

1. According to Castells' definition (1997: 11), network society can be defined as a 'systemic disjunction between the local and the global for most individuals and social groups', which has been facilitated by 'fast-expanding interconnections and interdependencies that bind localities, countries, companies, social movements, professional and other groups as well as individual citizens, into an ever more dense network of transnational exchanges and affiliations' (Cohen & Kennedy, 2000: 29).

global and historical forces, will now be addressed in conjunction with Castells' analysis.

i. Nationalist Identity – Nationalism
It is useful to define a 'nation' first, and then the 'nationalist identity' can be explained. According to Castells (1997: 51), nations may be defined as 'cultural communes constructed in people's minds and collective memory by the sharing of history and political projects'.

For Castells (1997: 27), nationalist resurgence, in the age of globalization, has been expressed both in the challenge to established nation-states and in the widespread (re)construction of identity on the basis of nationality, always affirmed against the alien.

At the same time it is apparent that the present phase of globalization involves the relative weakening of nation-states as in the weakening of the 'national economy' in the context of economic globalism and, culturally, the decline of patriotism. But this too is not simply a one-directional process. Thus the migration movements that make up demographic globalization can engender absentee patriotism and long-distance nationalism, as in the political affinities of Irish, Jewish and Palestinian diasporas and émigré or exiled Sikhs in Toronto, Tamils in London, Kurds in Germany, or Tibetans in India (cited by Pieterse, 1995: 49).

People in this group consider nationalistic patterns of behaviour and norms to be important. They maintain a particular dress code, eat special food, follow a certain social etiquette and hold to values inherited from their forefathers. For this substrata, nationalist identity is of paramount importance (resistant identity). Some of their most important characteristics are as follows:

1. Cultural Nationalistic roots of their identity are more important to them than other parts of identity like religion. They resist the disappearance of traditional culture and strive to maintain national traditions.
2. Their manifestation of their historical roots is based on national heritages.
3. Although they accept a major part of British culture, they emphasize their own national identity, which revives their historical nationalistic attachments in the form of dress, food, ceremonies and national art.
4. They identify themselves more in the form of their particular nationality (Indian, Pakistani) than in term of their religious belief.

ii. Traditional Identity – Traditionalism
This group constitutes a high proportion of the elder generation of the British Muslim community. It includes people who lead their lives in all of its cultural and social aspects according to the traditional religious norms and values. For

them religious rites and behaviours are of utmost importance. They insist on upholding them at all times.

These groups avoid any kind of change. The traditionalists among this group insist on upholding the social traditions of religion and avoid any political interpretation and implementation that puts them on a collision course with the centres of power. We can also include them under the 'resistant identity' title, because they insist on religious tradition against the modernist trends. For them the ritual aspects of religion are the most important. Some of their typical tendencies and social practices are as follows.

1. Like the Islamist Muslims they also emphasize the origin of Islam but they are not interested in the political aspects of Islam.
2. Traditionalist Muslims have also tended to display a degree of resistance to aspects of religious identity but they insist on the observance of the ritual and individual aspects of Islam and less on its social and political dimensions.

Due to the complexity and multiplicity of factors, in reality the above classifications appear to be more vague and ambiguous than clearly determined. However, the subdivisions help define the sphere of our study. For example, the Islamist group also consumes secular sciences and is influenced by Western culture, consumerism and media, as well as music; however, their response and the form of communication is different. They tend to spend their free time engaging in religious activities, to establish a close relationship with those of a similar outlook, and they are inclined to avoid British social norms. These inclinations influence their unique characteristics.

iii. Islamist Identity – Islamism

This type of identity emphasizes the ostensibly original foundation and principles of Islamic belief. In a general way, it can be argued that Islamists find it difficult to compromise, to adapt to changes that which are perceived as undermining not just the religion of Islam, but those features of sociopolitical identity, which are regarded as necessary expressions of Islamic integrity.

There is a similarity between this group and the previous group, in that both groups believe in the importance of religious principles and the necessity of adhering to them. There is, however, a fundamental difference between the two groups, in that this group looks at Islam as a political ideology. They endeavour to implement Islamic rulings in all parts of their lives, from private to social. They believe that nothing should be spared and no one should hold them back from implementing and practising these religious rulings (resistant identity). Some of their prominent characteristics are as follows:

1. They refer more to the 'original' rather than 'traditional' resources of religion: the 'tradition' is largely seen as a deviation from the 'origin'.
2. Political aspects of Islam impact upon the whole way of life – individual and social.
3. Although they are seeking justice and rights, their aim is to establish an Islamic state in which Sharia shapes all social life.

iv. Modernized Identity – Modernism

In this group, people struggle to adjust themselves to the prevailing cultural and social conditions. They try to have modern interpretations of religious concepts and reconcile them with the prevailing norms. These people struggle to alter their pattern of behaviour and fashion them according to modern cultural and social norms. They try to go beyond the norms that define their tradition. Their identity is a blend of traditionalism and modernism (projective identity). Some of their eminent characteristics are as follows:

1. They aspire to the modernization of Muslim community and religious understanding.
2. They are more concerned about pluralization of Islamic understanding than monopolization of Islamic knowledge by Muslim scholars (the *ulama*).
3. They are more concerned with the legitimization of social relationship in civil society, and therefore 'legitimizing identity' is the dominant part of their identity.

v. Secular Identity – Secularism

In the Muslim world the process of secularization has been embodied in different forms. In some Muslim countries, the establishment has attempted to modernize the country by secularizing the society in social and political arenas. Turkey during the regime of Ataturk (Niyazi, 1964) and Iran during the regime of the Pahlavis are standard examples in this regard. The main philosophy behind secularization is the freeing of society from any obstacles and boundaries – in particular, those rooted in religious tradition – that might impede social, political and economic developments.

Alongside globalization we are witnessing the expansion of secularization. Secular Muslims try to rationalize religion by separating it from politics and economic activities. Some of the characteristics of this type of Muslim are as follows:

1. Religion is a very minor feature of their lives.
2. They practise religion more in an individual and private manner.

vi. Anglicized Muslim (Westernized Muslim) – Anglicism

Those falling within this subdivision have been assimilated into the British culture and have adapted themselves to the norms and customs within Western societies. They have accepted the norms of Western culture in general and British culture in particular and adjusted themselves accordingly. They socialize and communicate like indigenous British teenagers. They communicate with English society freely, their friends are primarily from that community, they eat together and take part in the major celebration of the natives, like Christmas and Easter. In a nutshell, they behave just like ordinary English citizens. They prefer to be considered as British.

They have lost their original language and culture – their parents' language and culture. They cannot communicate on the basis of their mother's or father's culture. If they go to their country of origin they are somewhat alienated from that culture. For Anglicized Muslim youth, all the trappings of Western culture, rock music, dancing, watching various Western films, sexual relations before marriage, occasional drinking etc., are culturally acceptable norms, and religion is considered to be an old cultural fiction that has no relevance to their present lives.

Despite their efforts to reconcile themselves with the prevailing culture, their religious roots and cultural tradition create some ambiguity and conflict within them, leading to a pattern of behaviour reminiscent of the undetermined identity. We can crystallize some of the key characteristics of Anglicized Muslims as follows:

1. They have fully adapted to the Western culture.
2. Religious beliefs are replaced by secularization in their social life.
3. Typically their identity is a 'projective identity', which means that they have acquired a new identity as a consequence of social interaction with British society.
4. Mentally they have accepted British culture as a better culture, compared to their parent's culture.
5. They identify themselves first as British then as Muslim.

vii. Hybrid Identity

This is a type that lacks a distinct identity. We may categorize those falling within this category only in compounded or differentiated terms. Such mixed identities are in essence identities that have been influenced equally by two major factors. From one side they are affected by a deep-rooted attachment to everything that has been passed from one generation to the next throughout history. This dimension of identity is shaped and moulded within the environments of home, school, mosque and the general cultural domains that were important to the person.

In reality their religious personality is the outcome of these factors. The other dimension of identity is shaped by the newly created general environment that they live in and struggle with on a daily basis. This kind of identity can be seen within immigrant communities whereby the new generation, primarily made up of young people, have a mixed culture arising from a metamorphosis of the beginning culture and the end culture.

Contemporary society is also an amalgam of a traditional identity and a modern identity. This blend of the two identities forces them to have two completely different pictures of the same situation, just like a person that masters two different languages and is familiar with two different cultures. Such people are faced continuously with two roots, two beliefs and two ways of thinking. They find themselves ceaselessly swayed by two opposing waves, and torn between two forces that are at variance with each other. Such a mix in a character could be due to dual motives or due to the effect of the two major external sources influencing a person. In a recent study, Jessica Jacobson (1998: 153) has shown that the majority of second-generation[1] Muslims of Pakistani origin in Britain suffer such a paradox. We may characterize this group as follows:

1. They do not have monolithic values, principles or tendencies.
2. Sometimes they have great sympathy towards religious values and sometimes they lose their interest in religious activity or practices.
3. They are more often than not confused about where they belong.

viii. Undetermined Identity

This category embraces a group of the young generation who are not inclined towards any particular identity, neither traditional nor modern. They are not so much confused about their identity, they are disordered in terms of identity. We may characterize this group as follows:

1. They show no loyalty towards their motherland or to their country of birth, Britain.
2. They are substantially disordered in respect of both British and Muslim identity.
3. Their behaviour is unpredictable; it follows no definitive pattern, and shifts from one to another of the above modes of identity, in accordance with unforeseeable factors, both subjective and objective.

In this chapter we have offered a presentation of the research methodology that was used in this survey. We have also described the basic features of the sample group together with an overview of the cultural and religious aspects of the

---

1. That is, Muslims of Pakistani parentage born in Britain.

environment in which the sample group lives. The main hypotheses of this research have also been stated. Finally a typology of identity has been proffered, an eight-fold typology based on the three-fold distinctions defined by Castells.

In the next three chapters we will present our data both qualitatively and quantitatively in the light of the theories and concepts of globalization elaborated in the first two chapters, against the background of the periodization of Islamic history given in Chapter 3, and in the framework of our own hypotheses and the research methodology presented in this chapter.

FIVE

Global Forces and British Muslim Identity

In the previous chapter the methodology guiding this field research was presented. A research method, the four central hypotheses, as well as a typology of Muslim identity, were presented in general theoretical terms, following on from the discussion of historical processes of Muslim identity-formation and theoretical analysis in Chapters 1–3. The discussion now focuses upon the empirical aspects of the research, presenting concrete findings that will help to assess the validity, strengths or weaknesses of the theories given.

This chapter examines some of the processes of globalization that have contributed to the context within which the religious identity of British Muslims has evolved. We have examined the relationships between selected aspects of British Muslim identity: 'religious understanding', 'practice of religion', 'religious belief', 'social relationships' and 'day-to-day issues'. These dimensions of identity are assessed in relation to the process of globalization.

We earlier stressed that globalization can be understood as a new force,[1] which not only makes a serious impact on indigenous culture, but might arguably be said to rule over or dominate individual cultures. On the other hand, it can be shown that the very dynamics of globalization, in generating cultural diversity and new spontaneous forms of cultural expression, give rise to the strengthening of particular indigenous cultures or subcultures; the latter are able to express themselves in a new global setting thanks to the very processes that, in another respect, appear to be dominating over them. Therefore, alongside the process of centralizing globalization, there are countervailing tendencies that encourage the emergence of a multifaceted cultural milieu, where spontaneous diversifications of culture are accelerating.

---

1. Globalization as such is considered a new force because it is a result of the simultaneous emergence, on a global scale, of economic integration, telecommunications, transportation and, most significantly, cultural homogeneity. As Held *et al.* (1999: 327) said, 'There is no historical equivalent of the global reach and volume of cultural traffic through contemporary telecommunication, broadcasting and transport infrastructures.'

It is in the light of these transcultural processes that religious attitudes, orientations, interpretations, as well as modes of religious practice that are embodied in British Muslim identity, will be evaluated in the globalization era. Whatever we examine in connection with the contemporary situation of the British Muslim cannot be divorced from the dynamics of globalization, which has introduced new forms and dimensions within British culture, producing a multicultural society.

5.1. The British Muslim Respondents: Sunni and Shi'a

All those who answered the questionnaire were Muslim. They consisted of 108 Shi'a and 134 Sunni Muslims. Noticeable differences between the two sets of respondents emerged, and it might perhaps be useful to take note of some of the religious, legal and intellectual claims made on behalf of the two branches of the Islamic faith; for these may help to shed light on the different responses given in the survey.

On the Shi'a side, it is argued that the principal religiolegal characteristic that distinguishes this branch of the religion is the application of *ijtihad*, literally 'exertion';[1] in the field of jurisprudence; this term acquires the meaning of 'independent reasoning' of legal issues, on the basis of the principles (*usul*) of jurisprudence (*fiqh*).[2] It has been the traditional practice of Shi'a legal scholars of the highest rank to apply this principle to the constantly changing circumstances of time and place, thereby maintaining the capacity of Islam to meet the needs of successive generations, faced as they are with situations not explicitly covered by earlier jurisprudential rulings. For example, in 19th century Iran, faced with the damaging consequences – economical, political, social and ultimately religious – of the granting of a monopoly on the tobacco trade to the British government, the most senior *mujtahid* of the time, Ayatollah Mirza Shirazi, applied *ijtihad* to this situation, and decreed that today, tobacco consumption was forbidden (*haram*) (Martin, 1989). To give another example, music had always been considered *haram*. In 1984, Ayatollah Khomeini decreed that certain types of classical music were in fact permissible

---

1. See Hans Wehr's *Arabic-English Dictionary* (1976, Spoken Languages Service, Third Edition) : '*ijtihad*: effort, exertion, endeavour, etc ... (*Islamic Law*) independent judgement in a legal or theological question.' p.143. According to Rahman (1982: 8) the profound meaning of the term *ijtihad* is as follows: 'the effort to understand the meaning of a relevant text or precedent in the past, containing a rule and to alter that rule by extending or restricting or otherwise modifying it in such a manner that a new situation can be subsumed under it by a new solution.'
2. See for details, A. Ezzati (1976).

(Sahifeh Nour, 1986, vol. 12).[1] It is argued by the Shi'a that such decisions and decrees render Islam more flexible in its ability to adapt to changing circumstances without sacrificing any of its essential, immutable principles.[2] Furthermore it can be argued that the need in Shi'ism to follow strictly one *mujtahid* (religious expert) makes the Shi'a community a more closely knit one, more cohesive, with a stronger sense of collective identity as a particular community and a stronger sense of an individual belonging to that community of faith, allied with authoritatively prescribed actions; in this way, the individual in identifying so strongly with a Shi'a *mujtahid* can be said to have a stronger identity as a Shi'a, in contrast to the more loosely defined relationship between a typical Sunni and his juristic authority.

According to Sunni principles of *ijtihad,* which formally ended around the 10th century (4th century *hijra*)[3], the concept of *ijitihad* can and should be restored in the modern period; and that, as a rule, changing circumstances were in fact dealt with through recourse to *fatwas*, 'legal decisions', based on the principles of jurisprudence, as arrived at by *muftis*. However, this avenue remains open, providing scope for independent reasoning within the sphere of the law. The extent to which this parting of ideals impacts upon the identity and the nature of the responses given by the respondents in the survey remains an open question, but it cannot be denied that the above key differences play an important role. The salience of this factor will of course depend upon the

---

1. It is worth noting in passing that, according to Lewis, 'Music is a central component of ... youth culture' in the Muslim community in Bradford, the locus of his study, *Islamic Britain* (Lewis, 1994: 180). He notes the emergence of such groups as 'Nasib' and the 'bhangra' style of popular Asian music, in which Western motifs are combined with Indian rhythms and lyrics. The combination between Western popular styles and Islamic religious and cultural themes offers a clear example of the phenomenon of 'glocalization', the intensification of local themes through the medium of Western cultural forms that have become globally pervasive.

2. Although it should be pointed out that this difference has significance only in the measure that the individual has an initial religious orientation; only then will the greater flexibility of Shi'a *ijtihad* impact directly on the individual's life. Where this orientation is weak or lacking, it makes little difference whether the individual is originally Shi'a or Sunni. The influence of globalization will then operate in such a way as to deepen the secular tendencies that have replaced or marginalized the religious outlook.

3. Hashim Kamali writes in his book, *Principles of Islamic Jurisprudence* (1989: .386–91), that the beginning of what came to be called the 'closure of the gates of ijtihad' took place in the third to ninth centuries, with firm distinctions between 'unrestricted' and 'restricted' *ijtihad*, being set up in the 5th to 11th centuries: henceforth only the latter was to be practised, that is limited *ijtihad* within the framework of a particular, established school of law. This restriction is now being strongly challenged by modern Muslim scholars.

extent to which the respondents actually identified themselves as Shiʿa or Sunni. While the overwhelming majority did indeed so identify themselves (242 out of 247), the remaining five said they were confused about whether they were Shiʿa or Sunni. Although they are few in numbers, it seems that as a new phenomenon it has potential for proliferation within the coming generations. These Muslims identify themselves simply as Muslims.

Perhaps the idea behind this phenomenon is the wish to return to early Islam as a unified religion. This trend seems to be increasing gradually. This in itself may be due to the fact that globalization has increased awareness of diverse civilizations and cultures, while at the same time minimizing the differences between the branches of Islam.

Based on the findings of this research, there are many contributing factors that show that the Sunni community is inclined towards integrating within British society, which in turn renders them more open to liberal and secular forces than their Shiʿa counterparts.

Table 5.1 shows that in response to the question, 'Which country do you eventually wish to live in?', 55.6% of Shiʿas pointed out that Britain is their favourite place for permanent residence while 25.9% of them preferred their parents' homelands; 74.6% of the Sunnis would like to stay in Britain for life, while only 10.4% of them would like to go back to their parents' homelands.

Table 5.1: Country of Preference for Permanent Residence According to the Religious School

School	Country of preference for permanent residence				
	Permanently in UK (%)	Return to my parent's homeland (%)	Other (%)	United States (%)	Total (%)
Shiʿa	60 (55.6)	28 (25.9)	15 (13.9)	5 (4.6)	108 (43.7)
Sunni	100 (74.6)	14 (10.4)	15 (11.2)	5 (3.7)	134 (54.3)
I do not know	4 (80)	–	1 (20)	–	5 (2)
Total	164 (66.4)	42 (17)	31 (12.6)	10 (4)	247 (100.0)

As a footnote to the above findings it should be pointed out that all of the respondents surveyed here were born in the United Kingdom and as such had no other underlying restrictions or motives for living in the UK, that is, motives of a political and economical nature.

In response to the question about their preferred identity – whether they considered themselves first as British then as Muslim or vice versa – 7.4% of the Shi'as considered themselves first as British while 83.3% saw themselves first as Muslim. On the other hand, 20.1% of the Sunnis saw themselves first as British and 67.9% saw themselves as Muslim first. This indicates that the Sunnis may be more oriented than Shi'as towards a mode of self-identification that elevates the British dimension of identity above the Muslim dimension.

According to this research, British Muslims appear to have different religious understandings in terms of their perception of Islam and its applicability in modern societies. We can identify three different inclinations. Some believe that, in order to be a Muslim, it is enough to bear witness to the existence of Allah and the prophethood of Muhammad, which according to Shariah is the formal requirement for being a Muslim. A more demanding definition of Islam holds that Islam is a way of life – thus, that Islam should influence a Muslim in every aspect of life. One can refer to this as a 'maximalist' perception of the role of religion in social and political life. A third perspective claims that Islam consists entirely of ritualistic duties: praying, fasting, making the pilgrimage or paying religious taxes; this perspective minimizes or ignores the ideological and political dimensions of the religion. The first group may be said to have a more secular orientation in that they have attempted to limit the role of religion to one's personal belief in God and his message, without paying any attention to the social and political implications of religion. The second group are the Islamists and the third group's identity is closer to the traditionalists' mentality, which puts more emphasis on the ritual aspects of religion without being particularly concerned with its political and social implications. According to the results of this research, a high proportion of both Sunni (46.3%) and Shi'a (55.6%) respondents see religion as an all-encompassing way of life. The belief that religion can simply be defined as the notion of bearing witness to the existence of Allah and the prophethood of Muhammad was seen to be more common among the Sunnis (44.0%) than the Shi'as (29.6%).

Opinions regarding *hijab* (headscarf) differed significantly between the two groups also (see Table 5.2). While 84.3% of Shi'a respondents believe that the *hijab* is compulsory for all Muslim women, among the Sunnis only 60.4% of them believe in its necessity; 26.9% of the Sunnis stated clearly that they did not believe in the *hijab*, which is significantly higher than the Shi'a respondents (3.7%). There is no significant difference between males and female in this regard. The survey showed that 68.1% of the men believe that *hijab* should be compulsory for women, as opposed to 73.4% of the women.

Table 5.2: Views on Hijab *Among Sunni and Shi'a*

School	Believe (%)	Do not believe (%)	I have no idea (%)	It is not important to me (%)	No answer (%)
Shi'a	91 (84.)	4 (3.7)	2 (1.9)	5 (4.6)	6 (5.6)
Sunni	81 (60.4)	36 (26.9)	5 (3.7)	9 (6.7)	3 (2.2)
I do not know	3 (60)	–	–	2 (40)	–

Notable differences between the Shi'as and the Sunnis emerged on the question of *jihad*: 88.9% of the Shi'a respondents had a strong belief in the necessity of *jihad* as a principle of Islam, as compared with 75.4% of the Sunni respondents. Whereas 11.9% of the Sunni respondents expressed uncertainty about *jihad*, only 2.8% of the Shi'a respondents were uncertain. This difference, in addition to the different religious views noted at the beginning of this section concerning *ijtihad* and *taqlid*, should be interpreted in the light of the following fact: the Sunni community in Britain has a longer history of integration within Britain than the Shi'a community. The Sunni community's history in Britain[1] can be traced back at least to the 19th century[2]. This has made this community more inclined to assimilate within British society than the Shi'a community, whose major migration pattern to Britain only started some three decades ago[3]. The very nature of British political culture has meant that the longer established Sunni community has adapted itself more readily to the political system as compared to the more recently arrived Shi'a community.

In other words, the relative lack of violence and overt conflict in British politics, together with its relative stability arising out of a culture of accommodation and compromise,[4] might be said to have had an impact upon those migrant communities that have taken up residence in this country. Muslim groups who, to whatever extent, feel 'at home' or wish to integrate

---

1. See Mohammad S. Reza (1993) and also Nabil Matar (1998).
2. See Wahhab (1989: 6): Nielsen (1988: 53).
3. From the findings of this research 73% of Sunni respondents indicated that their parents had been residing in Britain for well over 20 years as compared to the parents of Shia respondents (36%), a substantially lower figure.
4. This is a political culture in which no violent revolutionary upheaval has taken place since the 17th century (the execution of Charles I occurring in 1688), and which has coped with the massive changes of industrialization and democratization peaceably, whilst the continental powers underwent violent revolutions in the process of adapting to the conditions of the system of industrializing, national sovereign states in Europe.

more closely into this society, are less likely to feel attracted by revolutionary causes in principle, whether in far-away places or within their newly established homes in British society. Furthermore, given the leading role of Britain in the globalization process, those groups who have been more integrated into this country may take upon themselves something of this global perspective; the likelihood of this taking place is increased since this perspective is expressed predominantly in the English language, and news pertaining to overseas events are also couched in terms, which make the typical form of anti-Western protests appear as 'fundamentalist', and hence irrational'. The question is often asked in Muslim circles: Are those Muslims who are fighting for their lands to be liberated from forces of occupation to be regarded as 'freedom fighters' or as 'terrorists'? The psychological impact of presenting Muslims in negative stereotypes in the media cannot be overlooked. A basically conservative outlook on the part of long-established Sunni groups in this country can easily merge into a perspective in which *jihad*, for example, is either marginalized or ignored altogether. This may not necessarily be because of any carefully thought out theological opinion, but simply because such concepts as *jihad* do not sit easily with the endeavour to integrate into British society, to be good citizens and to enter the new global age.

On the other hand, one does find that some of the young British Muslims, whether Sunni or Shi'a, are being attracted to revolutionary or radical movements in which *jihad* plays an important part. Paradoxically, this too can be seen as an expression of the impact of globalization, or in the words of Giddens (1999), as an expression of 'reverse globalization': the very immediacy of far-away events, the speed of their reporting, the massive flow of data, and its unrestricted expansion, allowing small groups and individuals to convey their own perspectives on conflicts and world events – all of this translates into a greater likelihood of a 'jihadist' mentality among at least some sections of the Muslim community in this country, those whose identity is primarily determined by Islam as a global ideology, rather than simply as a secondary aspect of identity. Also, the existence of a radical Muslim perspective, taking advantage of global communications, presents itself in sharp contrast to that image presented by the Western-controlled media, and gathers support amongst those most disillusioned with this media for this very reason. One can cite here the growth of and support for such radical groups as the Hizb al-Tahrir and al-Muhajiroun in recent years.[2]

Returning to the observation made in this research – that, as a whole, Shi'a respondents give greater importance to *jihad* than the Sunni respondents, as

---

1. See Edward Said (1993).
2. See Suha Taji-Farouki (1996).

noted above – one factor of significance that should not be overlooked is the strong role played by Shi'as in the radically altered political environment of the Middle East in the last two decades: principally, the Islamic Revolution in Iran, together with the resistance of the Shi'as in the Lebanon to Israeli occupation and incursion. The influence of the Islamic Revolution in Iran, for example, has mobilized other Islamic movements globally, leading to some extent to the radicalization of the British Muslim community, causing them to have a more global outlook. As a result, Muslims in Britain are more aware of the global dimensions of the Islamic struggles and conflicts throughout the world, and identify themselves more readily with oppressed or wronged Muslims in such areas as Palestine, Kashmir and Bosnia.

The inverse of the above can also be observed, i.e. the globalization of a local British Muslim issue. For example, the Salman Rushdie affair started as a local issue but subsequently it took on global dimensions, especially after the pronouncement of the *fatwa* against the author by the Ayatollah Khomeini (see Mowlana, 1996).

5.2. Globalization, Television, Film and British Muslim Identity

Globalization is governed by a set of processes which are intrinsic to the dynamics of a modern society, and as a cultural phenomenon one can see it in terms of 'global industries', such as transnational television and cinema, which play a significant role in the development of identity. With this in mind, emphasis will be placed on the critical role of transnational television, specifically in relation to religious identity.

In this section, aspects of TV viewing, such as favourite TV programmes and the influence of transnational television on British Muslims, will be examined. Secondly, the relationship between television as a global and local force and its effect on religious understanding, practice and belief will be elaborated. Finally, the debate on day-to-day issues in relation to the forces of globalization will be examined based on the findings of this research.

5.2.1. Television

Television as a major player both locally and globally has become a leading resource for the construction of 'identity projects' (Barker, 1999). For Barker (1999: 3) 'identity projects' is the notion that identity is not fixed but created and built upon. It is always in the process of 'moving towards' rather than 'arriving'. Barker suggested that, although television is not the only source of mass global and cultural capital, it is certainly the major one.

One of the major defining characteristics of an individual's life in the era of globalization, in contrast to the period prior to globalization, is that an individual in the preglobalization era had very limited choices. The choices available to individuals were limited to native commodities, while in the globalized world, choices have increased substantially, so that the individual has access to global markets and consumer goods. In the advanced industrial societies people can read, watch and listen across international boundaries. Consumers can consume native products as well as transnational ones. Therefore to understand something of the impact of globalization on British Muslim identity, we need to examine the level of engagement by British Muslims with global products, such as transnational television, as well as the internet. In this regard television is not the only vehicle for the process of globalization, but generally speaking, it is a major element that can be used in assessing the impact of globalization on religious identity.

In the course of this research we have examined different aspects of media consumption in relation to British Muslim identity. First of all the respondents were asked about the frequency of usage of the media, i.e. telecommunication systems. Secondly, questions were asked about their preferences as regarding programme contents. This will help us to gauge the impact of globalization in relation to British Muslim identity.

i. TV Viewing
Usually and understandably, the range of TV viewing is higher among the unemployed than among students and the working population, especially during weekdays (Dobrow, 1990: 71–83). Based on the findings of this research there is also a significant difference between the employed and unemployed British Muslims in terms of TV viewing: 55.7% of the employed Muslims in the survey are light viewers', which is significantly higher than that for the unemployed (35.8%). Also, those British Muslims who have higher levels of education watch less television: 63.6% of those who are postgraduates are light viewers, while 47.6% of GCSE and 45.4% of A level students are light viewers. A comparison between age groups and the rate of TV viewing confirms that the percentage of heavy viewers among younger generations is very high: 81.8 % of those who watch TV between 3 and 4 hours per day are between 15 and 24 years old; 73.7% of those who watch television between 5 and 7 hours a day are again in the 15–24 category.

The percentage of heavy viewers among males (55.5%) is higher than females (44.5%). This may be due to the fact that girls had greater restrictions (than

---

1.   Light viewers are those who watch TV for less than three hours a day; heavy viewers are those who watch TV for more than three hours a day.

boys) imposed upon them with regards to TV viewing in Muslim families (see Jacobson, 1998: 60). It may be argued that the domestic duties in the home will limit the amount of free time that the women (as wife and mother) and girls (as daughters and sisters) will have to spare in watching the television, although one must reflect on how the norms of the 'patriarchal' culture have greatly influenced the role of men in shielding and protecting the innocence and opinion of women from issues (portrayed on the television) that may corrupt family values within the home and the society (see Raza, 1991: 61).

It is interesting to note that, although most of the respondents were students, 43% of them are in the heavy viewers group. This is a high figure, and clearly reflects the fact that television has become the main source of entertainment during leisure time; but, more importantly, the content viewed on television can be regarded as playing a critical role in determining the kinds of activities that will be carried out at other times, in addition to having an impact upon lifestyles, family relationships and psychological and cultural perceptions. All of this is likely to have at least some influence on the nature of religious identity.

ii. Diversity of TV Channels

In response to the question: 'How many channels do you watch on a regular basis?', 67.7% of the respondents pointed out that they watch five to ten channels, with 17.4% watching more than 11 channels, and 13 individuals (5.2%) not watching television at all. The latter shows an unusual deviation from the norm, since in today's media communication age, we are witnessing a group of people who are attempting to isolate themselves from television completely. This is a type of 'identity resistance' against the general trend in the world. It is important to point out that 84.7% of this group who do not watch television are under 25 years of age.

Table 5.3: Gender and Favourite Channels

Gender	BBC1 (%)	BBC2 (%)	Channel 4 (%)	Channel 5 (%)	Sky Movie (%)	Sky 1 (%)	TNT (%)	Other (%)	No answer (%)
Males	36 (59.0)	9 (47.3)	8 (36.4)	15 (31.9)	31 (63.3)	1 (25.0)	1 (33.3)	6 (42.9)	12 (42.9)
Females	24 (41.0)	10 (52.7)	14 (63.6)	32 (68.1)	18 (36.7)	3 (75.0)	2 (66.7)	8 (57.1)	16 (57.1)
Total	61 (24.7)	19 (7.7)	22 (8.4)	47 (19.0)	49 (19.8)	4 (1.6)	3 (1.2)	14 (5.7)	28 (11.3)

Table 5.3 shows that BBC1 (24.7%), Sky Movies (19.8%) and Channel 5 (19.0%) are the most favoured (watched) channels for British Muslims in this research. There is a difference in the choice of channels between men and women in this respect: 63.3% of those whose favourite channel is Sky Movies are males. In contrast, 68.1% of those who prefer Channel 5 are females. The higher popularity of Sky Movies amongst men is most likely due to the level of excitement (i.e. action/violence) in the films of this channel. Psychologically, women normally prefer a movie in which they can become engrossed in a story-line or a film that portrays life (with its romance and tribulation), movies that are usually offered to viewers of Channel 5. These statistics also show that a favourite choice of channel for Muslims is not monolithic, but diversified. The diversity of channels that the young generation prefer today can be seen as a sign of the diversity of values, cultural affiliations and identities, or vice versa.

iii. Television Programmes
Usually, teenagers are more interested in exciting movie programmes but, because most of the channels showing such types of movies are expensive and some of them are considered as immoral, many Muslims do not subscribe to such channels. However, 52.2% of the respondents have access to movie channels such as Sky Movies either through cable or satellite TV. There is no significant difference between males and females in terms of the tendency to watch movie channels in general.

Table 5.4: Gender and Favourite TV Programme

Gender	News (%)	Films, dramas and serials (%)	Documentary (%)	Music and shows (%)	Religious programme (%)	Sport (%)	Other (%)
Males	33 (47.1)	60 (43.9)	4 (25)	5 (87.5)	–	6 (100.0)	2 (50)
Females	37 (52.9)	68 (56.1)	8 (75)	1 (12.5)	1 (100.0)	–	2 (50)
Total	70 (28.3)	128 (58.3)	16 (6.5)	6 (2.4)	1 (.4)	6 (2.4)	4 (1.6)

Table 5.4 shows that the most popular types of programmes are films, dramas and serials. Religious programmes were said to be the least popular; one reason might be that almost all religious TV programmes are either based on the Christian or Jewish perspective. It is also possible that religious TV programmes

are the least popular for most (if not all) communities, despite one's belief or religion. Additionally, the types of religious programmes (irrespective of the religion being portrayed) are normally very dry, unattractive and without any excitement, in contrast to the more thrilling nature of film, drama and music programmes. It is the nature and policy of these types of programmes to capture the imagination, attention and emotion of the audience so that the viewer will find difficulty in drawing their attention away from the programme.

The domination of the news by Western news agencies is significant because they supply 'spot news' and visual reports. CNN and BBC are two large Western television services that have a powerful influence in terms of data supply to indigenous television and newspapers in the 'South' and the 'North' (Barker, 1997: 102). In this survey, among the channels accessible to respondents, BBC1 (49.8%) and CNN (25.1%)[1] are the most favoured news channels whilst news channels from Muslim countries are not very popular (Table 5.5). These figures illustrate that Muslims will normally receive news about their motherland or the Muslim world through the Western broadcasting channels, which can greatly influence the political identity of Muslims in Britain. This trend is not indicative of the opinion that Muslims will necessarily assimilate to American politics, but the overexposure of Western broadcasting can create a sort of reactionary response in the form of resistance against the American/British politics.

Table 5.5: Favourite News Channel

TV channels	BBC1 (%)	BBC24 (%)	SKY News (%)	CNN (%)	Other channels (%)	Euro-news (%)	None (%)
Frequency	124 (49.8)	8 (3.2)	27 (10.9)	62 (25.1)	22 (8.9)	1 (.4)	4 (1.6)

The popularity of CNN can be related to the fact that this news channel professionally provides informative news for the interest of the global audience and that the choice of people has been monopolized by the America myth. On the other hand it clearly shows the transnationalization of local interest.

---

1. It is important to keep in mind that a minority of the respondents has access to CNN. Among those who do have access to this channel, 69.0% considered it to be their favourite channel.

iv. Transnational Television

Transnational television has significantly grown since the 1980s both in terms of global ownership and in the use of the distribution technologies of satellite and cable, to open up a new market (Barker, 1997). Barker (1997: 3) believes that: 'The globalization of the institutions of television raises crucial questions about culture and cultural identities, for television is a major disseminator of cultural maps of meaning and a resource for identity construction.'

Global television needs to be understood (historically and sociologically) in the wider context of the globalization of capitalist modernity, since global television is both a cause and a consequence of globalization. Television is itself a global consequence of the economic, cultural and political institutions of capitalist modernity, while at the same time contributing to the globalization of modernity through the worldwide circulation of images and discourses (Barker, 1997: 13).

Of the respondents of this research 38.5% have access to satellite TV and 28.3% of them are subscribers to cable television[1], while on average only 14.8% of the entire British audience are subscribers to cable television (*Screen Digest*, September, 1995). This may be due to the fact that satellite and cable are two of the major sources that make it possible for viewers to watch native programmes about their previous homelands. It may also be accounted for by the fact that TV viewing during the leisure slot, which is the optimum time for the majority of viewers, was also seen to substantially increase among British Muslims. This will be further discussed in the final conclusion. The amount of time devoted to TV viewing is greater than other possible activities such as sport, dancing or going to the pub. Another possible reason for the high rates of subscription (amongst Muslims) to the satellite and cable TV might be that Muslims as a minority within British society have fewer opportunities for social interaction with the main bulk of society, owing to racial, religious and cultural differences between Muslims and the majority of the British population. Therefore Muslims tend to build their culture more around their homes, and this naturally places a higher importance on the role of television as a conveyor of culture.

This has induced a specific type of socialization, one which takes its criteria and its modes of conduct more from the influences that are broadcast through the television than from influences that emanate from the home culture or the religious tradition into which the individual is born. This will be clearer from what follows below.

---

1. According to our sample group, 32.6% of those who have access to satellite TV are also subscribers to cable TV.

Transnational television and Muslim identity. In response to the question about the relationship between the programmes of satellite television and Muslim identity, 24.3% said that 'there are serious conflicts' between their perception of Muslim identity and what they watch on satellite television. Nearly half of the interviewees (44.9%) stated that 'there are some areas of conflict'. Among respondents, only 8.5% of the respondents answered with the statement, 'None, they are entirely different subjects.' There is also a significant proportion (22.3%) of the sample group that does not have any clear idea of the relationship between these two subjects, which indicates that they do not even have an understanding of the relationship between Muslim identity and television, i.e. the ways in which television content can influence one's moral outlook, one's cultural perceptions and one's religious outlook (Table 5.6).

Table 5.6: Views of Respondents Regarding Satellite TV and Muslim Identity

Relationship between satellite TV programme and Muslim identity	Frequency	Percentage
There are serious conflicts	60	24.3
There are some areas of conflict	111	44.9
None, they are entirely different subjects	21	8.5
I have no idea	55	22.3

The responses of different age groups to this question varies; the majority of those who are in the age group 15–24 see either serious or slight conflicts (68.8%) between what they watch on TV and their perception of Muslim identity. There is a small percentage (8.1%) of all the respondents who believe these two are unrelated subjects. It is interesting that a significant percentage (45.4%) of the older generation (over 30) seems to be confused about the relationship between existing television content and Muslim identity (Table 5.7).

Table 5.7: Age Group and Views on the Conflict Between Satellite TV and Muslim Identity

Age group	There are serious conflicts (%)	There are some areas of conflict (%)	None, they are entirely different subjects (%)	I have no idea (%)	Total (%)
15–19	25 (25.5)	44 (44.9)	8 (8.2)	21 (21.4)	98 (39.7)
20–24	22 (24.4)	48 (53.3)	7 (7.8)	13 (14.4)	90 (36.4)
25–29	8 (30.8)	10 (38.5)	2 (7.7)	6 (23.1)	26 (10.5)
30 and over	5 (15.2	9 (27.3)	4 (12.1)	15 (45.4)	33 (13.4)
Total	60 (24.3)	111 (44.9)	21 (8.5)	55 (22.3)	247 (100)

There is also a significant relationship between the academic status of the respondents and satellite TV viewing ($P = 0.002$ <0.01). A low proportion of those who achieved undergraduate or postgraduate education have access to satellite television: undergraduate (19.2%), graduate (24%) and postgraduate (0.0%); whilst 48.8% of those with GCSEs and 41.2% of those with A levels had access (Table 5.8).

Table 5.8: Academic Level and Access to Global (Satellite) TV

Access to global TV	GCSE (%)	A Level (%)	Undergraduate (%)	Graduate (%)	Postgraduate (%)	PhD (%)	Total (%)
Yes	41 (48.8)	40 (41.2)	5 (19.2)	6 (24.0)	–	3 (75.0)	95 (38.5)
No	43 (51.2)	57 (58.8)	21 (80)	19 (76.0)	11 (100.0)	1 (25.0)	152 (61.5)
Total	84 (34)	97 (39)	26 (10.5)	25 (10.1)	11 (4.5)	4 (1.6)	247 (100.0)

Although it can be argued that 'access' to satellite channels is itself a question of choice, and that the more educated individuals choose not to have access to such global television, it is self-evident that, as a whole, satellite technology has vastly increased the range and diversity of global television output and has consequently made available to the consumer a much greater range of programmes.[1]

According to this survey, 38.5% of the respondents have access to satellite TV; 86% of this group are between 15 and 24 years of age. It needs to be stressed that global television and satellite channels constitute an important facility, laying the foundations of transnational cultures, and as a corollary, weakening elements of national and religious identity in local ones. This is because transnational television can introduce more options and diversity for the viewer. This mode of new TV programming has the power to radically influence if not change completely the everyday lives, culture and identity of viewers.

There is a paradoxical relationship between the religiosity of British Muslims and access to satellite television. For example, 69.5% of those who have access to satellite TV pray five times a day, while only 55.3% of those who do not have access to satellite TV have the same disposition ($P = 0.028 < 0.05$). On the other hand, with regard to social relationships, 81.1% of those who have access to satellite TV pointed out that the majority of their friends are Muslim, while only 8.4% of those who do not have access to satellite TV said that the majority of their friends are Muslims ($P = 0.00 < 0.01$).

Why are those who have access to satellite TV more religious than those who do not? One answer that can be given is that this may be due to the fact that it gives them the opportunity to access and watch the programmes broadcast from the countries of their origin such as MBC, *Jam-e Jam*, TV Asia, etc. Therefore it plays a mediating role between Muslim viewers and their indigenous cultures. Given the fact that these indigenous cultures remain largely religious, it is obvious that the channels broadcast from these countries will have a relatively high proportion of religious content, and thus appeal to the type of viewer that already has a religious inclination.

In this respect, access to satellite TV is an expression of an inclination towards indigenous and religious identity. By contrast, access to cable TV can be read as a sign of less religiosity and expresses a different type of Muslim identity. In comparison to those who have access to satellite TV, subscribers of cable TV show less inclination towards religion. Regarding friendships, whilst 74.9 % of those who are not subscribers of cable TV stated that the majority of their friends are Muslims, only 50.0% of those who are subscribers said that the majority of their friends are Muslim ($P = 0.00 < 0.01$). Subscribers of cable TV

---

1. It is important to realize that the influence of transnational culture is not only dependent on satellite TV, but national televisions play an important role in propagating transnational film productions. National television itself broadcasts many imported films, documentaries, news and information from other parts of the world. The role of Western films, in particular Hollywood productions, is highly important with respect to transnational culture (see Tino Balio, 1990).

are on average less observant Muslims as compared to those who have access to satellite. For instance, regarding the five times daily prayer, just 40.0% of cable TV subscribers perform the five times daily prayers compared with 66.7% of those who have access to satellite TV, which shows quite a significant difference between these two groups ($P = 0.004 <0.01$ & 0.05).

However, in terms of religious understanding, for example, in response to the question about 'eternity and the applicability of religious values to all societies and times', there is a similar understanding between both groups. About 75% of each group believe that their religious values are absolute and applicable in every society and age. This shows that, whilst their religious understanding is almost the same, the level of observance of religion varies, as does the degree to which religious values and norms influence and shape the construction of social relationships.

Impact of transnational television. The perception of the respondents regarding television's influence on their lives varies. The extent to which the viewer feels influenced by film does not necessarily determine the effect of television and the cinema on religious identity. Quite often people do not recognize the extent of their influence.

Table 5.9: Gender and the Influence of Films

Gender	So influential that some have changed my values and behaviour (%)	Some may gradually change values (%)	TV is entertainment and that has nothing to do with values (%)	TV does not effect my value-judgements (%)	No answer (%)	Total (%)
Males	15 (57.7)	30 (46.9)	32 (59.3)	37 (39.8)	5 (50.0)	119 (48.2)
Females	11 (42.3)	34 (53.1)	22 (40.7)	56 (60.2)	5 (50.0)	128 (51.8)
Total	26 (10.5)	64 (25.9)	54 (21.9)	93 (37.7)	10 (4.0)	247 (100.0)

Nevertheless, 10.5% of the respondents believe that some films are so influential as to change their values and behaviour. Here males (57.7%) feel more influenced by television films than females (42.3%). While 26.9% believed that television has gradually altered their values, a higher proportion (37.7%)

believed that films have essentially had no influence whatsoever upon their beliefs. Again, one finds that there is a significant difference between males and females, with more females subscribing to this idea; 21.9% essentially viewed television programmes as recreational and unrelated to religious values and identity (see Table 5.9). Here, in contrast, males showed a greater inclination towards this belief.

5.3. Television, Cinema and Religious Understanding

In this section selected forces of globalization in relation to religious understanding will be examined. This will show that TV viewing is not simply a matter of spending leisure time; it also gradually creates a different type of understanding of religious identity as well as of cultural and social relationships.

5.3.1. Concept of Muslimhood (Islamicity)

The process of diversification and revitalization of everyday life through the mass media has also diversified world views and religious understanding. Today, people in a limited area do not think the same and do not necessarily have a shared understanding of the majority of social, cultural and political issues. The understanding of the 'relativists', as described in Chapter 2, of the process of globalization also supports the conclusions of the following discussion. Some of the findings of this research illustrate that British Muslims regard Islam and Muslimhood as two separate concepts.

Explicit questions were asked about what it means to be a religious Muslim. A high proportion of respondents (37.7%) believed that a religious Muslim is 'a person who believes in God and the prophethood of Muhammad'. Just one half of the respondents (50.2%) defined a religious Muslim as 'a person who believes that Islam is a way of life'; for them Islam dominated every aspect of life: political, economic, social and cultural. Among the respondents, only two respondents (0.8%) believed that 'all religions are the same'. Another small group (2.4%) believed in the ritualistic definition of Islam, in which the ritual aspects of Islam such as praying, fasting or attending the religious ceremonies are of central importance. The remainder (2.8%) either do not think it is possible to 'stay fully religious and live in the West' or do not have a clear idea of the definition of a religious Muslim (4.9%).

Table 5.10: Definition of a Religious Muslim

Definition of a religious Muslim	Frequency (%)
A person who believes in God and the prophethood of Muhammad	93 (37.7)
A person who believes that Islam is a way of life	124 (50.2)
Someone who prays, fasts and sometimes attends religious gatherings	6 (2.4)
Somebody who believes that all religions are the same	2 (0.8)
I do not think one can hold strong religious values and live in the West	7 (2.8)
I do not know	12 (4.9)
No answer	3 (1.2)
Total	247 (100.0)

On the other hand, in response to the question, 'Why are you Muslim?', views varied. A high proportion of them (38.9%) pointed out that they are Muslim because their families are Muslim; Islam for them is a cultural heritage respected by generation after generation as a normative value system. Just under half of the respondents (45.7%) pointed out that they are Muslim because they value their religious identity; apart from what their ancestors said about Islam, they themselves are fully aware of Islam. Another group of respondents (4.9%) said they are Muslim, because their strong faith 'controls their desires'.

5.3.2. Relativization of Religious Truth

The relativists reject convergence towards a single and unified culture as a result of homogenization of any particular dominant culture. They do not accept that as a result of globalization, homogenization of culture is necessarily going to take place. They suggest that variety and expanding religious and cultural pluralism are the main characteristics of the cultural response to the process of globalization. They believe that globalization leads to the relativization of truth and belief (Robertson, 1990, 1991, 1992; Turner, 1994).

Table 5.11: Plurality of Truth and Preference for Films and Programmes

Islam is not the only truth	Which films and programmes interest you more?			Total (%)
	Middle Eastern (%)	American and European (%)	No answer (%)	
No answer	3 (27.3)	5 (45.5)	3 (27.3)	11 (4.5)
Believe	10 (23.8)	31 (73.8)	1 (2.4)	42 (17)
Do not believe	34 (21.0)	92 (56.8)	7 (4.3)	162 (65.6)
I have no idea	–	19 (95.0)	1 (5.0)	20 (8)
It is not important to me	1 (8.3)	11 (91.7)	–	12 (4.9)
Total	48 (19.4	187 (75.7)	12 (4.9)	247 (100.0)

According to Table 5.11, the majority of respondents (65.6%) to this survey indicated that they 'do not believe in the plurality of "truth"', which means that they only believe in the truthfulness of Islam and not that of other religions. However, signs of pluralism and relativization of truth among the Muslims respondents have gradually emerged. A significant 17% of the respondents did not believe Islam to be the 'only truth'. A further 8% said that they had no idea and 4.9% felt that it was not important to them.

Table 5.11 illustrates that there is a significant interdependence between belief in the plurality of religion and preference for Western films and stars (73.8%). It also indicated that for those who seem not to have thought about religion or for whom religion is not a serious concern, there is a substantially greater attraction for Western films (95% and 91.7% respectively) than for those who do not believe in religious pluralism (56.8%).

Although television can have a great impact on religious attitudes and identity, nevertheless one should also consider the power of society and the environment as important factors in initiating changes as regards religious values, or creating a resistance movement in reaction to antisocial behaviour within particular cultures.

Table 5.12: Perception About Individual and Social Aspects of Islam in Relation to the Films and Actors Deemed Most Interesting

Islamic faith is an individual philosophy rather than a social philosophy	Favourite films and actors			Total
	American and European (%)	Middle Eastern (%)	No answer (%)	
Believe	48 (84.7)	5 (14.5)	1 (1.8)	57 (23.0)
Do not believe	68 (65.2)	34 (28.8)	7 (5.9)	118 (47.8)
I have no idea	42 (91.3)	2 (4.3)	2 (4.3)	46 (18.6)
It is not important to me	12 (80)	2 (13.3)	1 (6.7)	15 (6.1)
No answer	8 (72.7)	2 (18.2)	1 (9.1)	11 (4.5)

On the other hand, Table 5.12 demonstrates that those who see Islam more as an individual faith rather than a social philosophy are more interested in Western films (84.7%) than those who do not (65.2%). This indicates that there is a significant interdependence between the processes of individualization of Islamic faith and that of cultural consumption of products in relation to American and European cinema ($P = 0.002 < 0.01$).

5.4. Television, Cinema and the Practice of Religion

The findings of this research show that Islamic practice is more intense and restricted among those who have been educated in Islamic schools and colleges in Britain such as 'al-Khoei', 'Islamia' and 'Islamic College' and higher than among those who attend non-Islamic schools. For example, the proportion of those attending Friday prayers ($P = 0.00 < 0.01$) or congregational prayers ($P = 0.00 < 0.01$) and performing daily prayers ($P = 0.016 < 0.05$) among those who attend an Islamic school is significantly higher than among those attending non-Muslim schools, e.g. 68.5% of respondents in the Islamia school had said that they perform Friday congregational prayers every week, compared to 22.7% of respondents at British colleges or universities. Therefore schools, as one of the major sources of learning and socialization, seem to play a significant role in determining the Islamic form of British Muslim identity, as compared to those who are educated in a secular context.

5.4.1. Prayer

Performance of the daily prayer is and has been considered as one of the major features of the individual and social identity of Muslims throughout the history of Islam and even in the age of globalization. From the Islamic point of view, it is obligatory to perform the five daily prayers. Daily congregations and Friday prayers are also considered to be important congregational manifestations of Muslim identity. According to the findings of this research, 60.7% of the respondents perform all five daily prayers and a further 13% of the respondents perform all the daily prayers except the morning prayer; 21.5% pointed out that they just perform daily prayers occasionally and only 4% suggest that they do not pray at all.

Table 5.13: Relationship Between Praying and Perception on the Influence of Television on the Muslim Identity

How often do you pray?	The impact of television programmes					Total
	So influential that some have changed my values and behaviour (%)	Some may gradually change my values (%)	TV is entertainment and has nothing to do with values (%)	TV does not effect my values judgements (%)	No answer (%)	
Regularly, five times a day	23 (15.3)	40 (26.7)	28 (18.7)	53 (35.3)	6 (4)	150 (60.7)
All prayers except morning prayer	–	9 (28.1)	8 (25)	14 (43.8)	1 (3.1)	32 (13)
Occasionally	3 (5.7)	14 (26.4)	11 (20.8)	22 (41.5)	3 (5.7)	53 (21.5)
Never	–	–	6 (60)	4 (40)	–	10 (4)
No answer	–	1 (50)	1 (50)	–	–	2
Total	26 (10.5)	64 (25.9)	54 (21.9)	93 (37.7)	10 (4.0)	247 (100.0)

It is important to note that of those who do not pray, 60% believe that television is entertainment and has nothing to do with values, and 40% believe that television does not affect their value judgements. This shows a contradictory finding: as within the very group that claims that television does not affect values in a significant way, the fact that their observance of religion is minimal would appear to show the very opposite – that there is a strong, negative impact of TV programmes on religious identity and the practice of religious rites (Table 5. 13). Although, it can be expressed that, if a person is non-religious and more secular, this individual will watch more TV (rather than assuming that watching TV makes one less religious).

Congregational (*jamat*) Prayer is also highly recommended in Islam and it has become an important part of the social identity of Muslims all over the world.

Table 5.14: Relationship Between Attending Congregational Prayers and Frequency of TV Viewing

How often do you attend congregational prayer?	How much time do you spend each day watching TV?				Total (%)
	Light viewers (%)	Heavy viewers (%)	None (%)	No answer (%)	
Every day	23 (54.8)	15 (35.7)	4 (9.5)	–	42 (17)
Once a week or once a month	25 (53.2)	19 (40.4)	3 (6.4)	–	47 (19)
Occasionally	48 (40.3)	66 (55.5)	5 (4.2)	–	119 (48.2)
Never	20 (54.1)	16 (43.2)	–	1 (0.4)	37 (15)
No answer	1 (50)	–	1)	–	2 (.8)
Total	117 (54.1)	116 (47)	13 (5.3)	1 (0.4)	247 (100.0)

Table 5.14 shows that light viewers (54.8%) attend *jamat* prayer more regularly than the heavy viewers (35.7%). On the other hand the proportion of those attending *jamat* prayers only on occasion, as opposed to regularly, is higher amongst heavy viewers (55.5%) than lighter viewers (40.3%). One reason for the low attendance of *jamat* prayers among higher viewers is that a substantial percentage of their leisure time is usually taken up by television, leaving less time – and less inclination – for the performance of religious obligations, which are time-consuming. The perceptions shaped by high levels of television viewing appear to have a negative effect upon attitudes towards religious rites in general; however, in the light of the wider range of television channels provided by global networks, mentioned above, it is conceivable that those

viewers with an initial religious orientation select channels catering to religious needs, and thereby intensify the commitment to perform the ritual obligations of their religion. This fact must be taken into account as qualifying the general observation that, at present, religious activity appears to be negatively correlated with high television viewing.

5.4.2. Pilgrimage

From the Islamic point of view, the performance of the *hajj* to Mecca is obligatory for a person at least once in his or her lifetime, provided that he or she is financially able and healthy. The *hajj* is an expression of both the social and spiritual dimensions of the global Muslim *umma*. Millions of Muslims gather in Mecca annually to demonstrate the multicultural character of Islam, at the same time reflecting Muhammad's claim that all true believers belong to a single universal community (*umma*) transcending tribal bounds (Esposito, 1994: 10). Almost all British Muslims in this survey share a belief in the *hajj* (91.5%); only 0.8% do not believe in it being obligatory and the rest either do not have a clear idea about it (5.3%) or consider it unimportant.

A comparison between a propensity towards *hajj* and openness to globalization forces such as TV viewing indicated that, although light viewers (94%) are more inclined to perform *hajj* than heavy viewers (87.9%), there is no significant distinction between them ($P = 0.81 > 0.01$ and 0.05). There is also no substantial difference between those who are more engaged with different types of TV channels and those who are content with the national channels ($P = 0.25 > 0.01$ and 0.05). This reinforces Turner's theory (1994), which argues that the forces of globalization have not had a significant impact on religious values, understanding and practice. *Hajj* for example, is one religious ritual in which Muslims have retained – even reinforced – their belief; and they adhere to this belief and the rites that it entails, regardless of the strong influence of the globalization process.

5.4.3. Permissiveness

Here, our objective is to analyse the degree of permissiveness displayed by British Muslims in relation to the prohibitions of their religion. Amongst the respondents – who range between the devout and the minimally-religious poles – most commitment was shown with respect to abstinence from alcohol, non-halal food, abortion and sexual relations before marriage as the four most important prohibitions.

i. Alcoholic Drinks

Of the respondents 8% pointed out that they drink alcohol. These individuals belonged to different age groups. Ten of them were between 15 and 24 years old. Five of them were between 25 and 29 years old and the rest were over 30. Therefore, age group is not a significant factor.

Figure 5.1: Drinking Alcohol Among British Muslims in Brent

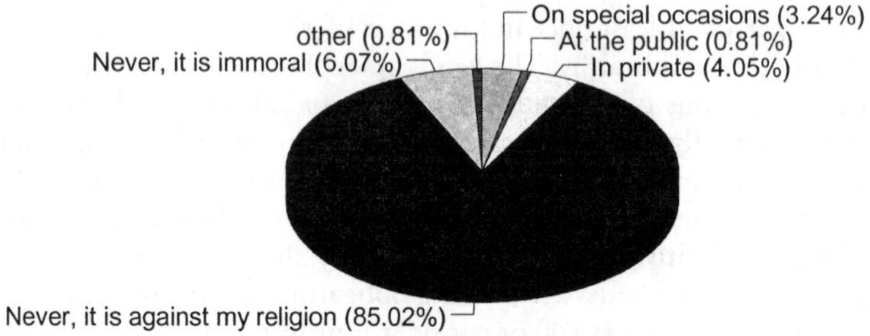

On special occasions (3.24%)
At the public (0.81%)
In private (4.05%)
other (0.81%)
Never, it is immoral (6.07%)

Never, it is against my religion (85.02%)

From the point of view of identity, drinking alcohol could be viewed as a sign of a critical shift from traditional, religious Muslim identity to an anglicized identity. This research shows that in many respects those Muslims who do not mind drinking alcohol are less traditional and religious than those who do. For example, in terms of choice of clothing, 70% of those who drink alcohol stated that their choice of clothing is influenced by film stars or other celebrities in the West and by contemporary Western fashion. Among them, only one person pointed out that her choice of clothing is based on religious tradition.

In addition, 35% of those who drink alcohol do not pray at all, while only 10% of all the respondents stated that they do not pray at all. This shows that there is a significant difference between those who drink alcohol and those who do not drink in terms of religious practice.

Another comparison shows interdependence between drinkers of alcohol and the way they introduce their identity: 55% of those who drink alcohol identify themselves first as British then as Muslim, while only 14.6% of all the respondents describe themselves in this way. This means that those British Muslims who drink alcohol identify with being British more than those who do not drink at all.

ii. Non-Halal Food

One of the central concerns for Muslims is the provision of halal food. This issue has been considered as a symbol of Muslim cultural identity. Many Muslim organizations engage local government and educational authorities in discussions regarding such provision, and this relatively new demand of Muslims has been given increasing attention in newspapers and public meetings. Although many of the British Muslims in this survey are not fully practising Muslims, a high proportion of the respondents have shown a great affinity for halal food (81.4%); 9.7% have had non-halal food occasionally, and the remainder had no particular views either way (8.9%).

Table 5.15: Relationships Between Consumption of non-Halal Food and Choice of Clothing

Have you ever eaten non-halal food?	Your choice of clothing is influenced by:					
	Stars of film and screen (%)	Contemporary fashion (%)	Ethnic tradition (%)	Religious tradition (%)	None (%)	Total (%)
Never	21 (10.4)	84 (41.8)	37 (18.4)	56 (27.9)	3 (1.5)	201 (81.4)
Sometimes	5 (20.8)	10 (41.7)	6 (25)	1 (4.2)	2 (8.3)	24 (9.7)
I do not ever think about it	2 (9.1)	11 (50)	7 (31.8)	1 (4.5)	1 (4.5)	22 (8.9)
Total	28 (11.3)	105 (42.5)	50 (20.2)	58 (23.5)	6 (1.4)	247 (100.0)

Table 5.15 illustrates a comparison between the views of respondents on the issue of non-halal food and choice of clothing. This shows that those who are inattentive to halal food are significantly ($P = 0.02 < 0.05$) less influenced in their choice of clothing by religious tradition (4.2%) compared to those who have never eaten non-halal food (27.9%).

iii. Abortion

Abortion is another gauge of permissiveness in the moral values of people who are brought up in either the Christian or Islamic religion. A small proportion

(5.7%) of the respondents believe in the legitimacy of abortion; a percentage among those believed that the choice of abortion is necessary to family planning. This group of respondents who favoured abortion are closely integrated within British society in terms of identity and culture; 57.1% of those who believe in abortion identified themselves first as British, secondly, as Muslim. The remainder of 35.7% of this group had placed Muslim identity before 'Britishness', whilst a small percentage of the respondents had not answered the question ($P = 0.00\% <0.01$).

The impact of American films and actors among those who believe abortion is an acceptable choice for family planning (78.6%), is significantly higher than those who do not believe so (59.3%). The rate for the heavy viewers among those British Muslims who believe abortion is an acceptable choice for family planning (64.3%), is also significantly higher ($P = 0.01 <0.05$) than those who believe it is wrong (46.4%).

iv. Sexual Relationships before Marriage

According to the results of this survey, 88.3% of the respondents believe that sexual relationships before marriage are illegitimate and immoral conduct; 7.3% believe that sexual relationships before marriage are normal and necessary. The rest of the respondents either do not have a clear idea about the subject (2%) or religious views are not important to them (2.4%). This correlation strongly suggests that what people watch on television impacts on their mode of behaviour within society.

In order to explain how permissiveness can be related to the process of globalization as well as the religious identity of the respondents, one can hardly overemphasize the acceleration of the process of secularization and liberalization in the postmodern world. The process of globalization, as has been discussed, intensifies and generalizes the social philosophy of Western liberalism; and central to such a philosophy is the concept of moral relativism. This is a process which marginalizes immutable, religious values and removes religion from sociopolitical institutions. Therefore, actions which were once regarded as sinful, such as sex before marriage, are no longer treated as negative phenomena'. On the other hand, a low percentage of such deviation from the religious norm indicates the strength of religious identity or resistance against Western culture. Both uncritical adoption and hostile rejection in the face of Western culture are responses to globalization.

---

1.   For example, the findings of this research further indicate that transnational films, Western films and actors are more influential among the group who believe in the legitimacy of sexual relations before marriage (77.8%) compared with those who do not believe such relations to be legitimate (59.9%).

5.5. Television, Cinema and Religious Belief

In the age of globalization, religious belief among British Muslims in Brent seems to vary between two poles, one that can be characterized as 'pious' and the other as 'minimally religious'. It is clear that the pole of atheism or unbelief is practically non-existent. Even if the practical application of religion is minimalist among some, belief in the essential tenets of the faith has not been shaken or dislodged by the phenomena associated with globalization. The strength of this association between belief and globalization is explained by Turner (1994: 78) in his theory of non-cognitive religious responses to the process of globalization. This theory explains the persistence of religious belief together with the weakening of religious practice partly as a result of globalization. Turner argues that people today do not adopt or reject religion directly for ideological or rational reasons – their belief has become 'relativized' or 'reproduced' according to whether or not it is relevant or irrelevant to their everyday needs and concerns.

Table 5.16: Attitude Towards Islamic Beliefs

Content	Believe (%)	Do not believe (%)	I have no idea (%)	It is not important to me (%)	No answer (%)
There is no God except Allah and Muhammad is His messenger	96.8	–	0.4	0.8	2.3
Our conduct in this world will have to be accounted for on the day of judgement	93.5	0.8	3.2	0.8	1.6
Nothing happens in life or in history without Allah's will; all is His work	86.6	6.1	3.6	1.2	2.4
Jihad is a duty for all Muslims	81.4	4.9	7.7	2.8	3.2

Table 5.16 clearly shows that a high proportion of the respondents believe in Allah and his messenger (96.8%). In addition, accountability in the afterlife for our conduct is accepted (93.5%) overwhelmingly by respondents. They believe in divine predestination – 'Nothing happens in life or in history without Allah's will; all is his work' (86.6%). The vast majority of the respondents also

believe in *jihad* (81.4%). Therefore, as Turner (1994: 78) suggests, one's deepest beliefs and ideals cannot readily be changed by global factors. The following cross-tabulations confirm this:

1. The relationship between TV viewing and belief in Allah and His Messenger is insignificant ($P = 0.99 > 0.01$ and 0.05).
2. The relationship between TV viewing and belief in accountability of our conduct in the life hereafter is insignificant ($P = 1.00 > 0.01$ and 0.05).
3. The relationship between TV viewing and belief that, 'Nothing happens in life or in history without Allah's will; all is His work' ($P = 0.93 > 0.01$ and 0.05).

This means that, whilst globalization forces have penetrated many elements of everyday life, including religious practice, they do not appear to have had a major impact on the basic religious and traditional beliefs prevalent among the British Muslims in this survey.

This becomes clearer if we compare belief in fundamental religious precepts with attitudes towards the social and cultural applications and implications of religion. While adherence to basic beliefs – such as belief in God or the life hereafter – has remained largely unaffected, a high degree of change and adaptation is visible when we look at attitudes towards other aspects of applied religion, such as: the sociality or individuality of Islamic belief (see Table 5.17); attitudes towards political Islam; necessity of *hijab* for women (Table 5.18); pluralism or absolutism of Islamic truth; and the belief in the necessity of reforming traditional Islam.

Table 5.17: Attitudes of Respondents Towards Hijab, *Plurality of Islamic Truth and Traditional Islam*

Content	Believe (%)	Do not believe (%)	I have no idea (%)	It is not important to me (%)	No answer (%)
Hijab is compulsory for all Muslim women	175 (70.9)	40 (16.2)	7 (2.8)	16 (6.5)	9 (3.6)
Islam is not the only truth	42 (17)	162 (65.6)	20 (8.1)	12 (4.9)	11 (4.5)
Traditional Islam should change	38 (15.4)	159 (64.4)	29 (11.7)	14 (5.7)	7 (2.8)

While a large (70.9%) majority of the respondents believed that *hijab* is obligatory for a Muslim woman, a significant minority (29.1 `%) either did not agree or are not particularly concerned. The importance of this data will be more apparent to us if we consider that a substantial percentage of the respondents (44.9%) have been educated in Islamic schools and belong to relatively religious families.

Different groups of respondents in this survey manifest divergent views on the issue of *hijab*.

Table 5.18: Different Viewpoints on Hijab *Among Different Groups*

Hijab is compulsory for all women:	Group code					Total (%)
	Khoei School (%)	Islamia School (%)	Islamic College for Advanced Studies (%)	Students in different colleges (%)	Muslims in the public domain (%)	
Believe	38 (21.7)	49 (28)	11 (6.3)	35 (20.0)	42 (24.0)	175 (70.9)
Do not believe	2 (5.0)	1 (2.5)	–	19 (47.5)	18 (45.0)	40 (16.2)
I have no idea	1 (14.3)	1 (14.3)	–	–	5 (71.4)	7 (2.8)
It is not important to me	–	2 (12.5)	1 (6.3)	9 (56.3)	4 (25.0)	16 (6.5)
No answer	3 (33.3)	1 (11.1)	1 (11.1)	3 (33.3)	1 (11.1)	9 (3.6)
Total	44 (17.8)	54 (21.9)	13 (5.3)	66 (26.7)	70 (28.3)	247 (100.0)

Table 5.18 shows that 92.5% of those respondents who did not believe in the necessity of wearing *hijab* were of the group who did not attend Islamic schools, with a very small percentage of non-observance of *hijab* for the students of al-Khoei (5%) and Islamia schools (2.5%). The majority of those respondents who suggested that *hijab* is not important to them are from the group of people who do not go to Islamic schools (81.3%). This shows that there is a significant difference between ordinary British Muslims and those Muslims who organize their life according to Islamic values and within a Muslim environment. Their religious identity and their response to the transnational culture are quite different. One can see this in terms of a division, with one group being the embodiment of cultural resistance, whilst

the other can be seen as a reproduction of the old and new culture, or assimilation into everyday culture.

However, the role of *hijab* is a pivotal one, especially in relation towards Muslim women's identity and in regard to the social responsibilities that differentiate them from non-Muslims. A Muslim woman who wears the *hijab* is immediately identifiable as a Muslim (see Murden, 1998). The discrimination faced by Muslim women who wear *hijab* in Western societies has received much attention in recent years.[1]

The findings here will be expanded upon in Chapters 6 and 7, so as to evaluate the importance and the role of *hijab* in relation to the construction of identity for Muslim women. The importance of this issue for Muslim women will be readily apparent from the forthright responses given by Sadaf, Mariam and Alireza, quoted below:

> My visual identity is my *hijab* (veil covering) which signifies my devotion and submission to my life according to Islam and this includes the *Qur'an* and *Sunnah*. I do not take part in anti-Islamic practices/trends etc. with the fear of upsetting my creator. (Sadaf)

> I think my *hijab* is my Muslim identity. (Mariam)

> Islam says to wear *hijab*, West says 'Dress how you like'; it is a question of prayers verses clubbing. (Alireza)

One can argue that the practice of wearing *hijab* for Muslim women especially in the West is a type of resistance against the general trend of Western global culture. It can be understood as a reverse phenomenon, one in which global Islamic norms impinge on local British Muslim identity, creating a radical contrast with the dominant or homogenizing forces of cultural globalization.

5.6. Global Information and British Muslim Identity

Today's informational networks are described in terms of a 'superhighway', with the implicit meaning that access to the informational infrastructure is free and universal. However, this information is channeled through three main conduits (cable, fibre optics and satellites), all of which are owned and operated by a small number of Western-dominated powerful partners in the telecommunications industry. Future developments promise to be even more

---

1.   See the report, *Islamophobia – A Challenge for us all* by the Runnymede Trust, 1997.

centralized; for example, Microsoft, Intel and Boeing are now working on an alliance to provide a low-level satellite blanket in the early years of this century (Steele, 1998: 1).

5.6.1. Internet

The expansion of the internet exemplifies the potential of this new technology. The internet has a number of different levels of use; email, chat groups, worldwide websites and online services. The last two of these are the most rapidly expanding and of most interest to commercial concerns. Yet the number of worldwide websites and internet users has recently expanded rapidly. The internet is a local/global communication system, which has come to have an important share in shaping a network society and 'possibly the most effective medium in accomplishing time–space compression' (Waters, 2000: 205).

Table 5.19: Gender and Access to the Internet

Gender	Yes (%)	No (%)
Males	47 (39.5)	72 (60.5)
Females	60 (46.9)	68 (53.1)
Total	107 (43.3)	140 (56.7)

According to this research, 43.3% of the respondents have access to the internet. There is a slight difference between males (39.5%) and females (46.9%) in terms of the usage of the internet (Table 5.19). Among them 39.3% have between 1 and 10 global contacts per week and 16.8% more than 10 contacts. This shows that the internet plays a central role as a global media tool amongst a component of British Muslims in Brent.

Among those respondents who have access to the internet, 60.7% of them spent 1–2 hours; 14.9% 3–4 hours and 11.2% more than 5 hours every week on the internet. The rest spend less than 1 hour every week. Their interest in the internet combines a variety of subjects. For 46.4% of the respondents, the internet is simply a communication tool. They use it for the purposes of electronic mail. Since the internet is a new phenomenon, many users look on it only as a general source of information, not for professional aims. Accordingly, 15.4% of the participants in this survey have said that the internet is like a shop window for different types of information, hence they were 'looking for a variety of information on the internet'. There is also a group of people (14.5%) who are fascinated by overseas news and information as well as 18.2%

of the participants who look for different websites of religious organizations. The rest are more interested in business and technical information on the internet (5.5%). There is a significant difference between males and females in terms of usage of internet in some areas. Compared to males (37%), females (63%) use the internet primarily for the exchange of email. There is also a substantial difference between males (35.3%) and females (64.7%) in relation to access to the internet for general information. Of those who seek economic information, 83% are men and 16.7% are women.

Table 5.20: Gender and the Main Areas of Usage of the Internet

Content	Male %	Female %	Total (%)
Exchange of email	62.7	37.0	51 (46.4%)
General information	64.7	35.3	17 (15.4%)
Overseas news and information	50.0	50.0	16 (4.5%)
Different religious websites	50.0	50.0	20 (18.2%)

This shows that the internet has become a huge global communications tool which can instantaneously create closer links between users exchanging information with the rest of the world. This has to a great extent created the potential for global awareness and wider shared commitments and values between Muslims around the world.

Apart from professional usage of the internet with regard to the job requirement or academic status of the users, one observes that general usage of internet is linked to the identity orientation of the users. For example, Table 5.21 shows a clear correlation between a tendency towards religious websites and the practice of religion: 90% of those who show an interest in religious sites pointed out that they regularly perform their five daily prayers. The proportion of the rest who do not seek such sites was seen to be lower as regards the performance of their regular daily prayers. This indicates that apart from the general uses of the internet, such as the exchange of email, other types of information that people search for can also be related to cultural, religious and sociopolitical characteristics of users of the internet. Comparison between those who have contact with Muslims from around the world and access to the internet shows that 62.6% of those who have access to the internet indicated that they have also close contact with other Muslims from around the world (P = 0.006 <0.05 and 0.01).

Table 5.21: Relationship Between Favourite Information in the Internet and Performing Daily Prayers

Favourite information in the internet	How often do you pray?					
	Regularly, five times a day (%)	All prayers except morning prayer (%)	Occasionally (%)	Never (%)	No answer (%)	Total (%)
Exchange of emails	25 (49.0)	9 (17.6)	13 (25.5)	3 (5.9)	1 (2.0)	51 (20.6)
General information	11 (64.7)	1 (5.9)	4 (23.5)	1 (5.9)	–	17 (6.9)
Overseas news and information	4 (25.0)	6 (37.5)	6 (37.5)	–	–	16 (6.5)
Different religious website	18 (90.0)	1 (5.0)	–	–	1 (5.0)	20 (8.1)
Economic market	2 (33.3)	1 (16.7)	3 (50.0)	–	–	6 (2.4)
No answer	90 (65.7)	14 (10.2)	27 (19.7)	6 (4.4)	–	137 (55.5)
Total	150 (60.7)	32 (13.0)	53 (21.5)	10 (4.0)	2 (.8.0)	247 (100.0)

5.6.2. Press

The printed word plays an important role in creating a common language as well as cultural and political links with a particular society. It can also map a common religious and cultural identity on the basis of shared values and ideas.

Table 5.22 Chosen newspapers

Gender	I am not interested in news-papers (%)	The Guard-ian (%)	The Sun (%)	The Daily Mirror (%)	The Indepen-dent (%)	The Tele-graph (%)	The Times (%)	The Daily Jang (%)	The Daily Star (%)	Other News-papers (%)
Males	11 (31.4)	28 (59.6)	7 (63.6)	19 (54.3)	12 (42.9)	—	32 (51.6)	5 (83.3)	2 (50.0)	3 (20.0)
Females	24 (68.6)	19 (40.4)	4 (36.4)	16 (45.7)	16 (57.1)	4 (100.0)	30 (48.4)	1 (16.7)	2 (50.0)	12 (80.0)
Total	35 (14.2)	47 (19.0)	11 (4.5)	35 (14.2)	28 (11.3)	4 (1.6)	62 (25.1)	6 (2.4)	4 (1.6)	15 (6.1)

Table 5.22 shows that the non-British press does not interest respondents of this research significantly. The press of their native homeland (e.g. the *Jang* newspaper) is no exception either. Their interests are quite diverse; however *The Times* is the most popular newspaper (25.1%) followed by *The Guardian* (19.0%). Then comes the *Daily Mirror* (14.1%); the *Sun* and the *Daily Star* are less popular.

Overall one can draw the following conclusion from the survey of respondents with reference to the impact of the press upon the day-to-day life of young British Muslims in the Borough of Brent: despite the influence of the press in global terms, its impact on the respondents was minimal. It is important to consider that the press does not have the same social and cultural function that television or even radio broadcasting has. In particular the foreign press (non-British) does not really play a major role in terms of the production of identity[1]. One reason could be that today's youth are not readily inclined to read newspapers, and this is due to a variety of reasons; one of these may be the fact that it is of little interest for them and it does not fulfil their actual needs. Furthermore, in contrast to television, newspaper text is

---

1. In the 19th century the press was the only medium capable of reaching a mass audience. It was a capability not fully realized until after the end of the First World War when other forms of social communication came to the fore, particularly broadcasting, which began to challenge the predominant position of the press as the main channel of entertainment and information in society. Today the visual media, such as television, takes up a greater proportion of the population's influence in leisure time, in particular the younger generations (see Ward, 1989: 21–57).

demanding; one needs to be motivated to read particular articles with interest and concentration. Newspapers do not attract the casual reader in the same way that television attracts the casual viewer.

5.7. Globalization, Social Relationships and British Muslim Identity

Globalization has enabled a juxtapositioning, a meeting and mixing of the people – within and outside the community at the local and global level. In other words, globalization industry has facilitated social relationships through telecommunication systems and the mass media. On the other hand, social relationships also reveal one's cultural isolation as well as one's multicultural and transnational cultural tendencies. The influence of the mass media on social relationships helps to show the relationship between globalization and religious identity. In this regard numerous questions were put to the interviewees.

Table 5.23: Contact with Other Muslims Around the World and Gender

Gender	Yes (%)	No (%)	No answer (%)
Males	80 (67.2)	30 (25.2)	9 (7.6)
Females	100 (78.1)	23 (18.0)	5 (3.9)
Total	180 (73.0)	53 (21.0)	14 (6.0)

As illustrated in Table 5.23 a high proportion (73%) of British Muslims in this research are in contact – via the electronic media, through news reports, etc. – with Muslims around the world. Such contact was not possible in the past and it is entirely a product of globalization. Chapter 7 will elaborate more upon the concept of the globalization of Islam and the recreation of 'the Muslim *umma*' through electronic media.

5.7.1. Friendship and Religion

As can be seen in Table 5.24, respondents were asked about their relationships with Muslims and non-Muslims. The objective here was to discover whether religion is a significant factor in determining tendencies as to whom one socializes with. If it is taken to be a significant factor, the extent of its importance must also be determined.

Friendships are among the most important forms of one's interaction within society. Traditionally Muslims have chosen other Muslims as their closest friends. This research has shown these boundaries are being transcended. Nearly half of the younger respondents do not make or break relationships because of the person's religion nor, usually, is religion taken into account when making friends.

Table 5.24: Friendship and Religion

Friendships and religion	Frequency	Percentage
I only establish friendships with Muslims	32	13.0
I prefer my friends to be Muslims	94	38.1
My friendship is not based on religion	107	43.3
I prefer non-Muslim friends	11	4.5
No answer	3	1.2

Of the respondents 107 (43%) pointed out that their friendships are not based upon religion. This clearly supports the suggestion that the secular attributes of individuals are not necessarily an obstacle when it comes to forming social relationships. Indeed only 13% of the respondents clearly stated that they specifically choose Muslims as friends. However a further 38.1% stated that they prefer Muslims as friends to non-Muslims; thus almost half of the respondents still tend to form friendships with Muslims. Data showed that 4.5% of the respondents stated that they prefer non-Muslims to Muslims as friends; 72.7% of this group have a longer background in Britain and they have chosen Britain as their permanent home. This shows that some of the norms and values in British Muslim society have changed as a result of living for a long time in the multicultural Western society.

5.7.2. Social Relationships with Non-Muslims

While Muslims, Christians and Jews may well have had relationships, even friendships, in the past, such associations were never so frequently encountered as to be regarded as a prevalent social norm. They were occasional, not normal. However friendship between peoples from different religious backgrounds established as a regular cultural pattern would appear to be a new social phenomenon.

A substantial percentage (75.3%) of those who chose Muslims as their best friends have close contact with Muslims around the world. British Muslims who are in close contact with non-Muslims as their best friends (65.9%) also have significant contact with Muslims around the world (Table 5.25). Therefore, those who have chosen Muslims as their best friends have a slightly wider network of relationships with Muslims in a global context.

Table 5.25: Friendships and Global Contact with Other Muslims

Best friend	Do you have any contact with other Muslims around the World?			Total (%)
	Yes (%)	No (%)	No answer (%)	
Muslim	149 (75.3)	38 (19.2)	11 (5.6)	198 (80.2)
Non-Muslim	29 (65.9)	13 (29.5)	2 (4.5)	44 (17.8)
No answer	2 (40.0)	2 (40.0)	1 (20.0)	5 (2.0)
Total	180 (72.9)	53 (21.5)	14 (5.7)	247 (100.0)

A comparison between different groups of respondents and the extent of their friendships with Muslims and non-Muslims shows that there is significant (P = 0.00 <0.01 and 0.05) difference between those who have been educated in Islamic schools and those who attend non-Islamic schools and colleges.

Table 5.26: Attitude of Different Groups of Respondents with Regard to Friendship with Muslims and non-Muslims

Group code	Majority of friends:			Total (%)
	Muslim (%)	Non-Muslim (%)	No answer (%)	
Khoei School	41 (93.2)	1 (2.3)	2 (4.5)	44 (17.8)
Islamia School	48 (88.9)	5 (9.3)	1 (1.9)	54 (21.9)
Islamic College for Advanced Studies	10 (76.9)	–	3 (23.1)	13 (5.3)
Muslim Students in different colleges in Brent	37 (56.1)	25 (37.9)	4 (6.1)	66 (26.7)
Muslims in the public domain	33 (47.1)	24 (34.3)	13 (18.6)	70 (28.3)
Total	169 (68.4)	55 (22.3)	23 (9.3)	247 (100.0)

According to data presented in Table 5.28 those who attend Islamic schools are more detached from non-Muslim society. This can be due to the fact that whilst the public sphere and wider culture, together with globalization forces, play an important role in the construction of identity, the religious commitment of the parents and impact of the Muslim environment at school can predominate over the influences stemming from the larger social matrix.

5.7.3 Marital Partnerships

Although endogamy is not recommended in Islam, it has been a vital element of boundary-maintenance for most Muslims in the past (Jacobson, 1998: 90). The tradition of marriage within kinship groups has also been the norm among many of the Asian communities.

Table 5.27: Preference for Marriage

Preferences	Frequency	Percentage (%)
From my parents' countries	83	33.6
A Muslim regardless of their parents' birthplace	107	43.3
A British or European person	1	0.4%
A Muslim who is a citizen of Western country	25	10.1
An open-minded person regardless of whether they are Muslim or not	8	3.2
No answer	23	9.3
Total	247	100

This research gives evidence of a significant shift of attitudes as regards choice of marriage partners: the conventional or traditional attitude in the past, when the majority of people preferred to marry either a relative or someone from their own locale, has been superseded by a more 'globalized' attitude towards marital partners. According to the findings of this research, while 33.6% of the core respondents said that they would prefer to marry someone from their parents' country of birth (see Table 5.27), 43.3% stated that 'they would prefer a Muslim regardless of their birthplace'. 10.1% pointed out that 'they would prefer to marry someone who is a citizen of a Western country'; this is due to the fact that European Muslims have come to accept many norms of their surrounding culture. This indicates that the place where marriage takes place, together with the question of the nationality of the couple, are not considered as major factors. A small proportion of the respondents have crossed the religious boundaries; they state that they would prefer an open-minded person irrespective of their religion (3.2%).

The observations by Modood *et al.* (1994: 64) on ethnicity and race and on mixed interracial marriages suggest that nearly half of the first generation group questioned had no clear views on the subject of mixed-race or mixed-ethnicity marriages, and several of the first generation respondents felt that relationships between different racial and ethnic groups were almost inevitable. He also expounds that over half of the second generation group that were surveyed expressed favourable sentiments about mixed relationships.

Mixed marriages and what we call 'transnational marriage' is an inherent embodiment of globalization. People are ready to marry with someone from abroad; hence a certain mode of 'delocalization' of marriage is taking place.

5.8. Globalization and Day-to-Day Affairs

Day-to-day matters like leisure time, clothing and eating are an important part of life and are highly affected by the process of globalization. This has an important role in the construction of identity as well. This section will examine the respondents' daily practices and their relationship with the processes of globalization.

5.8.1. Leisure Time

From the mid-19th century onwards, a massive leisure industry came into being in Britain. Indeed the whole leisure industry was ultimately connected with the distribution of commodities. With the exception of broadcasting, until commercial television brought it into line in 1955, the leisure industry had certain characteristics (Yeo, 1976). It was frankly commercial and often closely tied to advertising. It was specialized, having a long-term tendency to conglomerate with other specialists for financial advantage. It was largely based on a technological revolution, as significant for ways of life as the first industrial revolution. It was subject to the normal laws of the business game – where individual enterprises flourished they exploded into very large concerns thereby setting the context for others. Where they did not flourish they tended to die out. These constraints applied to shops or pubs as much as to the religious and voluntary groups (Yeo, 1976: 310-17).

The impact of television on leisure time has been sizable. Television has markedly increased its share of the media market sector. Television viewing as a primary activity, excluding very disrupted viewing while people are doing something else consumes more leisure time of Americans than any other activity. Among almost 40 kinds of primary exclusive categories into which the 24 hours of the day can be divided, television viewing falls behind only sleep and time spent at work. Despite the variations in total viewing attributable to sex, age group, ethnicity, education and socioeconomic status, it is a rare set of circumstances where television viewing is not the predominant leisure activity. Television's and now electronic games' most marked effects appears to have been to reduce time spent sleeping. It also appears to have reduced time spent in social gatherings away from home, in listening to the radio, reading books, miscellaneous leisure, conversation, travel related to leisure, movie-going, religious activities and household tasks (Becker, 1976; Comstoc, Chaffee, McCombs & Roberts, 1978).

Kubey & Csikszentmihalyis (1990: 148–70) suggested, in a variety of studies in different nations, that television has been shown to decrease the amount of time spent with friends and doing housework and hobbies, as has already been mentioned. They discovered that, although heavy viewers did not spend more time alone across all environments, they did spend substantially more time alone at home than light viewers. Because television viewing is a homebound activity, more viewing also means more time with family and less time with friends, in public and in transit.

Of the sampled population under study 54.3% preferred TV viewing as a first choice during their leisure time. In comparison to the viewers in the United States (31%) and the Republic of Ireland (19.7%), the degree of TV viewing as a first leisure-time activity among these British Muslims of this research is very high. The second and third priorities for the respondents is religious activity (13.8%) and visiting friends (11.7%), which again, in comparison to the respondents in the study of Kubey & Csikszentmihalyis (1990) and Ameli's research (1995), is significantly higher. This difference may be due to many structural factors, such as religious understanding, and cultural and social circumstances. Perhaps the lack of social choices for British Muslims is also one of the reasons for this difference (Back, 1996). For instance the IHRC (2000) has reported that there are currently extreme forms of social discrimination against Muslims; this has the effect of marginalizing them from the public sphere, thus restricting their scope for social and cultural activity within the wider community.

5.8.2 Choice of Clothing

In traditional and even modern society, choice of clothing is basically part of religious and ethnic provisions. In the globalization era, choice of clothing alongside other features of identity, has been influenced by transnational culture, which is heavily affected by contemporary fashion (42.5%) and displayed by film stars and other celebrities (11.8%). The choice of clothing for the remainder of British Muslims in this research has been influenced either by ethnic tradition (20.2%) or religious tradition (23.5%). There is a significant ($P = 0.00$ <0.01) relationship between choice of clothing and attending an Islamic school or college. Most of those respondents who are affected in their choice of clothing by religious tradition have been educated in Islamic schools or colleges in Britain.

Table 5.28: Views of Respondents on Traditional Clothes

Views	Frequency	Percentage
Embarrassed	28	11.3
Indifferent	80	32.4
Felt proud	45	18.2
Normal	3	1.2
Other	10	4
No answer	12	4.9
Total	247	100.0

Table 5.28 sheds light on the attitudes and inclinations of the respondents with regard to the wearing of traditional clothes. While 11.3% felt embarrassed wearing traditional clothes, a substantial proportion of them were indifferent to the idea (32.4%); 18.2% of the respondents said that they felt proud to wear traditional clothes. Resistance identity can be said to be more pronounced among those who feel proud of or honoured by wearing traditional clothes than those who are more interested in contemporary fashion.

5.8.3. Food Preferred

The last table (Table 5.29) in this chapter illustrates the priority given to different kinds of food by the respondents. Almost half of the respondents are interested in fast foods such as McDonald's (26.3%), Burger King (2%), Pizza (16.6%) and fish and chips (6.1%). However, a substantial percentage of the respondents still prefer their own traditional foods (49%).

Table 5.29: What Types of Foods Do You Prefer?

Food	Frequency	Percentage
McDonald's	65	26.3
Burger King	5	2.0
Pizza	41	16.6
Fish and chips	15	6.1
I prefer my own traditional foods	121	49
Total	247	100.0

As Featherstone (1995) has argued, McDonald's or any other American product not only entails economic efficiency, but also represents a cultural message. Therefore a McDonald's or a Burger King is not only consumed physically as material substance, but also culturally as an image and an icon of a particular way of life. Our survey suggests that the impact of American culture among the respondents in this respect is substantial.

What has emerged from the data of this chapter is a varied picture of the impact of globalization on British Muslim identity. In the five dimensions of identity that we have focused upon, a highly uneven, but nonetheless revealing, set of features are apparent. In respect of 'religious understanding', we have seen that the basics of the faith have not been substantially altered. Islamic belief, at least as regards the 'raw material' of traditional dogma and doctrine, does not seem to have been dislodged. What we cannot tell, however, with any degree of precision is the way in which the content of belief is psychologically or spiritually assimilated. What can be gauged, to some extent, is the extent to which the simple dogmas of the faith translate into political activism, Islamism or individualism. From the responses given, it appears that in this domain the impact of global forces is such as to render *jihad* an important concomitant of religious belief (see Table 5.16); this can clearly be attributed to two aspects of the global process of homogenization: on the one hand, a homogenized anti-Muslim slant in Western-dominated global media provokes a reactive mode of identity, a reassertion of the most forceful dimensions of identity; and on the other hand, the globalization of a relatively homogenous anti-Western Islamist ideology itself serves as a kind of shadow of the 'opponent'. This will be further explored in Chapters 6 and 7, which address the questions of homogenization and heterogenization.

Returning to the question of religious belief, the affirmation, for example, of belief in the 'existence' of God and in the hereafter can imply quite a wide variety of existential imperatives: to what extent will such beliefs actually determine one's inner imaginative life and one's outer active life? Such a question can be partially answered, as regards the area of outward manifestations of belief, by turning to the responses given in respect of the other more practical dimensions of identity.

In terms of the 'practice of religion', the data revealed that there was a wide spectrum of adherence to the normative rituals, ranging from the maximalists to the minimalists to the indifferent. Here, one observes the influence of the diversification of choice, together with the secular content of much of what is being offered as choices for the individual in the 'global market'. Even if the majority of the choices made accessible by the global media is not intrinsically contrary to religion, it is their very diversity, volume and density that constitutes an implicitly secular force; that is to say, a force that pushes religion into the margins of the field of attention. Religious belief may still remain, but the substance with which it works, the depth of the impact it has upon the active aspects of identity, will vary greatly as a result of this massive widening of choice. It is not only in the realm of religious practice that this diversity is manifest, but also in terms of 'social relationships' and 'day-to-day issues'. In these two realms also, the diversity of choice has clearly expanded the domain within which non-religious factors gain access to decisions that, collectively, manifest one's identity and in turn determine the way in which it will develop and evolve. What should be stressed above all is the rapidity with which these determinants of outward identity are evolving. As will be seen in the following chapter, the types of identity produced by these expanding conditions are themselves of a dynamic and not static order; the nature of the relationship between inward self-identification and outward expression of that identity will itself not be static, but will reflect the rapidly changing configurations of forces that are being given global expression and that are being filtered through the channels of local environment. An analysis of the reactions and responses of individual Muslims to these 'glocal' influences are the only means of obtaining a better picture of the nuances of identity in concrete contexts. The next chapter will distinguish various 'types' of British Muslims, in an attempt to identify for the purposes of analysis the different basic categories of reaction and response to the process of globalization.

SIX

Globalization and the Process of Homogenization

In this chapter we shall examine the way in which British Muslims in Brent are subjected to the forces of globalization. The premise of this study focuses on how 'global' culture can produce two processes that work concomitantly. On the one hand there is homogenization and, on the other, heterogenization. In both processes, it is a question of cultural forces expanding: becoming concentrated and diffused in a relatively monolithic manner in the process of homogenization, and becoming fragmented and diffused in diverse ways, in the process of heterogenization.

In the light of this two-fold impact, the concept of British Muslim identity will be examined in relation to the process of globalization. The notion of citizenship with regard to British Muslims will be considered as a phenomenon that has been affected to a large extent by the process of globalization. Then there will be a review of the process of homogenization, while the following chapter will elaborate on the issue of heterogenization. In particular, this chapter considers the concept of Americanization as the principal form of cultural homogenization. A critical discussion of the impact of this Americanization upon British Muslim identity in Brent will follow; then there will be an overview of the impact of globalization on the Muslim *umma* generally, the result of which has manifested itself in the form of 'reverse globalization'.

6.1. Globalization and British Muslim Identity

The issue of British identity is in serious question today. There is a continuing fierce debate over whether, and to what extent, any distinct elements of the British identity still remain (see Alibhai-Brown, 2000: 26).

6.1.1. *'Britishness' and British Muslim Identity*

In the context of any discussion regarding British Muslim identity, the actual notion of Britishness itself needs to be explored. The concept of Britishness rests upon the invention of the nation of 'Great Britain' itself, an entity that was 'invented in 1707 when the Parliament of Westminster passed the Act of Union linking Scotland to England and Wales' (Colley, 1992: 11). At the beginning of the 18th century, Great Britain was said to be like the Christian doctrine of the Trinity, both three and one, and altogether something of a mystery (Colley, 1992: 13). Colley makes a compelling argument to the effect that British national consciousness was built upon, and never completely eradicated, existing regional, local identities. She argues that the sense of being English, Welsh or Scottish remained stronger than the sense of being British.

In the 18th century the sense of Englishness, Welshness and Scottishness 'were cut across by strong regional attachments, and scored over again by loyalties to village, town, family and landscape' (Colley, 1992: 17). Despite the fact that many of these disparities would become attenuated as a result of technical advances in transportation, and by increased operation of free trade throughout the island, the key factor identified by Colley in the process by which an overarching sense of Britishness came about was a feeling of distinctness in relation to others, across the shore:

> Men and women came to define themselves as Britons, in addition to defining themselves in many other ways, because circumstances impressed them with the belief that they were different from those beyond their shores, and in particular different from their prime enemy, the French. Not so much consensus or homogeneity or centralization at home, as a strong sense of dissimilarity from those without proved to be the essential cement.
>
> (Colley, 1992: 17)

The binding force of Protestantism, together with the establishment of the British Empire, strengthened this incipient British identity; it might be said that British identity was at its strongest when the British Empire was at its strongest, and that, steadily since the end of the World War II, the elements that made for the distinctiveness of British identity have been waning. As Colley argues:

> The factors that provided for the forging of a British nation in the past have largely ceased to operate. Protestantism, that once vital cement, has now a limited influence on British culture ... Recurrent wars with the states of Continental Europe have in all likelihood come to an end, so different

kinds of Britons no longer feel the same compulsion as before to remain united in the face of the enemy from without. And, crucially, both commercial supremacy and imperial hegemony have gone.

(Colley, 1992: 374)

However, the extent to which the examination of Britishness is pertinent to the discussion in hand is largely determined by the extreme fluidity of the notion itself: Britishness means different things to different people.

All the varying markers that together comprise identity *per se* must be transposed onto the larger map of British identity as influenced by the processes of globalization and to a lesser extent, Europeanization. These processes must in turn be considered in the light of the two forces of nationalism, and national identity or citizenship. (Here, the term nationalism is to be distinguished from patriotism simply to avoid the confusing pejorative undertones that the term patriotism possesses [Raphael Samuel, 1989].) On the one hand nationalism and the resultant affiliation to a homeland is a question that has assumed growing political importance, correlative to the steady demise in nationalistic sentiment in postwar Britain. As the temporal distance from conflicts involving the efforts of all communities on the mainland of the UK has grown, the force of movements toward European integration has correspondingly grown, giving rise to many open debates on all levels about British national identity. On the other hand, the movement of peoples throughout the globe has shaped the notions of national identity as distinct from a sense of nationalism. The demands of border controls as well as economic markets are indelibly shaping how and in what ways people in the UK consider themselves British. The debate about the question of Britishness has assumed vital political importance, and has been fuelled by research findings, such as the report by the *Commission on the Future of Multi-Ethnic Britain* (Parekh, 2000), and a plethora of publications such as those by Paxman (1999), Marr (1999), Kearney (2000) and Alibhai-Brown (2000).

All have recognized the vital importance of socioeconomic grouping and generational factors in shaping individual notions of Britishness, and the only discernible consensus about the terms are their fluidity: 'Britishness is less unified, more diverse and pluralistic, than is normally imagined.' (Parekh, 2000: 36)

As Alibhai-Brown has stated, markers such as, 'The monarchy, love, sex and marriage, child-rearing and human rights ... [could] once be safely understood and where common ground within limits did exist, [these] are now far from settled. There is no package deal any more. Previously, if you were on the left or right, you knew what your thoughts should be on all of the issues listed above. Now there is no such safety ...' (Alibhai-Brown, 2000b: 270). Alibhai-

Brown cites globalization as a key factor likely to accelerate this trend, causing not only economic instability but mistrust, disorder and identity crises:

> While the old are still quarrelling about the European Union, multicul-turalism and globalization, the young appear to be making their own way in the world. Stronger identification by the young with the United States on the one hand and with Europe on the other, and a greater ease among many of them with the idea and reality of diversity, have caused a further weakening of attachment to that formerly venerated sense of national destiny.
>
> (Alibhai-Brown 2000a: 27)

The existence of 'pan-national virtual communities' means there is no longer any discernible distinction between British national identity, and other European or American identities. Paxman (1999) in the preface of his latest book: *The English: A Portrait of a People* said that: 'These four elements – the end of empire, the cracks opening in the so-called United Kingdom, the pressures for the English to plunge into Europe, and the uncontrollability of international business – set me wondering. What did it mean to be English?' Paxman (1999: 264) has clearly stated that, 'The English metropolitan elite now has more in common with Parisians or New Yorkers than it does with rural or suburban England. And so many of the other outward signals of Englishness, from clothing to language, are now universal property.'

If Englishness is itself unclear, then the notion of Britishness will be all the more unclear. It is clear that the calls for greater devolution of power away from London, towards the cities of Scotland and Wales, are evidence of a major diminution of the sense of British identity; they are not just to be seen as efforts to wrest political power away from the capital city. They are expressions of a breakdown of the sense of British as opposed to English or Welsh or Scottish culture and identity. 'What seems indisputable is that a substantial rethinking of what it means to be British can no longer be evaded' (Colley, 1992: 375).

If neither British nor English identity have clear-cut and easily defined characteristics, then the task of defining British *Muslim* identity will be even more elusive. Our task here, however, is not to enter into the abstract debate over labels and markers of identity, only to briefly state what appear to be the main obstacles in the way of reconciling Muslim identity with Britishness. It is not controversial to claim that Muslim identity and British identity can only be reconciled with considerable difficulty. The two forms of identity appear to be at opposite ends of the spectrum.

One may take belief in God as a key defining characteristic of identity. Many are of the opinion that at the heart of Englishness is the Protestant Christian conviction that, even if God exists, He really does not matter when it comes to everyday behaviour.[1] The dogma of almost unconstrained free will coupled with modern scientific knowledge is seen by many as having squeezed God out of the material Universe.[2]

In direct contrast, Islam says that God certainly does exist, that there is nothing else that can begin to rival this indubitable fact in importance, and that the exercise of free will is at best greatly limited by constraints imposed by external factors, and at worst illusory[3]. These two philosophies are, as said above, not easy to harmonize, so the individual is faced with a constant struggle to navigate a course between them. However, Englishness is not defined or definable exclusively in terms of religious conviction or theological principles; far from it. Indeed, it can be argued that today's 'Englishness' must be defined more in terms of a secular reaction to the religious worldview than in terms of religion itself. This makes it possible to conceive of a mode of receptivity to non-Christian forms of religion within contemporary English identity, much more so than was the case in the past.

It also means that Muslims born or brought up in England are not subject to a strict 'Islam versus English Christianity' dichotomy, but a dichotomy between Islam and a prevailing secular culture in which Christianity itself is on the defensive. Thus it can be argued that, in regard to such issues as personal morality, the British Muslim will have more in common with a British Christian than the British Christian will have with a British secularist. The question of British identity, however problematic in itself, does not directly affect the research here conducted, as the focus is not on how Islam impacts upon British identity, but on how identity is perceived and enacted by Muslims born or brought up in Britain, and thus being designated as 'British Muslims'. Thus, what should be addressed directly now is the nature, the components, and the implications of British Muslim identity.

One objective way in which British Muslim identity can be differentiated from Muslim identities elsewhere is by reference to the factors 'birthplace'[4] 'place of up-bringing' and 'language'. British Muslims are those who are born

---

1. See Colley, 1992: 11 and Letter to Melanchthon, Epistolae 1988: 345, Martin Luther, 1521.
2. The views expressed on such questions by Bertrand Russell can be taken as broadly representative of public attitudes to religion in 20th-century Britain (see his *History of Western Philosophy*); and for an account of the effects of secularization on urban Western culture, see Harvey Cox, 1965.
3. See, for example, the *Qur'an*, 10: 100; 82: 27–29.
4. See definition of Britishness in H. Kearney (2000: 15).

in Britain, or brought up in Britain, from a young age; they are also citizens of Britain and have grown up predominantly within the framework of the English language. Language indeed is the vehicle for the expression of culture in each and every society.

British Muslim identity, then, is the result of a combination of an Islamic cultural dimension, which has roots in a deep historical process, and a British cultural dimension, which is itself not of a fixed and immutable nature; both the Islamic and the British aspects of identity are subject to the complex and often paradoxical forces of globalization, so that this compounded identity is extremely difficult to define in a precise and objective manner. As outlined in the *Parekh Report*: 'Identity refers to who we really are, self-understanding as to who we think we are, and self-conception as to what we would like to be. The three are dialectically related, and both shape and are shaped by each other' (Parekh, 2000a: 5).

These dialectical aspects of identity were explored in Brent to the question, concerning the relationship between Britishness and identity, 'How do you describe your identity?'. Of the respondents 42.1% selected the response: 'A Muslim who is British'; 16.6% of them indicated the response: 'A British citizen who is Muslim'. On the other hand, 30.8% of them chose the response: 'A person whose identity is established first by nationality', and 3.2% said that they 'care more about humanity, so religion and nationality is all nonsense'. These figures show the importance of nationalism in the definition of identity amongst the Brent Muslims.

In the interviews conducted within the context of our qualitative research, a similar question was asked: 'What is your understanding about British Muslim identity?' The following different replies were offered:

It's a developing one. It still seems to be lacking in the areas of politics and social integration. (Abdul Rahman, aged 22)

I have no understanding of what is meant by the term British Muslim identity. (Homam, aged 16)

A British Muslim is one who ideally is at ease between his religion and his surroundings. (Haroon, aged 19)

A Muslim who lives in Britain and lives according to British norms and standards. (Nadia, aged 21)

To be a good Muslim, even though we are living in Britain. (Farah, aged 18)

British Muslim community has a multi-ethnic composition. This influx of culture adds to the diversity of the British Muslims' identity. Therefore as regards the British Muslim identity, this is an equivocal issue.
(Sadaf, aged 23)

My understanding is that British Muslims will embrace all elements of Western culture as long as it doesn't contradict Islamic teachings.
(Yakoub, aged 19)

As some of the answers explicitly show, many young British Muslims do not have a single clearly-defined perception of British Muslim identity. On the contrary, the concept is complicated, heterogenized and equivocal for them. Even those who attempted to define British Muslim identity did so in a general and vague manner, making it difficult to perceive the essence of the concept. However, the following basic elements can be put together: To be a 'British Muslim' is:

1. to benefit from the British standards of life;
2. to have a diminished commitment to religion in a social context;
3. to be attached to an identity that is still in the process of developing and has not yet crystallized; and paradoxically for some of them, it simply means
4. to be a practising Muslim, 'Britishness' not being a significant factor.

Having made this general statement, it is necessary to stress the heterogeneity of the concept and reality of British Muslim identity; this heterogeneity is rooted in a clearly observed diversification of social/global environments, cultural attitudes and religious tendencies, all of which are expressed in the range of different inclinations towards Western culture. The result, indeed is not a neatly identifiable British Muslim identity; rather, several types of British identities have emerged as being embodied in the responses given. Based on our findings, and as described briefly in the introduction and in Chapter 4, eight types of identity can be differentiated; these will be elaborated upon in Chapter 7.

6.1.2. *British Culture (Locality)*

According to Robertson's main theory on glocalization, one should consider both local and global forces in order to understand the impact of the latter on the former, and the way in which the local forces determine the way in which global forces will be assimilated. With regard to the local forces, one might view certain aspects of local British as themselves constituting a significant strand of the dominant forces within Western culture generally, and, to some extent, as one of the central forces of global culture. The way in which British Muslims interact with such a culture and the influence such a culture imposes on British Muslim identity can be examined on the basis of the following interviews.

In response to the question, 'To what extent has the British culture that you were brought up in affected your Muslim identity?', a range of different views was expressed. Some of the respondents such as Yasmin and Sara expressed the sentiment that British culture had a great impact on them:

> The effect of British culture on British Muslims has been great to the extent that they are searching to hold on to some form of identity and culture. (Yasmin, aged 21)

> The effect has been tremendous! I was brought up in this country and the British way of life, but at the end of the day I am an individual with my own ideas and views. (Sara, aged 17)

> It has made me to be more aware of my religion, because I am able to see the best and worst of the British culture. (Farah, aged 18)

> In a sense I have realized the importance of my religion from my un-Islamic background. (Saqib, aged 17)

These responses display differing degrees of acknowledgement of the impact of British culture on one's identity. What needs to be stressed is that this impact cannot necessarily be defined in negative terms; that is, it is not necessarily the case that British culture will weaken a sense of Muslim identity. The responses by Farah and Saqib should in particular be noted: Farah claims that she has become more aware of her religion because of her perceptions of 'the best and the worst' in British culture, implying that these poles of the local culture function as criteria for evaluating her own religion and its culture. Also, Saqib's response indicates an interesting, paradoxical impact on identity.

He is claiming, in effect, that living in a non-Muslim environment has helped, by way of contrast, to highlight the importance of his Islamic identity. One sees here a tendency that confirms to some extent the analysis of Giddens, when he argues that religious identity in a traditional environment is not 'traditional' in the sense that a consciously Islamic identity, in a modern, non-Islamic environment, is 'traditional'. The difference is important: in a traditional environment, there is no need to assert with vigour that one is 'traditional': one is traditional almost by definition, there being no modernity or secularity to pose an alternative. In a modern, secular, environment, on the other hand, one is forced to make a conscious decision, and with an act of will, adopt the characteristics of traditional culture in opposition to the prevailing secular culture. Thus, 'resistance identity' in a secular culture can be expressed in terms of the adoption of traditional Islamic identity, even if traditional Islamic identity, in the framework of a traditional culture, cannot be defined as 'resistance', rather, as a 'conformist' identity.

Saqib expresses a reaction to the secular modern environment, a reaction that, instead of conforming to the norms of that environment, on the contrary leads in the opposite direction, back towards religion, thus defining one's identity in contrast to the surrounding secular culture. This reaction can clearly be seen to lie at the root of two modes of what Castells called 'resistance identities', namely, Islamism and traditionalism; it can also lead, although less directly, to nationalism, because this shift to a nationalist identity linked to the country of one's origins, would depend on the degree to which the individual's perception of religious identity is bound up with the home culture of one's parents. In the case of Farah, it is evident that her heightened perception of religious identity has not led to a total reversion to her home culture, or to a reactive and extreme nationalism, as she says that she is able to 'see the best and the worst of the British culture'. If, on the other hand, there is a strong identification between one's home culture/nation and Islamic identity, then, this assimilation between the two elements would indeed give rise to a form of religious nationalism that might also be called a mode of 'resistance identity'.

Another batch of respondents (Homam and Tahir) indicated, on the contrary, that British culture had not affected their Islamic culture:

I think that my Islamic culture and upbringing has been so strong that I have not been affected by British culture. (Homam, aged 16)

British culture has greatly influenced the Muslim youth of today. However I feel that it cannot influence Islamic ideologies and belief since Islam is a perfect religion. God almighty states clearly in the *Qur'an* "Today I have perfected your religion". (Tahir, aged 20)

Tahir's answer seems paradoxical, and is representative of a view that is prevalent among a considerable number of young British Muslims. While he acknowledges the fact that British culture has greatly influenced Muslim youth, he also affirms strongly his conviction that British culture could not influence 'Islamic ideologies'. This contradiction in his position could be due to the fact that he has not been able to distinguish clearly between Islamic identity – that is, Islam viewed as a theological and relatively unchanging essence – and Muslim identity – the changing configuration of psychological, social, cultural and political attitudes that determine the precise constitution of 'Muslim identity'.

On the basis of this important distinction, we can reconcile the apparent contradiction between the two views expressed by stating the following: Tahir acknowledges the impact of British culture upon the *actual identity* of Muslims (that is, 'Muslim identity'), whilst simultaneously maintaining that 'Islamic identity' *as such* cannot be in any way affected by this culture. He views this essentialist Islamic identity in terms of ideology, although by this term we can also understand the notions of theology, given the extent to which the modern notion of ideology has come to encompass the whole spectrum of doctrinal and even conceptual schemas; one has to remember that the notion of an ideology is a 19th century construct.[1] Prior to that there were diffuse doctrines stemming from religious and secular thought, but nothing like a man-made 'ideology' that was formulated as a 'programme' for society to adopt. The fact that Tahir illustrates his point about 'ideology' by quoting a verse from the *Qur'an* shows that for him, there is a Qur'anic 'ideology'. But the response might also indicate the more specifically political connotation of ideology, and thus show the way in which a basic adherence to some notion of essentialist, or unchanging Islam – however ill-defined – can easily give rise to a politicized conception of Islamic identity.

6.1.3. Solidity of British Muslim Identity

As we discussed in Chapter 2, according to the relativists such as Featherstone (1990: 8), intercultural communication is one of the phenomena of globalization that exposes people to a variety of cultures, and which relativizes culture – in other words, it initiates a shift from absolutism to relativism. On the other hand, the post-structuralists point to a process of resistance against the dominant norms of society placing more emphasis on traditional identity. This phenomenon can be observed in some of the answers of respondents interviewed in this survey.

To the question, 'Is it vital for British Muslims to have a fixed identity in the age of globalization?', the respondents answers revolved around two themes. One group of respondents such as Sadaf, Abdul Rahman and Sabia believed that British Muslim identity should indeed be fixed and firm:

In order for Muslims to be unified as one *umma* we all need to have a fixed identity and worship Allah by adhering to the *Qur'an* and *Sunnah* of our

---

1. See the article on 'ideology' in the *International Encyclopedia of the Social Sciences*, vol. 7: 66–85.

beloved Prophet Muhammad. There is nothing wrong with incorporating a fixed identity into different cultures. (Sadaf, aged 23)

Muslim identity is absolutely fixed, it should not change at all. (Abdul Rahman, aged 22)

Yes, I think it is important for a British Muslim to have a fixed identity because when people who are non-Muslim look at us they should recognize the Muslim straight away. But if we are all different and twist and bend things here and there it will confuse those who don't already understand the Muslim identity. (Sabia, aged 17)

The second group of respondents looked at the issue of Muslim identity as a phenomenon that can be considered as relative and diverse, varying from one culture to another. This perspective was elaborated further by Mariam, Zahra and Yakob:

... I don't think it's possible to have a fixed identity, Muslims can come in any shape, colour, or nationality. A lot of Islam is mixed with old fashioned cultures. So it won't be possible for all Muslims to have a fixed identity because people and cultures are so different. (Mariam, aged 34)

No ... The strength and survival of any identity is shown by how flexibly it can change to its changing environment and society. (Zahra, aged 33)

No ... It is not important for Muslims to have a fixed identity because each one of us has different things to which we can identify with. (Yakoub Mohammad, aged 30)

Rizwan places more emphasis on the role of globalization and in particular nationalism as the main factors contributing to the heterogeneity of Muslim identity:

Islam has become fragmented due to globalization, and other factors especially that of nationalism. (Rizwan, aged 18)

From what we have so far discussed, one can conclude that: although many Muslims, traditionalist and Islamist alike, indicate a degree of stability and continuity in their Muslim identity, a degree of diversification and reformation of this identity cannot be avoided. This reformation or reconstitution is inevitable due to the fact that society and culture are themselves engaged in wide-ranging, dramatic changes. As Giddens puts it (1999: 45), 'In a cosmo-politan world, more people than ever before are regularly in contact with others who think differently from them.' Therefore people are forced to live a more reflective and flexible life. Identity as a multidimensional phenomenon is in one way or another in the process of reformation and reproduction; the end result of this process is not necessarily the 'detraditionalization' of identity, but rather, the re-articulation of traditional identity in a non-traditional context, and this is itself a 'retraditionalization', something quite different from a simple imitation of traditional markers of identity.

6.1.4. Globalization and British Muslim Citizenship

One of the consequences of globalization is the global 'movements of peoples across regions and between continents be they labour migrations, diasporas or processes of conquest and colonization' (Held, 1999: 284). Due to the advancement of the transportation industry and a global awareness about the social, economic and cultural domination of the West, huge numbers of people have migrated from the East to the West (see Held *et al.*, 1999: 281–326).

After the settlement of migrants in the 'host' society, they are faced with different types of nostalgia. Baudrillard (1983) and Robertson (1992) have both referred to the state of nostalgia, which has already been discussed in Chapter 2, with the claim that postmodern culture has created confusion about reality and unreality, true and false national representation, and local assertion of identity. As Robertson (1995) states, the concept of 'ideology of home' is also a serious challenge. Immigrants do not generally have clear ideas about their national identity. Mowlana (2000: 240–1), however, believes that globalization has not only created a serious challenge for the nation-state as a political authority, but has also 'crippled normal mechanisms of cohesion and power in the community' (Mowlana, 2000: 252) modifying the perception of citizenship.

i. Citizenship and Belonging
Generally migrant people have great difficulties in adapting to their new homes, especially when they are from a different culture and ethnic origin. They feel themselves as outsiders and cannot really integrate within the new social and cultural conditions. They engage with their new environment in diverse ways. According to this study, some of them may adopt the new cultural norms of the host society and even reject their native culture. Others may reject the dominant culture of the host society and insist on their own native culture. A further group of respondents show a hybrid tendency; they like Britain because they were born and raised in Britain but they also have

strong emotional ties towards their motherland or their ancestors' homeland. Still others reject both cultures. They seem to have no particular views or direction. These represent the *vagrant* identity.

There were diverse attitudes in response to the question: 'Do you consider Britain to be your main home?' Some clearly identify with Britain as their home because they were born here and they felt that they belonged to British society:

Yes ... in a way, having grown up here, we have not experienced any other way of life, this is our home. Our families are settled here and have died here, therefore we have emotional attachments with this country. (Eqbal, aged 19)

As I was born in England, I consider myself a British Muslim. Islam is my religion. I see England as my natural home, in the sense that it is where I can share my culture with other people who have a British culture. (Amir, aged 29)

I was born, brought up and I am currently living and studying in Britain, therefore it is definitely my home; my whole life is cantered around Britain. All my friends and most of my relatives are here. (Nadia, aged 21)

Yes, I was born here and I feel, that I belong to the British Muslim Community. (Haroon, aged 19)

Yes, I was born in Britain and I have adapted myself to the British mentality. (Sobia, aged 21)

The second group were more inclined to distance themselves from British society:

I do have British nationality but Britain is not my country. I may have lived here, but as a Muslim I cannot blend into a society that has no belief or religious values but has a lot of racism. (Abdul Rahman, aged 22)

No, I have no such consideration, I don't like Britain, I like to go back to my original country – Iraq. (Homam, aged 16)

No I don't consider Britain to be my home country even though I think it is the best place to be in order for us to understand the modernist culture and to utilize the best elements of it for our Islamic revival. (Yakoub Mohammad, aged 30)

I see Britain as a place that I am living in for a short term until *Insha-Allah* I have the means to make *hijrah*. I would consider 'home' to be a place where I can live under the rule of Islamic Shariah for I believe that there will never be justice, liberty or the means of equality given to Muslims here. Even if we do stay here then it should be solely for the purpose of *dawah* and to bring other peoples to Islam, but if one is not doing that then I really think they should reflect upon their current situation and reconsider. (Sabia, aged 17)

The third group consists of those who feel that they have two homes, one is Britain and the other is the place of belonging or the country of origin :

Yes, for I was born in the UK and I have a Muslim/British identity, but this is just my temporary home, my heart is set on Mecca and Medina and life after death, when I shall be blessed with Allah's grace. (Adil, aged 20)

I have two homes. Although I have lived for most of my life in Britain but I still consider Iran to be my natural home. (Mariam, aged 34)

I consider Britain as a country to make a living in. I was also born here and spent all my life in Britain. But I still feel that a part of my home is still in my country of origin. (Rizwan, aged 18)

The fourth group consists of those who are not sure about their national or cultural identity:

I am unsure of where I belong. 'Home' is near those that are dear to me. (Sobia, aged 21)

Unfortunately I have not had the experience of living in any other country, apart from a short visit to Pakistan at a very young age. I consider Britain to be my place of residence but not my home. Life is a journey and I just happen to be residing in Britain. I came to 'live' in Britain but that is all. I don't feel anywhere is my home. Maybe I have not found it yet! (Sadaf, aged 23)

No, I don't consider Britain as my home because of the traditional values in which I have been brought up. Even if British culture is definitely a part of my culture, traditional values are also present. So I feel that I belong to neither there nor here. I cannot consider any of these to be my home. (Homayra, aged 23)

Another group of respondents were questioned about their loyalties towards their native culture and their new home. The format of the question was along the lines of, 'If England were to play against a team from your motherland in a game of cricket or football, which team would you support in such a case?'. The majority of them (68.7%) said that they wished victory for their parents' native country; only 4.5% of them show partiality towards the English cricket or football teams; the rest either said that they would support the team that had played better (6%) or that they do not have nationalist tendencies or have no interest in sports at all. This shows that there are still strong feelings towards one's 'country of origin' amongst many young British Muslims (see Table 6.1).

Table 6.1: In a Hypothetical Situation, if England (Britain) Were to Play a Team from Your Parents' Native Country in, Say, a Cricket or Football Match, Which Team Would You Support?

Team	Frequency	Percentage
My parents' native country	46	68.7
Britain	3	4.5
I support the team that play better	4	6.0
Neither, I am not nationalist	7	10.4
I am not interested in football and cricket	4	6.0
Neutral		1.0
No answer	2	3.0
Total	67	100

Indeed, and somewhat surprisingly, the level of support among the third generation of British Muslims for the teams representing their original homeland (76%) is even higher than that among the second generation (65.1%). This shows that, to a moderate degree at least, a certain patriotic sentiment for one's distant, but cherished homeland, increases rather than decreases over time. One might venture to say that this increase in patriotism will be stronger if the contrast between the new and the original home culture is pronounced.

Another issue, which measures the loyalty of British Muslims to Britain, is participation in war. Respondents were asked whether, if Britain were to wage war against a Muslim or non-Muslim country, they would be prepared to fight as British soldiers. For the majority of respondents (92.5%) the answer was in the negative: they would not fight against other fellow Muslims. With regard to waging war against non-Muslim countries, while a few more respondents showed loyalty to Britain, the majority (85.1%) again said that they would not be prepared to fight against any country for the benefit of the British government (see Table 6.2).

Table 6.2: British Muslims and Support for Britain in the War

Views	If Britain were to wage war against:	
	a Muslim country, are you ready to fight as a British soldier? (%)	a non-Muslim country, are you ready to fight as a British soldier? (%)
Yes	7.5	9
No	92.5	85.1
Would depend on for what reasons Britain was waging war	–	4.5
I would not care	–	1.5
Total	100.0 67 (total number)	100.0 67 (total number)

In summary, most of the respondents who said 'no' placed religion before their nationality, with a few indicating their readiness to fight without giving any clear reasons as to why:

No, my religion is more important than my nationality.

No, Islam comes first, before my nationality.

No, because they are always in a position to destroy Islam.

No, I am a Muslim and no matter how long I live in a non-Muslim country, I won't be sucked into their traditions or ways – the least to say for them.

No, I would never, even if they killed me.

No, I would fight because I abide with the laws of the country that I live in.

In response to the question: 'If Britain were to wage war against a non-Muslim country, are you ready to fight as a British soldier?', again, most of the respondents indicated their loyalties to their religion first with a few indicating support for the idea of fighting for Britain for no other reason than being duty-bound to the laws of the land:

No, I would only fight for my religion and for no other reason.

No, I never supported Britain in any aspect of war.

No, for me to support a non-Islamic; non-Muslim country is not permissible because they will be fighting for that other than Islam, i.e. democracy, capitalist etc.

Although Britain is my home, I feel I have a duty to be faithful to my religion first.

No, I will only fight a war in the way of Islam 'holy war' and only when it is required.

No, I only live in Britain; I don't consider myself to be 'British' except in Citizenship.

No, I would not fight as a British soldier but, if I felt that war was the way to go (very unlikely), I would give them verbal support.

No, unless it was for a very genuine reason.

Yes, I have to abide by the laws of the country that I live in.

Yes, ... If Islam were to order me to do so, then I would fight for my religion.

Yes, because I would avoid becoming a refugee again.

It depends, I mean for what reason would Britain be waging war against another country.

Depends on what my situation is and what is fighting for.

Table 6.3: You Go on a Holiday to Where Your Parents Are from –
How do You Feel About Britain?

View	Frequency	Percentage
All the same – no specific feeling	87	35.2
I am proud to be where I am	106	42.9
I wish, I could go back to Britain	46	18.6
No answer	8	3..2
Total	247	100.0

In response to another question about whether they feel nostalgic when they return to their motherlands from Britain, 18.6% said that they were very happy to return to Britain; 42.9% were very happy to see their motherlands; and a proportion of the respondents showed no loyalties one way or the other. This phenomenon indicates the diversity of attitudes that are produced by the processes of globalization. Earlier, we discussed the importance of the diversification of choice that is brought about by the expansion of one's 'room for manoeuvre' in cultural terms. The proximity of 'home', whether this be in one's local environment, or one's original homeland, results in this diversification of loyalties (Table 6.3).

6.2. *The Impact of Homogenization on British Muslim Identity*

Homogenization as studied here is a process that can have two simultaneous outcomes: Americanization,[1] which has resulted in the integration of British Muslims into American culture and reverse-Americanization or, as Robertson (2000) refers to it, antiglobalization, which has had the result of British Muslims resisting the impact of American culture. These two paradoxical processes can also be explained by what Robertson (1992: 97–114) refers to as universalism/particularism, which on the one hand explains the homogenization of a dominant culture all over the world, and on the other hand accounts for the globalization of particular cultures, in the present case the

---

1. We should realize that Europe and America are not just a geographical site, 'but it is also an idea, inextricably linked with the myths of Western civilization and grievously shaped by the haunting encounters with its colonial Others' (Morely & Robins, 1995: 5).

subcultures of nationalists, Islamists or traditionalists in their various movements and forms of global outreach.

As we discussed in Chapter 1, American culture can be regarded as the tour de force of 'global culture', a view supported by *hyperglobalizers* (Held *et al.* 1999: 3–5). They hold the view that American 'popular culture' or Western consumerism will abolish all national and regional cultures. Whilst there are many indications showing the extent to which American culture has penetrated different societies, nevertheless there are also many signs of reverse Americanization in local as well as regional cultures. This is what Robertson (1995) proposed in his theory that rejected a monoperspective on the local or the global, but considered both the global flow of information and culture, and at the same time took into account local responses to transnational cultural production.

Before we can examine the impact of Americanization on British Muslim identity, we need to explore the role of transnational culture from the respondents' points of view. What does transnational culture mean to them? And what is their reaction to it? Based on this, we shall proceed to further analyse the position of American culture among British Muslims in this study.

6.2.1. *Responses of Indigenous Culture to Americanization*

One obvious perspective on the process of globalization is the export and import of culture (Jameson, 1998). This exchange, although in the majority of cases it is a one-way flow of culture, has created serious challenges for indigenous cultures in many aspects of life. Generally speaking, Muslims are suspicious of transnational cultures or alien cultures and, for many Muslims, transnational cultures mean colonial cultures in the form of cultural and media imperialism (Said, 1981, 1993).

6.2.2. *The Challenge of Transnational Culture to British Muslim Identity*

For the majority of British Muslims interviewed for this study, transnational culture means in essence Western culture. On the other hand there are also local forces that at the same time play the role of global forces within British Muslim society. Barker (1999: 41) refers to this as the global merging of two relative, local concepts that can co-exist together; or, as Robertson (1992: 176) would have it, local activities can be the catalyst for the introduction of global forces.

The notion of transnational culture for many of our respondents means a corrupted and destructive culture, which has devalued many elements of Muslim culture:

The West has destroyed Islam and is still doing it today like they did in 1924 when the Islamic state was destroyed. (Saqib, aged 17)

It has affected Islamic culture to some extent; foreign culture is more appealing to the Muslim world. (Adil, aged 20)

If we look at the nomadic Arab culture ... we see that transnational culture has affected their way of life completely. Although they led simple and yet fulfilling lives, nowadays their lives have become complicated. (Sadaf, aged 23)

Changing our views has tainted the minds of our youth and restricted our views on Islam. (Eqbal, aged 19)

While Homayra and Sabia have critical views about transnational culture, they have attempted to explain the reason why transnational culture or so-called Western or American culture could successfully change Muslim identity:

In a world where you can travel from one side to the other in less than 24 hours, it is obvious that any culture is going to face any other culture. The ease in which we communicate with other societies enhances the spread of other cultures easily. For example, a culture that has a lot of prohibitions will have fewer adepts than the one that says 'enjoy' in all ways. So transnational culture has had a lot of influence on indigenous culture, which deprives it from liberties and, if transnational culture offers these so called liberties, it will last. (Homayra, aged 23)

Indigenous culture is seen as 'backward' because of the vast changes that the disbelievers have brought forward to society today. They have played upon people's weaknesses by carrying out great detailed analysis to discover how they can affect them mentally and physically. I think that they have affected the indigenous culture a lot by showing people that you can be a better person by just being yourself and doing what you want. But that's not the case, we the Muslims have a *deen* [a way of life] to follow as this is the very purpose of why we are here today on Earth. (Sabia, aged 17)

Hanif (see quote below) has outlined three points regarding the influence of transnational culture over national and indigenous culture or inter-relationships between different cultures. One is that cultural attitudes, like other social and political perspectives, can be transferred from one culture to another; the second is educational training, which has a significant role in changing the direction of a society and this can give support to a particular understanding of a cultural condition; the third important point is that, when a new unfamiliar cultural product is imposed on a society, this will create fragmentation within the culture. This is due to the fact that there are many cultural elements belonging to other cultures with different historical backgrounds associated with that culture and perhaps irrelevant to the other cultures. For instance democracy without civil institutions can create 'cultural fragmentation', or industry without industrial institutions can lead to uneven and fragmented development.

> The effects of transnational culture upon the indigenous culture are evident as well as devastating. If we look at the present situation in Australia, it is clear that the largest ethnic group exposed to drugs are the Aborigines. The reason is that they have been encouraged to leave their habitat for the bustling cities. Since they are not used to city life, they fall into the abyss of confusion. If we take a universal appraisal of apartheid in South Africa (some forty years ago), it is evident that Black people were taught in their schools, by *law*, that Black people were an inferior race to their white counterparts. However from a broader perspective with regards to linguistics, there are more languages that will become extinct as a result of transnational culture and globalization. The results are sad, since language is a vital part of the cultural equation. (Hanif, aged 22)

6.2.3. The Challenge of Americanization and British Muslim Identity

As we explained in Chapter 1, the hegemony of American culture via the process of globalization is an important feature of the postmodern world. This can be further elaborated upon by the Frankfurtian, and post-structuralists schools of thought. In the following discussion, viewpoints of the respondents will be examined according to these two schools of thought.

i. The Frankfurtian Approach
As discussed in Chapter 2, the Frankfurtian view considers the homogeneity of American culture with special reference to its 'culture industry' – film industry, broadcasting system and global press domination (see Lowenthal, 1961; Adorno & Horkheimer, 1977).

In the globalization approach, however, the 'culture industry' is not only a local industry that can influence the masses, it is also a global network phenomenon that can instantaneously penetrate into different spheres of society globally. Americanization here can be viewed as a global culture being formed through the 'culture industry'. An example of this would be the

Hollywood film industry, a cultural industry that supports, and is supported by, the economic and political domination of the United States, which is thus able to impose its hegemonic culture at the local, regional as well as global level (Featherstone, 1995: 87)[1].

According to this research, some of the respondents have clearly manifested the importance of this 'industry of culture', in particular, with reference to Western television, in the construction of Muslim identity:

> Whatever school people have attended, one thing that they teach you is that the media is biased in whatever they show. So it is evident that, whenever the Muslims or Islam is shown on TV, the real facts are distorted and this is because they see so many people reverting to this religion and the state are trying to stop this as much as possible. So if people know that the media is biased then why do they not think to themselves for a minute that there must be another side to this story (i.e. Islam and the Muslims). Western television is very good at deforming the Muslim identity and no matter how many complaints people make they will never show the true side of Islam on TV because inside us we all believe that Allah has given us *hikmah* (wisdom) to know truth from falsehood. (Sabia, aged 17)

> TV has a very powerful influence on most people. Sometimes, it is the only way that people can interact with others and learn of different cultures or beliefs. Therefore it has the power to show Muslims in a good or bad light. (Haroon, aged 19)

> I think the media has a very big impact on Muslims, and they are not aware of this, because they use a subtle indirect approach. (Homam, aged 16)

> Youngsters in particular try to imitate singers and actors. They become these characters. In Middle Eastern countries, most young people are imitating what they see on satellite, dressing up like them or behaving like them. (Mariam, aged 34)

Consumption of American cultural industry among the respondents of this survey is also pervasive. According to our survey American cultural and

---

1. European culture, including British culture, has also been influenced widely by American culture. Kroes (1996: XI) has argued that 'American culture has penetrated ever more powerfully into the realm of European cultures'. Kroes (1996: 171) has also indicated that, 'In our century the tables have been turned. America has irresistibly moved toward centre stage, while Europe finds itself on the receiving end of a wave of American culture that washes across the globe'.

political views have enveloped the habits of many British Muslims particularly in the arena of television, cinema, food and code of clothing. In the major survey of respondents, 61.5% suggested that American films were their favourite, with 14.2% of them preferring European films and only 19.4% showing tendencies towards their native film industry. For 73% of those who had access to CNN, this news channel had a monopoly over all other news channels. As regards clothing, over half of the respondents questioned were followers of Western fashion (53.8%); 51% of the respondents also indicated their preference for American fast foods such as McDonald's, and Burger King, whilst 49% were still inclined to favour their own traditional foods. It is important to understand that the respondents were not asked directly as to whether they liked McDonald's or not, but what their preferences were, i.e. which was their favourite type of food.

It is appropriate that McDonald's should have been the subject of Barber's study (1996),[1] *McWorld vs jihad.* McDonald's has became a 'ubiquitous and immediately recognizable symbol throughout the United States as in much of the rest of the world' (Ritzer, 1993: 4). It has became globalized to the extent that 'McDonald's is now opening more outlets overseas each year than it is in the United States and half its profits come from overseas operations.' Ritzer had expressed that many people identify strongly with McDonald's to the extent that to some people it has become 'a sacred institution'(Ritzer, 1998: 83). One journalist described the opening of McDonald's in Moscow, as the 'ultimate icon of Americana'. Today many popular businesses looking for popularity such as McDentists and McDoctors are beginning with Mc in order to express that they follow the McDonald's mode to create representation of quick, competent and efficient types of work (Ritzer, 1998: 83).

As stated in Chapter 5 and in the work of Ritzer (1993, 1998) McDonald's as well as American and European cinema have become a 'transreligious phenomenon', which means people, regardless of whether they are Islamists, traditionalists, secularists, Muslim, Christian, communist, all consume McDonald's and watch Western films at cinemas, even if they have an anti-American orientation (see Tables 5.11 and 5.12).

Americanization, or specifically the term 'Hollywoodization' and 'McDonaldization', can be viewed according to the Frankfurt School of thought, which we have already touched upon earlier in Chapter 2. From this perspective

---

1. Barber (1996) argues that *jihad* is not necessarily in contrast with McWorld rather, it is 'in subtle counterpoint to McWorld and is itself a dialectical response to modernity whose features both reflect and reinforce the modern world's virtues and vices – *jihad* via McWorld rather than *jihad* versus McWorld. The forces of *jihad* are not only remembered and retrieved by the enemies of McWorld but imagined and contrived by its friends and proponents' (Barber, 1996: 157).

Hollywood and McDonald's productions can be regarded as a source for the global 'cultural industry', which is largely associated with mass culture'. With regard to the views of our respondents, their response to American culture can be seen as conforming to the Frankfurtian approach; that is, their views reflect the idea that culture has become something of a 'global industry', rather than an organic blossoming of authentic creative impulses. They put great emphasis on the crisis inherent within the cultural sphere; the values implied in culture are more clearly articulated than are those values explicitly associated with religious identity:

I think that Western globalization is messing up our culture.
(Ali Reza, aged 18)

Americanization has destroyed our culture in a big way, the way of dress, speech etc. (Farah, aged 18)

It is difficult to avoid the influence of this culture (American culture), especially for youngsters who have grown up only knowing this way of life. (Yasmin, aged 21)

... Huge impact on many peoples and their culture, thinking and practice. (Hamid, aged 26)

Zainab and Adil have formulated the idea that there is a close relationship between cultural consumption and homogeneity of identities:

American culture has penetrated into the mass culture ... Most Muslims are influenced by what they see with their eyes. (Zainab, aged 18)

Globalization is everywhere and affects the British Muslim identity as it affects other's identities. The creation of broad markets combined with a society of communication tends to make all identities – the same. (Adil, aged 20)

Shararit suggested the paradoxical functions of globalization. From his perspective on one side globalization has caused crystallization of British Muslim identity and global awareness as regards the Muslim *umma* all over the world

---

1. Barber (1996: 23) pointed out that 'McDonald's serves 20 million customers around the world every day, drawing more customers daily than there as people in Greece, Ireland and Switzerland together.'

(see Mazrui, 1999). On the other side, it may cause domination of a particular culture, i.e. American culture.

> Globalization etc. has had both extreme positive and negative effects on British Muslims. I feel that people have either become aware of their proper Muslim identity, or have instead fallen prey to globalization, and thereby completely forgotten Islam. (Shararit, aged 19)

Shararit reflects the views of the defensive/imitation theorists that many sociologists such as Castell (1996), Turner (1994) and Giddens (1999) follow. The variety of responses to globalization is a reflection of the fact that society itself has many different layers, tendencies and attitudes. Therefore social responses to globalization do not necessarily mean only homogenization and unification of cultures and identities according to American culture; it can also intensify native identities according to religious, national and cultural traditions. It can also be argued that these forms of indigenous identity will flourish more in a cosmopolitan society when it encounters a fuller diversity of races and cultures; therefore a multicultural society can be seen as a reference point for the crystallization of a particular identity – a background or 'scene' against which one's own identity is more acutely contrasted. This aspect of contrast will be highlighted in cases where the dominance of American culture globally leads to resistance from other local or native cultures. Therefore particularization, as Robertson terms it, can be seen here as a result of a confrontation between the peripheral and the central culture – a more radical delineation between local and global forces.

One can also give credence to the principle of the diversification of identities in response to the process of globalization with reference to the hermeneutic perspective. In his piece on cultural studies Hans-Georg Gadamer (1979) argues that an understanding of a cultural phenomenon is like taking in a text; even the image of the text and the tone of the voice reading it are part of the overall hermeneutic of the reader. According to Gadamer (1998, 1999) meaning is not necessarily inherent in a text, image and voice (an unchanging essence); meaning is always something a person makes when he or she reads a text or watches an image or listens. The social and individual understanding of a person depends on many factors, such as historical background, local and global forces that construct one's religious tendencies, cultural habits, national and transnational perceptions, as well as religious and national identity. In this perspective, the individual's response to the global cultural 'text' will be dialectically determined by the specific 'context' just as much as, if not more than, by the globally dominant force. That dominance, or homogenization, will be filtered through the prism of local perceptions, and all the innumerable contextual variables that determine those perceptions. Therefore, it can be argued that the so-called 'essence' of Westernization that dominates the global cultural 'text' is not going to predetermine any specific outcomes: those outcomes will be the result of the interaction between the 'text' and the 'context'. Either the one (homogenization through the dominant 'text') or the other (heterogenization through the local 'contexts') will in fact be the result of the complex dialectical interplay between the two sets of factors.

ii. Post-structuralists' Approach

The post-structuralists look at the American cultural, political and economic domination with critical reasoning. From their point of view periphery cultures as well as minority groups (in response to the one-way flow of American culture), have tended to isolate themselves, so that they often remain frozen in the traditional ways, this makes them more susceptible to hold on to their traditional values[1] (see Turner, 1986).

For post-structuralists, there is nonetheless an influential pessimist tradition, which looks at the way in which the dominance of certain cultures in the global economy leads to a *de facto* cultural imperialism. The asymmetries in the availability of, and access to, production equipment, distribution networks, venues etc., leads to a structural bias that favours some producers at the expense of others. This bias brings to mind a system of colonialism and notions of cultural colonialism (Shiller, 1992).

From the post-structuralists' perspective, American cultural domination has established a matrix with all of its elements intact. However, responses to the American cultural and economic production is not expressed in terms of fixed and monolithic behaviour.

Table 6.4 portrays three examples of Muslim behaviour: The first group consists of those who choose their way of dressing according to Western film stars and contemporary fashion. This group is more inclined to watch American films (85%), indicating a link between the choice of viewing and clothing. This brings to mind what Philo (1990) said on the influence of television as a process of 'seeing and believing', which means what people see does influence further choices.

The second group choose their clothing according to their native ethnic traditions and compared with the first group showed a lower tendency to watch American films (74%). Whilst this may be an obvious finding, it is important

---

1. It is important to note that Americanization has not only been discussed as a challenge for Eastern culture and in particular Muslim identity but it has been also argued as a great source of identity crisis within European culture (see Kroes, 1996: 162–78; Andrews, 1997: 72–101; Cvetkovich & Kellner, 1997: 1–30).

to note the concordance between such markers of identity as clothing, and the receptivity to Western films, carriers of modern, secular icons and role models.

Table 6.4: Relationship Between Choice of Clothing and Interesting Films and Actors

Your choice of clothing is influenced by:	Which films and actors interest you more?			Total (%)
	No answer (%)	American and European (%)	Middle Eastern and Arabian (%)	
Stars of film and contemporary fashion	5 (3.7)	113 (85.0)	15 (11.3) (	133 (53.8)
Ethnic tradition	4 (8.0)	37 (74.0)	9 (18.0)	50 (20.2)
Religious tradition	3 (5.2)	33 (56.9)	22 (37.9)	58 (23.5)
None	–	4 (66.7)	2 (33.3)	6 (2.4)
Total	12 (4.9)	187 (75.7)	48 (19.4)	247 (100.0)

$P = 0.001$

The third group affirm their loyalties towards religious traditional values as regards their choice of clothing. In comparison this group showed less inclination towards watching American and European films (56.9%). This indicates that what people watch on TV or in the cinema affects their everyday lives such as choice of clothing and eating. Secondly, one can show that partiality towards religious tradition can be very effective in terms of cultural orientation, such as showing interest in American or Arabic films. The final finding in Table 6.4 shows that resistance against Western cultural products (such as films) is more dominant amongst those who have stronger religious tendencies than those who only possess a national and ethnic partiality. More specifically, one might argue that a traditional Muslim is more defensive as regards the process of Americanization than a Pakistani, Bengali or Arab nationalist who is influenced only, or predominantly, by ethnic or national values. The reason for this should be clear: a traditionally inclined Muslim will resist all perceived threats to the integrity of the elements that make up the culture that define his or her religious outlook. A nationalist, on the other hand, is not necessarily going to resent such forces of Americanization, as the nationalist mentality is by nature competitive: as America stands for material power and prestige, and a nation that needs both power and prestige, any culture – secular or religious – will further that power and prestige to the glory of the nation. Thus what will be perceived as a threat by a 'Muslim' can be perceived as a useful tool or instrument for the nationalist.

One should bear in mind that among those respondents who showed strong inclinations towards their native culture, as reflected in the form of nationalist or Islamist ideology, over half of them manifested an interest in watching American films. This indicates that while people are subsumed within a particular culture and that culture influences their every day lives in myriad ways, they nevertheless will manifest, in differing degrees and in diverse ways, a certain resistance to that culture. This trend can be considered in terms of what we would call *the dialectical identity in the age of globalization*. This type of identity refers to a phenomenon in which people may well consume all things American, but simultaneously oppose American culture, either in part or wholly, on the ideological plane. This 'dialectical identity' expresses a certain contradiction or at least a polarity, as between cultural behaviour and ideological orientation; culturally, a degree of 'Americanization' might be tolerated, even encouraged; ideologically, the political values for which America and the West generally stand, are to be rejected. This ideological opposition is then taken as a sign of cultural resistance to America, and also of loyalty to one's own culture. This diverse and occasionally contradictory response is clearly visible in the understanding of a component of British Muslims in Brent in regard to the challenges of Americanization to British Muslim identity (see Table 5.11).

Post-structuralists such as Kroes (1996: 175) hold the view that: 'America has replicated itself into icons, clichés of itself that leave an imprint everywhere, on T-shirts, in commercial images, and in our heads.' Some of the respondents in our survey harbour similar views to those of the Islamists, that Islam influences their whole way of life and that Americanization has penetrated and corrupted the culture not only of the wider society but also the lives of British Muslims:

... I think Americanization has integrated deeply into the lives of many peoples living in the west, and it has become a normal way of living. (Saqib, aged 17)

... Tremendous, influences on our way of life ... Taking away from Muslims the realization of their 'true' identity. Trying to make us 'globally friendly' through the civil way of life, when in fact Islam and Muslims already can provide this. (Eqbal, aged 19)

Some of the interviewees hold very pessimistic views. They see the impact of globalization as an American conspiracy waged against the Muslim community. From this perspective globalization is an American conspiracy, which has been planned and designed to make America a global power:[1]

> Americanization has acted as a barrier, which slows down or stops the Muslim mind from developing (academically and spiritually) into the ideal Muslim. (Sohaib, aged 19)

> From the start America has always been against Muslims, but Muslims are slowly recognizing this and soon an identity will be established. (Asad, aged 28)

> I think globalization has had a great impact on the Muslim identity because the way the Muslims are today has been the result of this very process. The non-believers (Americans) have been working very hard to change the way in which we all think. They want us to have the same goals and objectives as them and this goal and objective is full of corruption. However, it has worked because they know what people in today's society want, and they have been providing that, and this has resulted in the destruction of the Muslim identity. As Muslims are being shown that they can be different and so this has caused many peoples to be Muslim but in a modern way, which has lead many to commit *bid'ah* [innovations] in the *deen* [religion] since they conform to the new way of being a Muslim and not the way of the *Qur'an* and *Sunnah*. (Sobia, aged 21)

> ... effects our belief and faith through the Americanization of the media. (Nazem, aged 31)

Many of the pessimistic views of the respondents are similar to the post-structuralists perspective as relating to their concerns about the media and cultural imperialism. For them, for example, television can be seen as an extension of US cultural influence – a kind of cultural imperialism as in the form of purchasing US programmes, international coproductions dominated

---

1. The idea that American government has planned Americanization for domination of the world has been discussed by Albrow (1996: 71–4). He argues that the election campaign of Bill Clinton and his running mate Al Gore in 1992 portrayed how the United States attempted to impose their domination all over the world by using the pollution of environment around the World as a serious threat for American children. From this perspective, global becomes local, and then serves as the code for a political campaign and the 'environment' serves as a signifier for everything that had gone wrong in society. Such circumstances enable the United States to establish a New World order in which America is a central power for the rest of the World.

by American themes, US-dominated information services and local adaptations of American formats for domestic consumption. The outcome is said to be both the limiting of indigenous production capacity and the domination of local culture by foreign values (Barker, 1997: 183).

In contrast, there are those who don't see globalization as a dangerous American plot, Homayra believes that globalization does not pose a serious threat for Muslim identity:

> It has no serious repercussions on the Muslim identity. The theories of globalization conflict with the traditional Islamic teachings ... Modern Muslims can adapt with the global age ...(Homayra, aged 23)

Yaqob sees Americanization as a political phenomenon that seeks to increase its global power. Due to the fact that power still rules society, it still shapes and dominates every aspect of social and cultural activity (see Castells 1997: 359). According to Yaqob's definition of America, the main cause of the cultural identity crisis is the force exerted by the global political powers, it is these forces that pose the most serious challenge for indigenous identity and culture.

> America means power, and power is what everyone wants. So it means America has a great impact everywhere. (Yaqob, aged 19)

Amir, Yaqob and Yakoub Muhammad see American culture as a culture that has become normative within society. For them American culture is the major prevalent culture due to the fact that it has been legitimized via social institutions. Therefore people who do not have a choice will either ultimately follow the American style of life or become isolated from social life.

> Americanization has brought its own culture and dominance into the sphere of British life, i.e. McDonald's. The British Muslims would have to either accept it, otherwise they may be left behind in society therefore struggle for survival. (Amir, aged 23)

> America is the most powerful country in the world. Every person feels that by referring to himself as an American, he will feel superior to other citizens who are not American. This is what the Americans have done to people. 'Power means everything', the one with the power is in control. (Yaqob, aged 19)

> People will always imitate the dominant culture in a society. People will always want to be recognized and to be somebody. This is why people will

prefer American Western culture because it gives them an identity, a position in this modern global village. (Yakoub Mohammad, aged 30)

According to Castells (1997), what's known as 'legitimizing identity' can explain how dominant institutions of society introduced American culture to the extent that its domination via the mass media, as well as through the educational and political systems, was enforced over all other subcultural values. Therefore integration into an American or so-called Western culture arises from the very civil institutions that gave legitimacy to the idea of social as well as cultural structures. Such an expansion of American culture into the social spheres has created the right type of conditions for the global hegemony of the United States (Giddens, 1990).

In response to the question 'Why do people prefer American popular culture?', a diverse range of replies were given. Some answers portrayed the views of the Islamists and traditionalists, as well as the nationalists who are more inclined to resist the general trend of globalization. They harbour many negative views of American culture:

... because it allows all the *haraam* [prohibited] acts. The world is a paradise for the non-believers and a hell for the believers. (Ali Reza, aged 18)

Because it's all the work of the devil. It contradicts everything Islam stands for. (Saqib, aged 17)

Some of the respondents place more emphasis on the professional way of presentation and richness offering more freedom of choice and enjoyment:

Most people prefer American Western culture due to the fact that the demand for the products of American Western culture exceeds that of any other culture in the world market. The success is a direct result of the trillions of dollars wasted and used by the media especially the immoral themes of Hollywood movies as well as the exploitation of sexual themes especially in the world of advertising. (Hanif, aged 22)

... Probably because there is so much fun. There's not much else to do, it seems. (Haroon, aged 19)

It's a bigger richer nation, technologically advanced therefore people look up to them. (Nadia, aged 21)

Material wealth, intellectual calibre and achievement, global position, maturity of thought, pride in identity, country and ideology, self confidence. (Hamid, aged 26)

... Because ... it offers more freedom. (Homam, aged 16)

They find it modern, attractive and free of restrictions which religion imposes. (Farah, aged 18)

American culture appeals to people because it is an easier route away from reality. It indoctrinates views, which appeal to the youth's nafs. America is more technologically advanced thus the youth are attracted to it. (Suhaib, aged 19)

Sadaf questions the idea that American culture is really a first choice for most people:

I think the answer to the question depends on who 'most people' are. But those who do prefer American culture I would assume they do so for the following reasons. People tend to admire American attitudes such as confidence and positive outlook. (Sadaf, aged 23)

Tahir believes that American culture is popular especially for children who have been brought up in social institutions that to a large extent demonize their Islamic way of life and socialize them into new types of identity. For Tahir Americanization is more deep-rooted within the social structures, not simply as a result of McDonaldization or Hollywoodization but as a result of tremendous changes within the fabric of social life and institutions:

The most fundamental reason is that children have been socialized to think and behave in a certain manner. Institutions such as public schools with their own agendas and other agencies contribute to create this deviance from the Islamic way of life. (Tahir, aged 20)

Homayra, Adil and Mariam highlight the accessibility of American products. This gives American goods worldwide distribution:

American Western culture or McWorld and MTV culture has spread everywhere because it is *cheap* and *fast*. In this new millennium people are looking for anything that is entertaining at the condition that it is cheap and fast. American Western culture is answering these two criteria that will please every one. (Homayra, aged 23)

More advanced in some ways. Also they class themselves as free agents, they know about Islam but do not abide by it. Also America is more technologically advanced. (Adil, aged 20)

I think because people spend so much time in front of TV, watching videos and satellite. Most of the popular songs and films are from the US, so they are brainwashed into preferring it. (Mariam, aged 34)

Sabia, Shararit and Amir have made the connection between Americanization and liberalization. For Sabia, American culture has became global owing to the fact that it has been able to offer unlimited freedom in every aspect of life. They recall views of Legenhausen (1999) and sociologists such as Habermas (1975) and Berlin (1996)

They prefer American Western culture because it teaches them that you can be who you want, when you want and do what you like and no one has the right to control your mind whether it be a particular person or 'religion' because the times have changed and so have ideas. So be 'free' they call it and make the most out of your life while you have the chance. All the evil that surrounds us today has been beautified and made to look 'fair-seeming'. We the Muslims today are not referring back to the book of Allah, and the role our parents are playing is not very positive because many of them do not even encourage the practice of Islam. As long as they see that we are 'good' and not doing anything bad then everything will be all right. All this leads to the individual to follow their whims and desires that American Western culture has to offer, and as soon as they see that their child is getting out of hand, that's it, they can't control them any longer, and the parents wonder what went wrong? (Sabia, aged 17)

American Western culture provides freedom of enjoyment. There are no rules and regulations except fun and enjoyment. Whether we like it or not, everybody in the majority, even Muslims, prefer freedom of enjoyment rather than pertaining to rules and regulations of a sublime life. (Shararit, aged 19)

It's an open culture, there is no restriction, no family values. Americans have achieved enough. They have utilized many different methods such as the media to brainwash the masses psychologically thinking that 'move on' (progress in life) is to accept their culture. (Amir, aged 23)

Yasmin and Eqbal both believe that American culture does not have a substitute culture that would introduce new and equal options for the consumer:

... Because there is no other substitute. (Yasmin, aged 21)

There is not any other 'ideal' presented to them, it seems exciting but in reality it is all evil and full of ways to make you enter into hell, given people the false belief that through this culture they will have a peaceful life. (Eqbal, aged 19)

As explained in Chapter 4, Islamophobia portrays itself in the form of discrimination and hostility towards Muslims. It depicts them as fundamentalist terrorists possessing antihuman values. Our respondents believe this portrayal to be an attempt to isolate Muslims from the public domain. Some of the interviewees believe that Western media, in particular American media, has attempted to portray Islamophobic images of Muslims all over the world:

It has a great tendency to highlight events that occur in the name of Islam but unfortunately it fails to mention that Islam may not agree with the things being done, i.e. bombing of innocent civilians ... American media portrays Muslims as nothing more than terrorists. (Sara, aged 17)

We are seen as terrorists and fundamentalists. This idea has come about from the Western media. (Ali Reza, aged 18)

Western media has portrayed Islam in the majority of cases as being very repressive. (Rizwan, aged 18)

It hides the truth about Muslims and claims we are terrorists. (Saqib, aged 17)

The media (including television) are partly responsible for causing stereotyping and propagating Islamophobic ideas against Islam. Fly on the wall documentaries, growing fanatics and fundamentalist. (Sadaf, aged 23)

Yasmin is content with the fact that for the last few years Western media has devoted more programme time to Muslims. For her this is a positive sign, regardless of whether or not the images of Muslims that are portrayed are positive or negative:

> TV – has more recently devoted more air time to the coverage of Muslim programs. Whether this is positive or negative – I feel that at least it conveys the idea that Muslims are not being ignored. (Yasmin, aged 21)

6.3. Reverse Globalization: Homogeneity of Muslim Umma

Reverse globalization portrays the global movement of non-Western and even to some extent Western culture, as a general trend in the opposite direction to the Americanization of the World. In the following section we will discuss this trend from two perspectives. First we look at the response of Muslims to the process of globalization. Then the formation and development of the notion of the global Muslim *umma* will be explored.

6.3.1. Reverse Globalization: Muslim Resistance

Giddens (1999) has questioned the idea that globalization has constituted a monolithic one-way flow of cultural ideals from the West to the rest by raising the issue of 'reverse globalization' or, as Barker (1999) refers to it, 'reverse flow': the impact of non-Western ideas and practices on the West.

Following Castells (1997), it may be suggested that this 'reverse globalization' has been generated among those groups that are in positions /conditions devalued and/or stigmatized by the logic of domination. Thus they build trenches of resistance and survival on the basis of principles different from, or opposed to, those permeating the institutions of society (Castells, 1997: 8). The views of one of the respondents of this research reflects Castell's view with regard to 'resistance identity'. Castells (1997: 66) sees Muslim resistance as an attempt against the general trend of globalization simply because he considers its output as unfulfilling:

> In some ways globalization ... has made Muslims into people who are trying to escape from such an unfulfilling way of life. (Haroon, aged 19)

Those who have a resistance identity are very suspicious about the process of globalization, which means to them, basically, the expansion of American culture:

... American culture has starved the Muslims from their resources. (Nazem, aged 31)

In most cases American culture has eradicated their culture and in other cases there has been created a rebel culture, .i.e. terrorism for survival; the Americans use globalization as a weapon to destroy the integrity of Muslims. (Amir, aged 23)

As was pointed out earlier, this kind of identity is similar to that sense of identity felt by Muslims in an earlier part of Islamic history. The reason for this similarity could be the common perception and feelings that are shared by both periods. These perceptions can be summarized as a sense of scorn and humiliation, a sense of losing all values (religious and humanistic), a sense of being deprived of peace and tranquillity, and a sense of danger (see Chapter: 3).

One can say that resistance identity in essence originates from the insecurity and danger felt by Muslims when faced with an alien culture – Western culture. This feeling of insecurity forces one to return to the old traditional ways. This type of identity is an inherent part of Islamic communities, especially as relating to migrant communities living in Western countries. One can argue that the religious resistance of Muslims around the world has set the foundations for a strongly traditional religious movement within European and North American societies; the black Muslim uprising under the banner of the nation of Islam is a chief example of this type of identity that emerged as a result of a strong reaction in response to the profanities directed against everything considered sacred in religions.

One could cite the protest against Salman Rushdie's book *Satanic Verses*; the protest against the use of the word Mecca for bingo halls, and derogatory films that have been made about Islam, as contemporary examples and manifestations of a reverse globalization process. These also portray a revival of the Muslim *umma* all over the world[1].

There are numerous similarities, for example, of the resistance movements among earlier Muslims and those of the postmodern period. In the initial period of Islamic history, Muslims found themselves trapped between two opposing forces. From one side they suffered the most appalling humiliation, and from the other side the highest honours and reverence were bestowed upon

---

1.   One must remember that objecting to profanity directed against religious values is not exclusively a Muslim trait. One can find such examples within the Christian world. Now more and more of the pure traditionalist Christian concepts are rising to the fore. Parekh (1995) raises the point that, in the face of an advancing global culture, many societies display an understandable tendency to return to the security of the traditional ways of life and to romanticize a past age.

them. The depth of their conviction, gave them clarity of purpose and strength in their will and determination to overcome their enemies. In their endeavour to achieve reverence they were prepared even to give up their lives and in the process become martyrs.

Currently, Muslims are in a state of agitation and change. Resistance towards the Western culture is profound. They have found themselves in an environment where their religious and cultural values are subjected to daily ridicule. With the advent of the 21st century – because of new technology provided by the process of globalization – this feeling of subjection and humiliation is shared by many group of Muslims all over the world.

Since the beginnings of Islam up to now, the belief in the oneness of God, the *Qur'an*, the role of Muhammad, and the *umma* have continued to be the central pillars in the continuity and unity of Islam amongst Muslims (Voll, 1982: 1–23). The term *umma* was first used by the Prophet in the Covenant of Madinah negotiated with the Jewish minority, wherein the Jewish community was recognized as an autonomous *umma* having its own law, religion and institutions (al-Faruqi, 1981: 102).

The concept of *umma* as a social expression of the worldwide Muslim community is derived from the *Qur'an*, and is encapsulated in the concept of *tawhid* according to which there is no absolute separation between the individual and the community, between the social and the spiritual, between the temporal and the eternal.

The Divine imperatives, the prescribed norms of Man's conduct and the means of salvation are all defined in terms of society. It follows, therefore, that there can be no incompatibility between the individual and collective interests. In the Islamic framework, the necessity of society is seen to derive, at least in part, from what Faruqi has termed 'the insistence that ethics is concerned with action, rather than intention' (al-Faruqi, 1981:96). While this view is no doubt true as regards specifically the social or communitarian aspect of ethical behaviour, it needs to be qualified. The stress on inner virtue, which pertains to intention, greatly outweighs, in spiritual terms, the whole realm within which outward action takes place; were it otherwise, the notion of hypocrisy would be deprived of all meaning, for hypocrisy is precisely the correct outward action, accompanied by the wrong inner intention. The concept of *tawhid*, again, entails this union between the inner state of the soul and the outer quality of action.

The effort to initialize a properly Islamic society necessitated the formation of a new concept and ideal of what the bonds and the norms of society actually are: the *umma*, the new community of believers, was to be established on the basis of an ideal capable of holding within its embrace, people belonging to different races, colours and historical traditions.

As we discussed in Chapter 3, historically, the concept of a global Muslim *umma* has been formed in three distinct epochs throughout the history of Islam, initially in the era of the revelation and the subsequent caliphate period. During this time, tribalism, and other negative forces in society along the lines of colour and ethnic discrimination, were overcome, in principle if not always in practice. Secondly, the reversion to tribalism during the Umayyad Empire weakened once again the principle of an overarching ideal of a global *umma*; during this period the central state became the main force for the unification of the community of believers, empowering the Muslim *umma* as an integrated community and creating close understanding and a homogenized consciousness amongst Muslims. After the demise of the Abbasids, the Muslim lands were divided up into different territories, ruled over by such overlords as the Mongols, the Safavids, the Ottomans and the Moghuls (see Nicholson, 1930). This prefigured the subsequent further division of power that was the concomitant of the victory of the Western nation-states, whereby the *umma* was split up into competing, often hostile, politically sovereign entities. This paradoxically resulted both in the homogenization and the heterogenization of the Muslim *umma*. It homogenized Muslims through the influence of antinationalist movements – those who seek to purify the essence of Islam from alien values as well as alien power; it circulated all over the Muslim world through revivalists such as Jamal al-Din Astarabadi and Muhammad Abduh. This tendency to throw off the ideological yoke of nationalism persists to this day, and has found significant support among the educated classes, even if they are clearly in a small minority. On the other hand it has had a heterogenizing impact on the Muslim *umma* through the empowerment of the latest form of tribalism, that is, nationalistic ideology in subjective terms and the formation of the nation-states in objective terms.

Anwar Ibrahim (1991) further elaborated the concept of *umma* – Muslim and non-Muslim alike. For Ibrahim (1991: 306), 'The *umma* is not a cultural entity patterned on the norms of any one dominant group or groups' but it 'exists within and is expressed through diverse cultural groups – diversity within unity'. In this model, he refers to the migration of the Prophet to Medinah. He pointed out that the *umma* in this approach has 'necessitated that the Muslims became more engaged with other people, nations, worldviews, religions and ideologies to work for a set of moral objectives that we can and must define together. But it takes us much further. It requires that we respect the *umma* of other people ... The history of the *umma* has presented exemplary, almost unique models of multiracial, multicultural, multireligious, pluralist societies' (Ibrahim, 1991: 309). Such an understanding is likely to produce amongst young British Muslims a grounded legitimacy in Islam, which would nonetheless allow for the construction and exercise of a new social identity among Muslims in Britain.

Our review of Muslim identity by means of periodization in history (see Chapter: 3), and its relevance to the research carried out here, is two-fold: first, an awareness of the historical background and events that have led to the formation of Muslim identity furnishes us with useful information for this study; any effort to understand the processes by which identity is being formed in the present cannot dispense with at least a preliminary understanding of how identity was formed in the past. History is thus an important factor. Secondly, even if, subjectively the respondents may be ignorant of their own history, this history nonetheless has an impact upon them, whether they know it or not. This is due to a set of circumstances formed by the past, and they respond to these circumstances by means of ideas and principles that are equally the products of the past, their historical background; so even objectively, this history can be said to have an impact on their life today.

Returning to the first factor, that of objectively discernible processes of identity formation, it can be seen that, throughout the history of Islam, there has been a dialectical tension between the spiritual essence and cultural forms. The way in which this tension has worked itself out in history gives us an insight into the possible forms that this tension might take in the contemporary world, alerting us to various possibilities. It is of course true that the processes of globalization have imparted to this dialectic unique characteristics. One could say, for example, that the ideal of a unified Muslim *umma* has become, in purely objective terms, more concretely visible today than ever before; and yet it seems as elusive a reality as ever. This is because the globalization process has had two, apparently contradictory, consequences for the formation of the identity of contemporary Muslims. On the one hand, the notion, the ideal and also the objectively measurable dimensions of the *umma* have been 'globalized', i.e. given a more homogenous, unified content, one to which the global community of Muslims can in fact relate; they relate to it as both a subjectively posited ideal, and an objective fact: an ideal to be realized, and a fact that cannot be denied. The ideal of a Muslim *umma* that is united is now an ideal that many Muslims will strive to realize; but they do so, in today's world, on the new objective basis of an actual community of worldwide Muslims that are acutely aware of their identity as Muslims and of the existence of countless other Muslims, who similarly define themselves in Islamic terms, whatever be their actual national, cultural, or even sectarian, affiliation.

To speak of these differences, however, raises the second feature that apparently contradicts the first, or at the very least, conditions and qualifies the feasibility of the ideal stemming from the homogenization wrought by the forces of globalization, i.e. the very distinctiveness of the various groups and subgroups that make up the Muslim world are accentuated, deepened, made even more exclusive as sources of identity, competing with, if not overriding, the sense of belonging to a community of faith, a spiritual reality, transcending all outward differences on the lower, cultural plane. Hence, the critical question becomes: to what extent do the forces of heterogenization, leading to particularity and exclusivism, predominate over the formation of an *umma*-oriented identity; and to what extent will the forces of homogenization lay the foundations for an objectively defined *umma*, as a universal and inclusive reality? The research undertaken below will help to shed light on the relative weight of these two forces and their concomitants upon the way in which Muslims in Britain actually identify themselves.

6.3.2. Development of the Muslim Umma

The globe has become the real frame and field of operation for movements of all kinds; particularly in relation to the regional and local definitions of values and approaches. In this respect the Muslim *umma* has become the counterpart of, and seeks to influence, institutions that operate at the global level in the form of Islamic worldwide movements[1].

Some of the respondents in this research have pointed out that globalization plays a major role (all over the world) in the reformation tactics of the Muslim *umma*:

> Like I mentioned before, media has had both a positive and negative effect. Also new technology plays an important role in mass communication. In a way it has contributed greatly in making the Muslim *umma* more integrated. (Zahra, aged 33)

> Globalization has affected all elements of culture. Muslims are allowed to accept this new culture and become diffused and be destroyed or Globalized with its own identity and culture and to make others to integrate into Islam. (Amir, aged 23)

---

1. See Islamic Human Rights Commission's Press Release on the 24th April 2001 which launched the results of the survey in relation to the views of Muslims on the issue of global Islamic communities. The findings of this survey indicated that Muslim communities who showed greater zeal and commitment suffered escalating levels of injustice being perpetrated against them, i.e. Bosnia, Kosovo, Chechnya, Palestine, Kashmir, which has outraged other Muslims, mobilizing them into speaking out against injustice.

Globalization has pulled together all of the Muslims scholars and ordinary Muslim. This will help in resolving most of the problems.
(Yakoub Mohammad, aged 30)

I believe globalization has been of benefit in allowing greater communication between Muslims worldwide. (Yasmin, aged 21)

Globalization has brought Muslims closer. (Homam, aged 16)

Today, Muslims are more aware of their social position, cultural and economic power around the world. This awareness highlights exactly the conceptual meaning of globalization that was put forward by Robertson (1992) in his analysis of human consciousness of the 'compression of the world'. Sadaf's views also reflect Robertson's theory:

Islam is about unity. And looking at the Muslim *umma* at a global level has raised Muslim awareness; however, it is also adding to the immigration of Muslims, who are also fragmented. (Sadaf, aged 23)

On the other hand, globalization can create a global awareness within particular circles of any nation, as seen among diasporic culture around the world. Eqbal makes this point:

Problems have arisen to some extent. Globalization has raised the awareness of nationalism. (Eqbal, aged 19)

This research shows that the majority of British Muslims (72%) have some sort of global contact with Muslims around the world. Nevertheless this global communication is not necessarily based on face-to-face contact but mainly through telecommunication systems. It appears that advanced technology has preoccupied the individual with the convenience of modern lifestyle, which has greatly reduced human interaction.

This chapter has addressed two sets of themes. In the first section, we elaborated in analytical terms upon the concept of British Muslim identity. The very existence of such an entity as 'British identity' was put into question by Paxman (1999), Marr (2000), Alibhai-Brown (2000) and Parekh (2000). It was proposed that, with the impact of globalization, whatever was left of British identity was in the process of gradually exhausting itself. Whatever the actual degree to which this hypothesis is true, the fact remains that the concept of 'Britishness' is undergoing severe strain; apart from language and geography, it is difficult to identify any particular elements that might differentiate

Britishness from many other cultural characteristics in Western countries. This unity of culture is even more pronounced when one takes into consideration the acute contrast between identifiably 'Western' culture and non-Western cultures, even though, under the weight of globalization, the pockets of Western culture in the rest of the world are rapidly expanding also, hence the very term globalization. In the British milieu, British Muslim identity can be differentiated from other Muslim identities elsewhere by reference to factors such as one's birthplace, place of upbringing, and language. In this section different perspectives of respondents in relation to defining elements of Muslim identity were also examined. The points of view of respondents with regard to British society as a local force, together with the nature of identity as fixed or relative – considered both in terms British identity and as a response to the process of globalization – was also examined.

The impact of globalization ultimately demonstrates the fragmentation of Muslim identity. In Albrow's (1996: 144) terms, 'Globalization restores the boundlessness of culture and promotes the endless renewability and diversification of cultural expression rather than homogenization.' In fact, as Ritser (1998: 86) argued, it is homogenization that tends to bring forth heterogenization as a response to it. However, globalization has not operated in a single dimension, nor is it a process that has altered in a uniform manner every discernible tendency in culture and society; therefore, another key consequence of this trend to be discussed in the next chapter is the process of the heterogenization of identities.

In the second section of this chapter, the principal focus was on the Americanization and globalization of Islam. It was observed that resistant Muslim movements were established in reaction to the process of homogenization. In this respect, homogenization can be viewed as the McDonaldization or Hollywoodization of cultures more commonly referred to as Americanization. Just as this can be considered as a global phenomenon that transcends local boundaries, so the movement or tendency that is defined as the inverse of the dominant trend of globalization – that is 'reverse globalization' – likewise transcends local boundaries, serving as a mirror-image of what it opposes. The resistance movements of Islamists or 'jihadists' throughout the world fall into this category of groups tending towards 'reverse globalization', but doing so in a 'globalized' manner themselves.

Seven

Globalization and the Process of Heterogenization

As discussed in Chapter 6, globalization implies a dichotomy of homogenization and heterogenization. In the previous chapter, homogeneity of Muslim identity was examined in accordance with the process of globalization. In this chapter the heterogeneity of British Muslim identity will be the main theme of discussion.

One of the central, if paradoxical themes of globalization, is the generation of two simultaneous processes, heterogenization, which has induced the fragmentation of identities, and homogenization, which has created domination by Western culture, in particular American culture, all over the world. Many globalization theorists such as Featherstone (1991) and Pieterse (1994) argue that contemporary society is witnessing greater heterogenization, whilst the spread of Western culture and in particular American culture around the world points towards increased homogenization. In the following discussion different aspects of heterogeneity regarding British Muslim identity will be elaborated.

In Chapter 4 we discussed Castells' theory regarding identity formation. To summarize, he basically identified three *modes* of identity in response to the process of globalization, which, when applied to British Muslim identities, may in fact be integrated into eight different *types* of identity. Each one of these types of identity can be seen to correspond to one of the three modes of identity. The typology we proposed in Chapter 4, based on the influences of local, global, and historical forces, will now be elaborated in conjunction with Castells' analysis. According to Castells' theory 'resistance identity' includes what we call here the traditionalist, Islamist and nationalist types of identity. All of them 'resist' in accordance with a particular aspect of what we call 'the original culture'. 'Legitimized identity' includes what we call here the Anglicist, secularist and modernist types of identity, which have adapted themselves according to the norms and culture of the day, or what we may call 'the new culture'. 'Projective identity' is a combination of what is known as 'the original culture' and 'the new culture', which contains within it what we call here hybrid and undetermined identities. Considering the above typology, all these eight types of identities will be explained in terms of the globalization process in the following section.

7.1. Traditionalist Identity

Traditionalists are taken here to refer to those who emphasize the necessity of continuing the specifically religious aspect of the Islamic tradition, and who do not have any strong inclinations or serious attitudes regarding Islam as a political ideology. They give primacy to the formal, conventional and ritual aspect of Islam.

Giddens (1999) suggests that the concepts of tradition and traditionalism have emerged as a result of social processes initiated subsequent to the appearance of modernism – before the advent of modernism, everything in life was 'traditional'. In the age of globalization, however, it becomes increasingly difficult to maintain religious traditions as unchanging entities; the dynamics of consumer preference is introduced into the religious sphere. Religious ideals and beliefs become subjects from which to pick and choose.

Table 7.1: Views of Respondents Regarding Traditional Islam

Should Islamic traditions change or not?	Frequency	Percentage
Yes	38	15.4
No	159	64.4
I have no idea	29	11.7
It is not important to me	14	5.7
No answer	7	2.8

Table 7.1 illustrates that, whilst nearly two-thirds believe that Islamic tradition should remain as they were (64.4%), the remainder either believe in the necessity of reform or fundamental change in traditional Islamic values (15.4%) or seem indifferent (11.7%) or else consider the subject to be unimportant (5.7%). The category of 'traditionalist' is a general one, embracing various strands of those who believe that Islam should not change. There are those who believe in the continuing validity of traditional Islamic doctrine, alongside a belief in the necessity of militant social activism, and these are not to be regarded as 'traditionalist' in the strict sense, rather they fall into the category of 'Islamist'. There are others who oppose such activism but support nationalist attitudes,

and are thus closer to the nationalists. In other words, the determining factor is not so much traditional doctrine as such, but the manner in which this doctrine is translated into practice, in terms of conventional ritualism, in terms of patriotism or in terms of political militancy. Also, it has to be said that, for the Islamist type, a belief in traditional doctrine may well be acknowledged or affirmed, whilst that which is taken to be 'traditional doctrine' may in fact be the appendage of a political or ideological programme, and thus far from 'traditional religious doctrine', which comprised principles of a social or political order, but which cannot be reduced to those principles alone.

According to the findings of this research we can demarcate three distinctive characteristics for those who can be referred to as traditionalist. These characteristics are defined in terms of conservatism, ritual orientation and indifference to politics.

7.1.1. *Conservatism*

Traditionalists are on the whole more prone to identify themselves with the forces of conservatism; there is a marked tendency to avoid any sort of hazardous and risky social commitments and ventures, and this trait is usually more noticeable among the older generation. In contrast, Islamists willingly open themselves up to high-risk activities in the realm of politics, with the stress on *jihad* and other related social activities. This trait is manifested more especially among the younger generations.

Table 7.2 displays the attributes of conservative traditionalists, those who answered both that traditional Islam need not change, and that they are indifferent to the plight of their fellow Muslims. This group believes in the continuity of religious traditions with particular emphasis being placed on non-involvement in risky and dangerous ventures; this non-involvement going so far as to refrain from supporting Muslims who are in difficulties. Table 7.2 shows that 50% of the respondents who indicated their indifference to Muslims who are in difficulty also believed in the continuity of religious tradition. On the other hand, only 9.1% of those who were indifferent towards Muslims in difficulty believe that traditional Islam should change.

Table 7.2: Risk and Tradition

How do you feel if you observe a Muslim being treated with disrespect?	Traditional Islam should change:					
	I believe so (%)	I do not believe so (%)	I have no idea (%)	It is not important to me (%)	No answer (%)	Total (%)
Indifferent	4 (9.1)	22 (50.0)	9 (20.5)	8 (18.2)	1 (2.3)	44 (17.8)
I go to help	34 (16.7)	137 (67.5)	20 (9.9)	6 (3.0)	6 (3.0)	203 (82.2)
Total	38 (15.4)	159 (64.4)	29 (11.7)	14 (5.7)	7 (2.8)	247 (100.0)

According to Figure 7.1, one can consider another combination of the values discussed earlier, that is, a belief in the need to change the tradition going hand in hand with a certain courage in the face of risk – values that characterize the modernist identity. This trait takes on an Islamic colouring to the extent that there is any considerable readiness to come to the aid of Muslims in need; 16.7% of those respondents who asserted their readiness to help Muslims in need believed in the necessity of changing traditional Islam. This group can be seen to correspond to that type of modernist who makes a decisive effort to introduce structural changes within a definitely religious framework, that is, to modernize religion as part of the endeavour to modernize society.[1]

1. We have in mind here the kind of efforts pioneered by such individuals as Abduh (see Abu-Zahra, 1998: 99) and Fazlur Rahman (1982: 82), who argue for the gates of ijtihad to be reopened, and for the Sharia to be creatively adapted to meet the needs of modern society. This approach is to be carefully distinguished from the Islamist one, despite certain overlaps as regards ijtihad, and other areas, in that the Islamists are prepared to take the 'risk' of change much further, that is, in the direction of political militancy and violence, if necessary.

Figure 7.1: Combination of Tradition and Risk

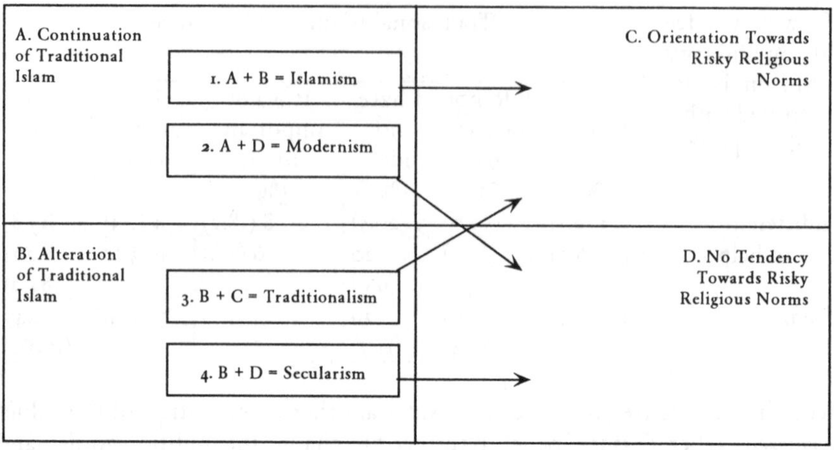

A. Continuation of Traditional Islam	C. Orientation Towards Risky Religious Norms
1. A + B = Islamism	
2. A + D = Modernism	
B. Alteration of Traditional Islam	D. No Tendency Towards Risky Religious Norms
3. B + C = Traditionalism	
4. B + D = Secularism	

Belief in the necessity of change in traditional Islam is in itself a risk-laden value to uphold, owing to the fact that it requires non-conformity to many of the prevailing social norms and values of the day. Secondly, it can lead to an opposition to many of the changes taking place within the social fabric of society – changes that weaken the Islamic orientation of society, and that neither traditionalist Islam nor Islamism as a political ideology are adequately addressing, in their view. These social transformations, however, are viewed as ambiguous phenomena, their positive content being seen as possible instruments for the modernizing of their society and thus of social and economic improvement within Muslim societies, their negative content being their detrimental impact on the Islamic character of society.

There is observable a certain paradoxical fusion between tradition and risk that gives rise to forms of Islamism, i.e. some of those who uphold the Islamic tradition, and who do so with intensity, are willing to take the element of 'risk' so far as to wage war on society – 'Western', 'imperialist' or any other – in order to bring about greater conformity to their perceptions of traditional Islamic norms. They cannot be properly referred to as 'traditionalists' because of the radical, and indeed, it might be argued, 'antitraditional' methods they employ in order to establish Islamic 'tradition', this tradition now being viewed through the perspective of a radical political ideology, the most extreme examples of such tendencies being the *jihad*-style movements.

A completely opposite fusion can be seen in regard to secularists: that is, they are opposed to Islamic tradition and are not prepared to take any kind of risk in the effort to introduce religion into social institutions for the benefit of the religious community. (They may, however, be prepared to take risks in other areas, unrelated to religion.)

The attitude towards political activity and the attitude towards the continuity of religious tradition are two critical factors that help to distinguish the four different types of identity: traditionalists, modernists, Islamists and secularists. The manner in which the boundaries between politics and tradition are crossed and how these key elements interact will be further discussed in the conclusion.

7.1.2. Partiality towards Ritual Aspect of Islam

Traditionalists are inclined to put more emphasis on the ritual aspects of religion. Historically, Islamic ritualistic aspects flowered in the midst of congregational traditions, such as the Friday and *Jamat* prayers, in line with the performance of individual prayer.

Table 7.3: Relationship Between Inclination Towards Tradition and Performing Daily Prayers

Traditional Islam should change	How often do you pray?					
	Regularly, five times a day	All prayers except morning prayer	Occasionally	Never	No answer	Total
Believe	16 (42.1)	6 (15.8)	11 (28.9)	4 (10.5)	1 (2.6)	38 (15.4)
Don't believe	115 (72.3)	20 (12.6)	22 (13.8)	2 (1.3)	–	159 (64.4)
I have no idea	12 (41.4)	3 (10.3)	11 (37.9)	3 (10.3)	–	29 (11.7)
It is not important to me	2 (14.3)	2 (14.3)	9 (64.3)	1 (7.1)	–	14 (5.7)
No answer	5 (71.4)	1 (14.3)	–	–	1 (14.3)	7 (2.8)
Total	150 (60.7)	32 (13.0)	53 (21.5)	10 (4.0)	2 (.8.0)	247 (100.0)

Table 7.3 illustrates the frequency in the performance of daily prayers as an individual ritual. There is a sharp difference in the views between those who pray regularly (i.e. five times a day) who believe that traditional Islam should change (42.1%) and those who perform prayers with great regularity (72.3%) and hold the opinion that there should not be a change in the religious tradition. Again, within the category of those who never performed their daily prayers, 10.5% believe in changing the religious traditions, this being considerably higher than those who supported the continuity of religious tradition (1.3%). This indicates that those who believe in the continuity of traditional Islam bear a stronger affinity with ritual aspects of the religion.

7.1.3. No Orientation towards Political Islam

As discussed earlier, the concept that distinguishes between secularists and modernists as well as traditionalists and Islamists is the notion of political Islam: 48.3% of those who do not believe in the 'politicization of Islam' at the same time did believe in the necessity of the continuity of Islamic traditions – a key difference between the traditionalists and the Islamists.

Table 7.4: Political Islam and Traditional Islam

Islam is a political ideology which should dominate government and all social institutions	Traditional Islam should change					Total
	Believe	Don't believe	I have no idea	It is not important to me	No answer	
Believe	13 (10.0)	103 (79.2)	9 (6.9)	2 (1.5)	3 (2.3)	130 (52.6)
Don't believe	12 (41.4)	14 (48.3)	2 (6.9)	1 (3.4)	–	29 (11.7)
I have no idea	6 (11.1)	28 (51.9)	16 (29.6)	4 (7.4)	–	54 (21.9)
It is not important to me	6 (24.0)	10 (40.0)	2 (8.0)	7 (28.0)		25 (10.1)
No answer	1 (11.1)	4 (44.4)	–	–	4 (44.4)	9 (3.6)
Total	38 (15.4)	159 (64.4)	29 (11.7)	14 (5.7)	7 (2.8)	247 (100.0)

$P = 0.00 < 0.01$

As Table 7.4 shows, the number of young Muslims who consider themselves as traditionalists is very small (14 out of 247), but the percentage of those who believe in totalist Islam, which includes traditional and political Islam, is substantially high (103 out of 247).

7.2. Islamist Identity

Islamists, or as Shepard (1987: 308) named them, 'Islamic totalists', are committed to making Islamic ideology pervasive in society. Radical Islam, or what Turner termed 'fundamentalism'[1] should be regarded as a religious response to globalization, multiculturalism and postmodern pluralism (Turner, 1994: 186). This 'reaction' may be attributed to the harsh labelling of Muslims as extremists and terrorists – thus creating an Islamophobic environment, which, in turn, promotes extremism – and to the fact that cultural globalization is seen as antagonistic to Islamic culture.

American and European media, which over the last two decades have focused on the worldwide Islamic resurgence, have portrayed Muslim identity in the context of two major themes. One is the notion of Islamic fundamentalism, linked strongly with violence, and the other is the presentation of Muslims as an ethnic group. The Balkan War, for example, was seen as a conflict between Bosnian Serbs, Bosnian Croats and Bosnian Muslims. Bosnian Muslims were labelled according to their religious affiliation whereas the non-Muslim residents of Bosnia – Serbs and Croats – were described by their nationality, and not by their religion. In contrast, in the current crisis in Kosovo, for a variety of reasons that are not yet clear, the global Western media has retreated to the old concept of ethnic identity. This time the majority of the people of Kosovo, who are Muslims, are identified simply as ethnic Albanians thus ignoring their Islamic identity (see Mowlana, 1998). One possible reason for this might be that the conflict in Bosnia, which seized the conscience of the world's Muslims and highlighted the oppression of a defenceless Muslim population by an overwhelmingly powerful enemy, gave rise to severe criticism of the Western powers by Muslims all around the world. The damage done to the image of the 'New World Order', and to relations between the West and the Muslim world, as a result of the Bosnian genocide and the inability or unwillingness of the Western powers to intervene until global opinion forced it to do so, might be one factor in explaining the

---

1. According to Mowlana (2000: 260), American observers borrowed the label of 'fundamentalism' from the history of Christianity, and applied it in their news reports on the revival of Islamic fundamentalism in Iran and elsewhere.

shift from Bosnia to Kosovo in terms of the definition of the groups and the portrayal of the conflict by the Western media.

However, this shift may be explained also by other factors, and it may also be a short-lived phenomenon, more the exception to the rule. For it cannot be denied that the trend in the dominant global media is towards the portrayal of Muslims as a religious community, first and foremost. The point here is that the identification of Muslims as a religious group rather than in terms of their nationality increases the global perception of a single Muslim worldwide community, and thus might be seen as one of the reasons why Muslims have a greater sense of solidarity with other Muslims around the world, and are beginning to possess a more defined 'Muslim' rather than nationalist identity.

Numerous analyses have shown that from the Islamic revolution in Iran to the Gulf War and from the occupation of Afghanistan by the Soviets to the ethnic cleansing in the Balkans, the mainstream international media have contributed more than their share to the already confused state of public opinion about Muslim identity in the West with their adverse publicity and propaganda waged against Islamic movements (see Said, 1981; Mowlana, Gerbner & Schiller, 1992; Kamilapour,1994). Fundamentalism may be interpreted as a response both to modernization and to postmodernity, since fundamentalism has been considered as a process of dedifferentiation (Lechner 1985a, 1985b; Roberston & Chirico, 1985).

The Western hegemony of the Muslim world has led to Islamophobia with stereotyping and the labelling of Muslim movements around the world as terrorists and fundamentalists. This has created radical reactions among Muslims. The perception of Islam as a political ideology is, of course, another critical factor involved in the construction of Islamic movements, especially among young Muslims all over the world and, in particular, young Muslims in Britain. This trend can readily be seen in the emergence of such organizations as the al-Muhajiroun and Hizb-ut-Tahrir that have been established in the last decade calling on Muslims to rise up in resistance against Western culture or what they call the domination of *kufr*, heathen disbelief.

It would be useful to state here, in the briefest terms, the basic aims and objectives of these two highly active and militantly Islamist groups. In the light of these aims, the 'Islamist' character of some of the responses below will be more readily apparent.

The aim of the al-Muhajiroun group is to revive the *umma* from severe decline, and to liberate Muslims from the clutches of the 'heathen' system of *kufr*. It also aims to restore the notion of Islamic statehood (*Khilafah*) so that the one true state is governed by the rules of God. Al-Muhajiroun also believe that Muslims in the West are responsible for the preservation of their Islamic identity, i.e. their belief and their Islamic personality.

Hizb-ut-Tahrir has similar views: to restore the Islamic way of life and to convey Islamic *da'wah* to the world. In essence this is a way of bringing Muslims back to living in an Islamic way in *Dar al-Islam*, particularly in relation to Islamic societies, such that all of life's affairs in society are administered according to *Shari'ah*, under the auspices of *halal* and *haram* parameters with the banner of Islamic Statehood, which can be regarded as the Khilafah State. This is a state in which Muslims appoint a Khilafah and give him *bay'ah* (the oath of allegiance) to offer him obedience, on condition that he rules according to the *Qur'an* and the *Sunnah* of the Prophet, to convey the message of Islam to the world through the concept of *da'wah* and *jihad*. It also aims to bring back the notion of Islamic guidance for all mankind and to lead the *umma* into the struggle with *Kufr*, its systems and its ideals, so that Islam comes to dominate the world.

The respondents' views in this study *vis-à-vis* 'the role of young Muslims' who consider themselves as Islamists in the age of globalization can be summarized as follows:

… To follow the *Qur'an* and *Sunnah* and to further spread Islam.
(Ali Reza, aged 18)

… To carry out *jihad al-nafs* [the war against the soul] to its full extent, and later on pass both this knowledge and all other things gained to others.
(Sara, aged 17)

… Striving for the re-establishment of an Islamic state and revival of our *umma*. (Saqib, aged 17)

… A Muslim's role involves social and environmental responsibilities. For example, a Muslim has a role as an individual and a member of the local community; in addition to this at a macro level he or she is part of a growing international community with an overall aim to live in harmony under Allah's law or example of the Prophet. (Sadaf, aged 23)

The role of a Muslim in today's society should be to ensure that he remains firm upon his Islamic belief and practices while simultaneously adhering to the duties and respect owed to individuals of other faiths and walks of life in order to illustrate the beauty of Islam. (Tahir, aged 23)

… To remind and encourage one another in holding to the ethics and values of Islam whilst progressing materially in the global village.
(Hanif, aged 22)

... A Muslim should try to maintain some type of Islamic identity in a multicultural society. It is important that Muslims uphold this sacred Islamic identity. They should strive to maintain Islamic morals and ethics. (Suhaib, aged 19)

As far as is discernible, most answers given in this survey emphasize the responsibility of Muslims within non-Muslim communities or, as Suhaib said, in a multicultural society. They adhere to the framework of maintaining traditional Islamic values whilst putting a strong emphasis on the positive qualities of Islam, especially geared to those Westerners who have a phobic picture of Islam (see the *Runnymede Trust Report on Islamophobia*, 1997). Another important point that has been portrayed by many of the above respondents is that of the 'globalization of Islam'. Considering their belief that Islam had been addressed to all societies, aiming, in essence, to universalize its message, these followers of Islam also believe that Islam should be globalized.

The findings of this survey have also shown that a large number of the Islamists share the same values as the nationalists and traditionalists, but their views on Islamic movements and the political ideology of Islam are what distinguish them from others. They can also be differentiated from the secularists, modernists, Anglicists, as well as those who consider themselves as having a hybrid and undetermined identity, in that they have a deep empathy with the programme of perpetuating traditional Islamic values, and resisting the tide of Western culture, by radical means. According to results of this research, Islamists have four distinct characteristics which differentiate them from the rest of the British Muslims.

7.2.1. Emphasis on Islamic Politics and Movements

Modernists and Islamists share similar views on the politicization of Islam. Nevertheless, the ideals of these two groups differ with regard to the role of Islamic movements and the perpetuation of traditional Islam. While modernists believe that the 'Islamization' of societies should take place via gradual social reformation, Islamists favour a more rapid transition in social change, which, if necessary, may be achieved through *jihad*.

Table 7.5: Relationship Between Islamic Movements and Political Islam

Your views on Islamic movements around the world	Islam is a political ideology, which should dominate all social institutions and governments					Total (%)
	Believe (%)	Do not believe (%)	I have no idea (%)	It is not important to me (%)	No answer (%)	
Most are illegal and create problems for society	15 (36.6)	6 (15.4)	11 (26.8)	9 (22.0)	–	41 (16.6)
I do not believe in the politicisation of Islam	9 (39.1)	1 (4.3)	8 (34.8)	4 (17.4)	1 (4.3)	23 (9.3)
It is necessary to enable people to decide their own future	74 (56.1)	15 (11.4)	32 (24.2)	9 (6.8)	2 (1.5)	132 (53.4)
Social justice cannot be established outside of an Islamic state	32 (74.4)	5 (11.6)	3 (7.0)	2 (4.7)	1 (2.3)	43 (17.4)
No answer	–	2 (25.0)	–	1 (12.5)	5 (62.5)	8 (3.2)
Total	130 (52.6)	29 (11.7)	54 (21.9)	25 (10.1)	9 (3.6)	247 (100.0)

Table 7.5 shows relatively the correlation between belief associated with political Islam and Islamic movements ($P = 0.00 < 0.01$). The results show that over half (56.1%) of those who believe that Islamic movements around the world are necessary to enable people to decide their own future believed also to Islam as a political ideology,. The survey also shows that 74.4% of those who believe that social justice cannot be established outside of an Islamic state, also support the establishment of Islamic State, which is a substantially higher proportion than that having an opposing opinion (11.7%).

The attributes of the Islamists can be subdivided into two important components: one is sympathy towards the Muslim *umma* around the world – this can be seen as a social phenomenon that has been facilitated by the process of globalization; the second component relates to the ideological impact of the notion of political Islam upon one's religious beliefs.

7.2.2. Radical Muslim (Practice and Understanding)

The findings of this research suggest that the generation of Muslims who have imigrated (Stalker & Rienner 2000: 163) from their native homelands to Britain, establishing families here, seem to adhere to Islamic traditions and values with tenacity. It is to be expected however that, regardless of where one might migrate to, it is assumed that one is more likely to hold more strongly to their fundamental beliefs. This can be due to the fact that when one's traditions and values are threatened by, or defined in relation to, an alien way of life, the reaction is to hold on to the old traditions with more intensity. This can be viewed as a religiocultural resistance against the tide of the surrounding cultural system.

Table 7.6: Different Views on Islamic Values

Views	Frequency	Percentage
Islamic values are absolute for every society	186	75.3
Some Islamic values are absolute and some should be updated	36	14.6
There is no eternal good or bad	23	9.3
No answer	2	0.8
Total	247	100.0

As can be seen from the Table 7.6, the majority of respondents (75.3%) still believed that 'Islamic values were absolute for every society' regardless of differences that exist between traditional, modern and postmodern societies. Some of the respondents disagreed and suggested that certain Islamic values were absolute whilst others needed to be updated (14.6%). The rest of the respondents had no clear convictions on the matter one way or the other with 9.3% indicating their inclination towards a more liberal understanding of Islam.

The following comments made by Yakob and Sabia show the general nature of the Islamist line of thought regarding responsibilities of Muslims in a global world:

The role of a Muslim is to understand the modern society the way it functions and to apply the injunctions of the *Qur'an* and the *Sunnah* in order to establish the *Khilafat Rasulullah* [governance according to the Prophet]. (Yakoub Mohammad, aged 30)

I believe that Muslims should not lose their identity, as this leads to corruption of the heart and belief. A Muslim in today's society should be motivated to learn the *deen* (religion) and implement it in their lives whatever the age, sex or occupation that they have. We're here for a reason as Muslims and that is to implement the word and command of Allah to the best of our ability. I believe that another one of our missions is to act as good Muslims and set a positive example to people who have many misconceptions about Islam today. So our role is to fight the pressures that face the youth today and show that Islam really is the way and not the short enjoyment of this *dunya* (world). (Sabia, aged 17)

For Islamists every aspect of life should be constructed according to religious law. Religion should dominate every aspect of our individual's social and political life. Their philosophy of life is obedience to the commands of Allah. From their perspective, Western culture is based on man-made laws and there are important differences between Islam and what we know to be Western culture:

Muslims are bound to follow the divine order set down in law. This is in direct opposition to secular man-made laws which Western culture is based on *vis-à-vis* following and establishing the New World Order and the free-Masonic movement. (Adil, aged 20)

There are many differences ... Firstly the dress code. Family values and social behaviour. A Western person can leave home at the age of 16, get a boy/girl friend become a single parent. Stay out late to go clubbing and drinking. (Mariam, aged 34)

I'd say the major conflicts arise in the way Muslims and [those in] Western culture behave. What I mean is that the way a Muslim person behaves and thinks is totally alien to the way they think in the West. I think Western culture has made people to question certain aspects in Islam in a haphazard way without prior knowledge or in-depth appreciation of the subject at hand, e.g. why Muslim women wear the *hijab*. The suppressed role of women; why we have to pray five times a day, etc. ... the fact that Western culture has emphasized the right of freedom for all the paradox being that they are prisoners of their own liberation! Consider the fact that there is more racism, stereotyping, sexism and dishonouring of women in particular. Their man-made laws protect no one, especially children who are today victims of sexual abuse, etc. Western culture refuses to understand that real equality only lies in Islam, the belief in the one true God and the

Prophet, and following his ways, which is the best of ways. No racism, nationalism, sexism or dishonouring of women and children.
(Sabia, aged 17)

All these differences, which have been expressed by Adil, Mariam and Sabia, in essence refer to conflicts between Islam and Western culture as understood by the Islamists in the age of globalization.

7.3. Modernist Identity

In contrast to the secularists, modernists conclude that Islam does indeed provide an adequate ideological base for public life (Shepard,1987: 311). al-Azmeh (1993: 39) suggests that modern history is characterized by the globalization of the Western order. The modernists' approach can be thought of as a combination of modernization and Islamic ideology. Modernization has opened up to scrutiny many elements contained within the traditional norms of Islam. This process has been fostered by Muslim modernists who wish to apply the traditional norms in novel ways in order to integrate the Muslim ethos more fully within modern society, in response to the actual needs generated in the modern world.

According to Turner (1994) the issue of Islamic modernization can be understood initially within the framework of Weber's sociological analysis of the process of rationalization, with particular focus upon the paradoxical relationship between the process of rationalization and the problem of meaninglessness. The argument here is that Weber's sociology provides and anticipates the current contrast between the program of modernization and the condition of postmodernism. Within this framework, Modernism is an attempt at dedifferentiation (Turner, 1994: 77). However, Turner's analysis does not sufficiently take into account the important distinctions that must be made within his category of 'Islamist/modernist'. For the two elements are clearly different in meaning and implication. For, while it is true that Islamists, by the very fact of using Islam as an ideology, are acting and thinking in 'modernist' terms, not every 'modernist' can be regarded as an 'Islamist': for there are many modernists who are passionately anti-Islamist, seeing in the ideologization of Islam something that is fanatical, backward and therefore distinctly antimodernist. Islamists tend to stress the necessity of a return to the tradition – even if they do so in ways that are far from 'traditional' – whereas the modernists stress the need to go forward into the modern world with a minimum of cultural and religious 'baggage' from the past – even if they still wish to maintain the basic Islamic obligations. This minimalist approach to the practice of Islam does not make modernists Islamists; nor does Islamists' use of modern tools of expression and thought make them 'modernists'. There exists a critical difference between the modernists of today, and those of the preglobalization era. Today, the West's civil institutions, which embody Western social and political thought, penetrate the formers' method of thinking, thus making them more liberal and pluralistic than before. The main target of the modernists, in the past, was the traditionalists while modernists, today, are equally opposed to traditionalists and Islamists alike.

The two critical components of the modernist identity are: the desire to reform society through modernization and to reform religious thinking in accordance with modern modes of thought. These are the criteria that we have adopted in this research in order to distinguish and gauge the modernist dimension of identity.

7.3.1. Social Reformation

Modernists believe that Muslims should review their previous history in order to reproduce a new model of thinking that can be answerable to the actual demands and needs of society. They believe that the Muslim world should develop and change within the modern age in order to join the global community, which can be hindered by the Muslims' wish to return to the past, preferring traditional values over forward-looking ones, and failing to adapt the *Sharia* to contemporary social conditions (see Abu-Zahra, 1998: 83).

The interviewees that we can refer to as 'modernists' describe the role of Muslims in the globalization age as one which should make them more aware of their actual social environment in which the Muslim community currently finds itself, and out of which solutions to its problems must be found. The attitude of modernist Muslims should be to question themselves in these turbulent and fluctuating times, i.e. initially refining the 'self', with the aim of, eventually, reforming and, thus, concentrating their exertions upon the difficulties present within their own societies. From this perspective, globalization is not the pivotal challenge facing Muslim society:

I feel that Muslims are unsuccessful because of themselves and not Western globalization. They are far too busy with petty problems and differences, such as one's nationality, and don't consider all Muslims as one people; rather, they do not like someone because they belong to a different country than themselves. (Farah, aged 18)

... A Muslim should be allowed to be whatever he/she wishes to be ... This is actually popular attitude in the global age. (Hussain, aged 18)

There are two main aspects of the modernists' approach to reforming religious thought:

1. The belief in the necessity of serious change within traditional Islamic discourse.
2. The belief in the applicability of reformed and modernized Islam in the modern and postmodern world.

Table 7.7 shows that 52.6% of those who believe that traditional Islam should change also believe in the applicability of Islam in every society. It is this group that gives precise form to the category of 'modernist'.

Table 7.7: Traditional Islam and Applicability of Islamic Law
in Modern and Postmodern Society

Traditional Islam should change	Islamic law is applicable even contemporary societies					Total (%)
	Believe (%)	Don't believe (%)	I have no idea (%)	It is not important to me (%)	No answer (%)	
Believe	20 (52.6)	11 (28.9)	5 (13.2)	–	2 (5.3)	38 (15.4)
Don't believe	135 (84.9)	4 (2.5)	11 (6.9)	6 (3.8)	3 (1.9)	159 (64.4)
I have no idea	17 (58.6)	3 (10.3)	7 (24.1)	2 (6.9)	–	29 (11.7)
It is not important to me	9 (64.3)	1 (7.1)	1 (7.1)	3 (21.4)	–	14 (5.7)
No answer	3 (42.9)	–	–	–	4 (57.1)	7 (2.8)
Total	184 (74.5)	19 (7.7)	24 (9.7)	11 (4.5)	9 (3.6)	247 (100.0)

$P = 0.00 < 0.01$

Table 7.7 shows also that a substantial percentage (84.9%) of those who do not believe in any sort of alteration in traditional Islam, simultaneously believe in the applicability of Islam in modern and postmodern society, thus demonstrating that, for them, traditional Islam can be applied, with little need for substantial change, within every society and in every age.

7.3.2. Modernization of Religious Understanding

According to Shepard (1987: 311), the Islamists show strong tendencies to propagate the flexible side of Islam within the public domain. This flexibility implies interpreting Islam in terms that can be congruent with Western ideologies. He refers to the Sunni modernist view that the 'gate of *ijtihad*' should be reopened, so that Muslims do not just rely on the 'medieval synthesis' as represented by the four schools of jurisprudence, but they should go back directly to the *Qur'an* and *Sunnah* in order to seek a fresh interpretation of these sources, thus making Islam more practicable in modern times. The Shia Modernists argue that they have always believed in and practised *ijtehad*, and that, as a consequence, they are able to formulate solutions to the new problems faced by the *umma*. For them Islam needs to restructure itself according to the modern age (see Shariati, 1979)[1].

The above view is further expounded upon by Homayra:

Muslims evolving in modern society should not only follow ancient and traditional values but also follow certain aspects of modernity. In a world where high technologies prevail, they must be ready to grasp the 21st century. (Homayra, aged 23)

7.4. Secularist Identity

To understand secular identity, we need first to discuss the phenomenon of secularization. Secularization is one of the consequences of the process of modernization in the West, and essentially entails the separation of church and state and, by extension, the exclusion of religion from social and political institutions and its confinement to the private domain. Protestantist movements are regarded as the epistemological driving force behind the evacuation of social consciousness from religion. Robinson (1999) refers to and creatively applies the important analytical distinction drawn by Berger between *structural* and *subjective* secularization. Structural secularization is a process that

---

1. The new modernists in Iran are introducing a sort of religious democratic doctrine, which gives the main authority to the people's will. From their viewpoint religion needs to be refurbished in a way that can be answerable to the demands of the young generation. The orientation of the new modernists seems to be different from the doctrine of the modernists in 1940–1980, such as Afghani, Abduh, Muhammad Iqbal and Mawdudi. The new modernists look for democratization of religion and de-ideologization of religion, whilst the early modernists' approach was more ideological (see Soroush, 2000).

evacuates religion from *society's institutions*. This means that religion is driven out of the frameworks of *law*, of *knowledge*, and of *power*. Subjective secularization is the evacuation of religion from the consciousness of man, which disentangles the religious vision from the consciousness of human beings. However, Giddens has suggested that secularization does not seem to result in the complete disappearance of religious thought and activity. While this is no doubt true – religious consciousness has not disappeared, but simply taken on different forms – it cannot be denied that, as regards public 'space' within society, religion has been effectively excluded. Most of the situations of modern social life are manifestly incompatible with religion as a pervasive influence upon one's day-to-day life (see Cassell, 1993: 301).

Shepard (1987) believes that the Muslim world has witnessed moderate secularism, which seeks to separate religion from politics and other areas of public life. The most extreme case of secularism in the Muslim world is Turkey, which in 1928 removed from its constitution the clause that made Islam the state religion. At present the relevant article reads: 'The Republic of Turkey is a democratic, secular and social state governed by the rule of law ... loyal to the nationalism of Ataturk and based on the fundamental principles set forth in the Preamble' (Article 2).

In the globalization era, the secularization model has been developed in different modes and degrees all over the world. Secularization has been expanded such that it now penetrates nearly all aspects of life structurally and subjectively. This process has become increasingly similar across the world through, for example, the influence of secular education. Similar course syllabus and content, comparable term units and semesters, and increasing professorial similarities are part of the global homogeneity in the education system. Also, the process by which society is 'rationalized' according to the programme of conventional modernization, through democratization, liberalization, and bureaucratization of the political and social system, has successfully 'evacuated' religion from the whole social system, i.e. from the domains of law, education and power, as well as art, broadcasting and other media. The whole way of life in Islamic countries has been influenced by this secularizing process. Although most policy-makers in Muslim states have actively participated in this process, they have been opposed by significant numbers of Muslims who have tried to uphold Islamic values and laws, seeking to apply the *Shariah* in all aspects of social and political life.

In the type of society in which a multitude of choices in diverse domains is available, it might be argued that individuals are deprived of that mental 'space' that allows them to focus on religion. In other words, religious consciousness has, traditionally, functioned within a social and psychological framework that was less cluttered by multifarious items, all seeking attention and consuming time. Traditional rhythms of social life and intercourse were modulated according to religious norms, whereas the rhythms and demands of modern life, on the contrary, relativize religious practices by relegating them to the margins of social and professional interaction.

Accordingly, in the globalization era, what has been called 'subjective secularization' is much stronger and more influential than ever before. Today, people have access to hundreds of global TV channels and millions of internet sites, which connect them to the news, economics, music, fashion, sports, sciences, pornography, the different religions and cults, and forms of entertainment found throughout the world. It is not just global TV and the internet that have given consumers the opportunity to access images or texts visually: all these materials have been repackaged in the form of videos, CDs, journals and books, and are available in the cities and even villages of the world.

Britain, which is considered by some as the upholder of Christian values, is also regarded as the vanguard of secularism. This paradoxical state of affairs has left little room for the direct role of religion within social and political institutions, the media, the educational system and the law. In this context, the local environment, and not just the global one, plays a highly significant role in influencing or changing the views of British citizens, including British Muslims, *vis-à-vis* the construction of a secular identity. Therefore, global Western culture and local British forces have come together to create conducive conditions for the secularization of British citizens. Needless to say, however, this has caused its own reaction: young Muslims in Britain are clearly resisting the tide of secular and modern forces or, as Robertson (2000) termed it, 'antiglobalization'.

Secularity in itself can be examined from a subjective and objective perspective in its relationship with individual and social life, but the main characteristics of the secularists can be subjectively examined as regards their attitudes and behaviour in everyday life and objectively portrayed as one that involves the applicability of religion in social and political institutions and processes (Robinson, 1999).

7.4.1. Attitudes towards Political and Traditional Islam (Subjective Secularization)

The secularists and traditionalists share similar views with regard to the idea of the politicization of Islam: they both reject it quite forcefully. They also share common values with the modernists who reject the traditional aspects of Islam, but they differ from the traditionalists in that the secularists are active in secular politics and social activity, but traditionalists avoid any involvement with politics. According to the findings of this research, 28.9% of those who do not believe in traditional Islamic values also hold the view that Islamic law is not applicable in modern and postmodern society. This group of respondents included only 4.5% of all the respondents questioned in this survey. This indicates that, while local and global forces can be seen as the main architects in the construction of the social and political framework with a secular mandate, the majority of respondents in Brent reject the restriction of the role of religion to the domain of individual experience. However, in practice, British Muslims have great difficulties in implementing Islam within British social institutions, including that of education.

Table 7.8: Relationship Between Belief in Traditional Islam and Views of Respondents on Islam as an Individual Rather than a Social Philosophy

Traditional Islam should change	The Islamic faith is an individual philosophy rather than social philosophy					
	Believe (%)	Don't believe (%)	I have no idea (%)	It is not important to me (%)	No answer (%)	Total (%)
Believe	21 (55.3)	13 (34.2)	3 (7.9)	–	1 (2.6)	38 (15.4)
Don't believe	31 (19.5)	94 (59.1)	22 (13.8)	6 (3.8)	6 (3.8)	159 (64.4)
I have no idea	4 (13.8)	7 (24.1)	12 (41.4)	5 (17.2)	1 (3.4)	29 (11.7)
It is not important to me	1 (7.1)	1 (7.1)	8 (57.1)	4 (28.6)		14 (5.7)
No answer	–	3 (42.9)	1 (143)	–	3 (42.9)	7 (2.8)
Total	57 (23.1)	118 (47.8)	46 (18.6)	15 (6.1)	11 (4.5)	247 (100.0)

Table 7.8 shows that over half of the respondents (55.3%) who believed that traditional Islam should change also see Islam as an individual philosophy rather than a social philosophy. The idea, implied or explicit, of the individualization of religion is, in itself, an inherent part of the secularization process. Therefore, one can interpret this conception of Islam as an individual quest as forming part of the secular orientation towards religious identity.[1]

---

1. It is true, however, that in traditional Islamic contexts there were always 'individualists' whose quest was personal, mystical and somewhat divorced from the
(continued...)

7.4.2. Space for Religion in Social and Individual Life (Objective Secularization)

Given the extent to which social institutions in Britain operate according to secular principles, there remains one other outlet for British Muslims through which they practise their religion, and that is during their leisure time. On the one hand, the activities engaged in these times seem to correlate with their perception of religion; and, on the other hand, the way in which Muslims spend their leisure time could gradually change their religious understanding and practice.

Table 7.9 below shows that among those who spend more time watching TV in their leisure time than doing anything else, a majority (57.9%) believe that 'Islam is an individual rather than social philosophy', as compared with 43.2% who do not. It also shows that the proportion, of those who do not have a clear perception of the question, and watched TV, was high (76.1%), as was the percentage of those who answered that religion was not an important issue for them (73.3%). On the other hand, involvement with religious activities among those who do not believe Islam to be an individual philosophy is significantly higher (22%) than those who have held such a view (10.5%); and for those to whom Islam did not matter, involvement with religious activity during leisure time is almost negligible. This close correlation was to be expected.

The overall result concerning the manner in which individuals spend their leisure time demonstrated that religion has been evacuated from British Muslims' leisure time. Only 13.8% of the respondents give priority to religious activities in their leisure time. Watching TV (54.3%), visiting friends and family (11.7%) and sport (7.7%) were stated as the primary leisure activities by the majority of the remainder of the respondents. Consequently, it can be inferred that the vast majority of the respondents neither observe religion within social institutions nor during their periods of recreation. This leaves little room for religious involvement within society, thus accentuating its secular orientation.

(...continued)

communitarian aspects of religion. But the 'individualization' of religion in question here is of a different order: it implies restricting religion to the individual order even while the individual as such continues to play an active role in society, a society that is dominated by secular norms.

Table 7.9: Individualism and Leisure Times

How do you spend your leisure time as your first choice?

The Islamic faith is an individual philosophy rather than individual social philosophy	TV	Radio	Sports	Religious activities	Cinema or theatre	Reading	Visiting friends and family	Voluntary work	Playing various electronic games	Other	Total
Believe	57.9%	1.8%	5.3%	10.5%	1.8%	1.8%	19.3%	–	1.8%	–	57 (23.1)
Don't believe	43.2%	–	8.5%	22%	0.8%	6.8%	12.7%	2.5%	1.7%	1.7%	118 (47.8)
I have no idea	76.1%	–	–	4.3%	6.5%	–	6.5%	–	6.5%	–	46 (18.6)
It is not important to me	73.3%	–	13.3%	–	–	6.7%	–	–	6.7%	–	
No answer	36.4%	–	36.4%	–	9.1%	18.2%	–	–	–	–	11 (4.5)
Total	134 (54.3)	1 (0.4)	19 (7.7)	34 (13.8)	6 (2.4)	12 (4.9)	29 (11.7)	3 (1.2)	7 (2.8)	2 (2.8)	247 (100.0)

7.5. *Nationalist Identity*

The term 'nationalism' was most probably used for the first time in 1798 by Augustin Barruel when, in a history of Jacobinism, he recalls that 'Nationalism, or the love of nation (*L'amour national*) took the place of the love of mankind (*L'amour général*)' (Kamenka, 1976: 8). Basically, nationalism became a serious movement after the establishment of nation-states in the 19th century (Giddens, 1989: 303). Nationalism as an ideology both set the scene for the development of the nation-state and was further deepened by that system. According to Reece (1986), the idea of the nation-state is a relatively recent phenomenon in European history. The nation-state concept comprises a notion of a people who share a common language, ethnic background, culture and historical experience, organized as a sovereign state possessed of full independence in the management of its internal and external affairs. Such is the concept that currently dominates the international system, despite the fact that it is also said to be under threat by globalization.

On the other hand, Anthony Smith (1991) insists that globalization and its corollary, regionalization, will not affect nationalism at all. He even believes that a growing cosmopolitanism does not in itself entail the decline of nationalism; the rise of regional culture areas does not diminish the hold of national identities. He sees some of the changes in the level of national identity as being due to the variations of time and place. He believes that pan-Europeanism is strengthened through political federation, but at the national level nationalism is still very deeply rooted. It can be argued that what Smith did not realize is the extent to which globalization has in fact reduced the power of the nation-state, and destabilized national culture and national identity through the diversification of the everyday life of the people and the ever-growing interdependence and cross-fertilization of cultures and civilizations. People may still be proud of their nationality, but the distinctively *national* elements of sovereign power and authority are not so easy to distinguish in the growing regionalization that is taking place. Along with this change in the objective elements of the nation-state environment, there is a corresponding diminution in national identity. However, among certain groups, there remains a clear resistance to this tendency, as one finds signs of increasing nationalism as a conscious opposition to any regional or transnational identity.

Fred Halliday (1997: 363–4) stresses this aspect of the situation by explaining nationalism as both an ideology and social movement, giving rise to processes which are contradictory to globalization. For him, the very creating of a world market and the transnational flows of goods, technology and people, itself provokes responses, and resistance, by those who feel their interests are threatened. Therefore nationalism can, in the first instance, be seen as a mode of collective resistance to the general trends of globalization. In another respect, however, he presented nationalism as a product of globalization. As key examples of the impact of global forces on the state system, he referred to the fragmentation of nations that has come about through the collapse of Soviet Communism in the 1990s. Four states disintegrated along national lines – the USSR, Czechoslovakia, Yugoslavia and Ethiopia. The impact on the hitherto insulated communist world of social and economic pressures from the West was the (re)establishment of 22 new states.

Mowlana (2000: 245–7) has also described nationalism as one of the outputs of the globalization process. In particular, he sees Islamic nationalism as a product of the nation-state system, which was imported into the Muslim world by Western global forces. From his perspective, the so-called decolonization under the nation-state system drew political frontiers in the Islamic world where none existed before. It created competing national leaderships among a people with a long common history and, like Arabs, even a common language and culture. Having said that, however, decolonization from imperialism and the imperial powers became the beginning of recolonization by the same powers, but through indigenous elites, under the banner of nationalism.

One important notion with regard to nationalist identity is the difference between *patriotism* and *nationalism*.

7.5.1. Nationalism or Patriotism and Religion

Patriotism is defined as the love for one's homeland as opposed to one's nation. This is infused in Islamic culture and is even considered as part of one's religious belief.[1] But nationalism has been considered as an ideology juxtaposed with religious ideology, competing with it for the loyalty of the masses. Therefore, nationalism as an ideology can be seen as a form of resistance against both alien and Western culture, but nationalism as part of religious 'ideology' is a relatively recent phenomenon. Patriotism, on the other hand, as mentioned above, can be considered as a part of one's religious belief.

Alongside the emergence of nationalistic movements, antinationalistic movements have also developed among Islamists, which, in spite of there being no contradiction between patriotism and Islam, in turn have caused the weakening of patriotism among Islamists.

The findings of this research show that, although the nationality of all of the participants in this survey is British, nonetheless a substantial number of

---

1.   'Love of one's homeland is part of faith (*iman*)' [Prophet of Islam] (Morteza, 1995: 333).

them identify with the culture of their parents' homelands, not necessarily connected with any ideologically defined nationalist inclinations, but, in many cases, as an expression of their patriotism.

Answers given by respondents on issues such as marriage, codes of dress, food and country of settlement in relation to religious belief, understanding and practice indicated that they possessed a great degree of patriotism and religiosity. As stated in Chapter 5, 33.6% of the respondents preferred marriage with someone from their parents' country of birth. This group of respondents is significantly composed of religious people and in many respects shares its values and attitudes with the religious views and habits of Islamists. Of the respondents, 60.7% stated that they performed the five daily prayers; 80.7% of those who preferred marriage with someone from their motherland said that they performed the five daily prayers as a rule. This high degree of commitment to the formal prayers can readily be linked to the respondents' preference in marrying partners from their own faith, regardless of their own or their parents' birthplace (49.5%) (see Table 7.10, $P = 0.00 < 0.01$).

With reference to Table 7.10 below, those who preferred to marry Muslim citizens of Western countries (44%) showed less commitment in performing their regular daily prayers as compared to those who showed loyalty toward their parents' native land.

The strength of religious attitude and affinity towards one's 'motherland' can be seen as a crystallization of diasporic culture within the global culture. As Cohen & Kennedy (2000: 353) have argued, 'Among many peoples there is a renewed search for "roots", what Hall (1991: 21–2) has called a "reach for groundings". Yet this inclination need not imply a narrow localism, a retreat from global realities, an incapacity to respond to the challenges of the ever widening marketplace and to the new ethical and cultural demands stemming from globalization.'

*Table 7.10: Relationship Between Preference of Marriage and the Extent of
Performing Prayer*

Preference for marriage	How often to do you pray?					
	Regular five times a day	All prayers except morning prayer	Occasionally	Never	No answer	Total
From my or my parents' country of birth	67 (80.7)	8 (9.6)	8 (9.6)	–	–	83 (33.6)
A Muslim regardless of their own or their parents' birthplace	53 (49.5)	18 (16.8)	30 (28.0)	5 (4.7)	1 (0.9)	107 (43.3)
A British or European person	–	–	–	1 (100.0)	–	1 (0.4)
A Muslim who is a citizen of a Western Country	11 (44.0)	3 (12.0)	9 (36.0)	1 (4.0)	1 (4.0)	25 (10.1)
An open-minded person regardless if they are Muslim or not	2 (25.0)	1 (12.5)	3 (37.5)	2 (25.0)	–	8 (3.2)
No answer	17 (73.9)	2 (8.7)	3 (13.0)	1 (4.3)	–	23 (9.3)
Total	150 (60.7)	32 (13.0)	53 (21.5)	10 (4.0)	2 (0.8)	247 (100.0)

7.5.2. Nationalists and Day-to-Day Affairs

There is a significant correlation between the way people spend their daily lives
and the way in which the essential rites of religion are practised. We can take
the choice of food as one indicator of lifestyle, and measure preferences in this
domain against the degree of observance of the daily prayers, the most
important rite amongst the obligations of religion. First of all, those who were
more inclined towards traditional foods showed more commitment in to the
performance of the daily regular prayers (78.5%) (see Table 7.11, $P = 0.00 < 0.01$).

Table 7.11: Relationship Between Choice of Food and Observance of Prayer

Which of the following types of foods do you prefer?	How often do you pray?					Total
	Regularly, five times a day	All prayers except morning prayer	Occasionally	Never	No answer	
McDonald's	56.9%	12.3%	20%	10.8%	–	65 (26.3)
Burger King	–	20%	60%	20%	–	5 (1.6)
Pizza	31.7%	24.4%	39%	4.9%	–	41 (16.6)
Fish and chips	33.3%	13.3%	53.3%	–	–	15 (6.1)
I prefer my own traditional foods	78.5%	9.1%	10.7%	–	1.7%	121 (49.0)
Total	150 (60.7)	32 (13.0)	53 (21.5)	10 (4.0)	2 (0.8)	247 (100.0)

Table 7.12 ($P = 0.00$ <0.01) also shows the significance of religious attitudes among those who value the patriotic dimension of identity. Views of respondents on the choice of clothing clearly reflect the depth of commitment to one's religious identity as regards films and fashion. Those who are more influenced by films (53.6%) and contemporary fashion (61%) show less inclination towards religious commitments (e.g. *hijab*), as opposed to the group whose clothing was governed by the dress codes of their ethnic (82%) and religious traditions (91.4%). Although this might appear to be an obvious point, and reinforces what one would presume to be the case, in advance of any empirical research, it does sharpen one's perception of the important role played by Western cultural forces, mediated especially via film, on the immediate self-expression of the individual. For one's choice of clothing is a highly sensitive, and value-laden preference, indicating a great deal about a person's self-perception and identity; it is not simply an outward question of choosing this or that fashion, it is more a question of manifesting an orientation towards this or that lifestyle.

The question may be asked whether one is influenced by Western films because one already identifies with Western culture, or whether one identifies with the culture because of the influence of films. This is like asking which came first, the chicken or the egg. In practice, it is difficult to discern to what degree the identification with Western culture is the cause or consequence of susceptibility to Western films; we would conclude by saying that it is part cause and part consequence, the one cannot be separated entirely from the other. The important point to make is that the correlation between the two sets of attitudes is strong, and this reinforces and empirically confirms the assumption that one of the principal ways in which Western culture is transmitted to and impacts upon Muslims in the West is through the imitation – conscious or otherwise – of Western cultural icons in the film and fashion products of the global 'culture industry'.

Table 7:12: Relationships Between Ultimately Preferred Homeland and Cultural Attachment

Which films and actors interest you?	Country in which one wishes to live permanently				Total (%)
	Permanently in UK (%)	Return to my parent's homeland (%)	United States (%)	Other (%)	
American and European	134 (71.6)	25 (13.4)	9 (4.8)	19 (10.2)	187 (75.7)
Middle Eastern and Arab	22 (45.8)	16 (33.3)	1 (2.1)	9 (18.8)	48 (19.4)
No answer	8 (66.7)	1 (8.3)	3 (25.0)	–	12 (4.9)
Total	164 (66.4)	42 (17.0)	31 (12.6)	10 (4.0)	247 (100.0)

As Table 7.12 illustrates, 75.7% of the representatives were positively predisposed towards American and European films and actors, compared with 19.4% who showed interest in Middle Eastern and Arab ones; 134 of the 187 (71.6%) respondents who preferred American and European films and actors wished to settle in the UK – a much higher proportion than that of those who watched Middle Eastern and Arab films as well as wishing to settle in the UK. However, this figure was still higher – 22 out of 48 – than the number of those who wanted to return to their parents' homeland (16 out of 48).

This indicates the extent to which the behaviour of immigrants as regards cultural adaptation is determined by a continuing attachment to the original home culture. What emerges is that people who have been conditioned to consume the cultural products of a particular nation continue to receive a degree of satisfaction from the life and culture of that country, even when they no longer live there. The persistence of the 'locality of culture' in relation to cultural products can be seen as a serious challenge to the process of globalization. On the other hand, when the consumption of the artefacts of a particular culture is high, this induces a positive orientation towards that culture itself, and creates a correspondingly high desire to migrate to the land where that culture originates. This could be one contributing factor for the migration of people from around the world to the United States and European countries.[1]

7.6. Anglicized Identity

Anglicized Muslims are those who do not have any serious inclination towards their original culture and have been influenced entirely by the native culture in Britain. First of all, the majority of them are unable to reassimilate themselves into their culture of origin, for they cannot understand their parents' culture and have absorbed British culture to the point that their attitudes, values and norms are indistinguishable from those of their 'native' counterparts. Secondly, they seem to be involved in multiplex secular social relationships with non-Muslims and, as compared with the rest of the Muslims, this group is less orientated towards religion.

7.6.1. Anglicized Muslims, British Culture and Culture of Origin

Anglicized Muslims are those who have fully and culturally integrated into British society. They communicate in English, think in English terms and are almost totally detached from their previous background.

---

1. Peter Stalker and Lynne Rienner (2000) conclude that present trends augur even greater migration pressures owing to the disruptive impact of differential capitalist development and media's lubrication of the flow.

Table 7.13: Identity: Combination of the 'Original' Culture and the 'New' Culture

As a British Muslim, what do you regard yourself primarily?	You go on a holiday to where your parents are from; how do you feel about England?				Total (%)
	All the same – no specific feeling (%)	You are proud of your parents' country of origin (%)	You wish you were going back to England quickly (%)	No answer (%)	
British	5 (13.9)	13 (36.1)	18 (50.0)		36 (14.6)
(Muslim	73 (39.5)	84 (45.4)	23 (12.4)	5 (2.7)	185 (74.9)
Confused about identity	8 (33.3)	9 (37.5)	5 (20.8)	2 (8.3)	24 (9.7)
No answer	1 (50.0)			1 (50.0)	2 (.8.0)
Total	87 (35.2)	106 (42.9)	46 (18.6)	8 (3.2)	247 (100.0)

Table 7.13 suggests that whilst just 42.9% of the respondents would feel proud of their parents' home country, over 35% of the respondents felt that they would have no special feelings and almost a fifth would wish that they were back in the UK. The vast majority of these respondents identified themselves as Muslims with just under 15% regarding themselves as British.

This reveals that Muslim respondents have become 'anglicized' to varying degrees with a continuing strong attachment to their Muslim identity at the same time, perhaps displaying a weakening of the bond with their parents' country of origin.

7.6.2. Friendship and Religiosity

According to this survey, there are, as will be seen below, some indications that point to the existence of a category of Muslims in Britain who have assimilated themselves so completely with British society and who have entered into communication with the British people in such a way that they have come to show a preference for native non-Muslim British people. Once this degree of social interaction and assimilation with British people is attained, many significant elements of British Muslim identity start to change. For instance, viewpoints on Islamic values, social communication and even the performance of religious rituals such as the daily prayers, all of this shows significant divergences from the orientations and practices of other groups of British Muslims, especially those who uphold, defend and promote what has been called 'resistance identity'.

Table 7.14: Relationship Between Friendship-Affiliation and Views on Islamic Values

Islamic values	Best friends			Total (%)
	Muslims (%)	Non-Muslims (%)	No answer (%)	
Islamic values are absolute	166 (89.2)	17 (9.1)	3 (1.6)	186 (75.3)
Some Islamic values are absolute and some should be updated	19 (52.8)	15 (41.7)	2 (5.6)	36 (14.6)
There is no eternal good and bad	11 (47.8)	12 (52.2)	–	23 (9.3)
No answer	–	2 (100.0)	–	2 (0.8)
Total	198 (80.2)	44 (17.8)	2 (0.8)	247 (100.0)

Table 7.14 shows a significant relationship between friendship affiliation and viewpoints of respondents on Islamic values ($P = 0.00 < 0.01$). As expected, the vast majority of respondents believe Islamic values to be absolute. Of the 186 respondents who believe Islamic values to be absolute, a mere 17 had non-Muslim 'best friends'. In contrast, of the 36 respondents who consider only some of the Islamic values to be absolute, with others requiring updating, 15 had non-Muslims as best friends. The proportion with non-Muslim best friends was even higher (52.2%) among those respondents who believed that there was no eternal good or bad. This shows that there is a significant relationship between changes on social communication and Islamic values ($P = 0.00 < 0.01$).

Table 7.15: Relationship Between Friendship-Affiliation and Social Communication

Best friends	Visiting the house of non-Muslim friends						Total (%)
	Several times a week (%)	Once a week (%)	Once a month (%)	Occasionally (%)	Never (%)	No answer (%)	
Muslim	6 (3.0)	6 (3.0)	16 (8.1)	93 (47.0)	75 (37.9)	2 (1.0)	198 (80.2)
Non-Muslim	6 (13.6)	8 (18.2)	8 (18.2)	21 (47.7)	1 (2.3)	–	44 (17.8)
No answer	–	1 (20.0)	1 (20.0)	2 (40.0)	–	1 (20.0)	5 (2.0)
Total	12 (4.9)	15 (6.1)	25 (10.1)	116 (47)	76 (30.8)	3 (1.2)	247 (100.0)

Table 7.15 shows that the social relationships of those who choose Muslims as best friends are significantly different from those who choose non-Muslims as best friends ($P = 0.00 < 0.01$). This is most evident in the category of those who 'never' visit non-Muslim friends (in this case, one would understand by 'friends' something more like 'acquaintances'): only 2.3% of those who had non-Muslims as best friends would 'never' visit other, non-Muslims, whereas 37.9% of those who had Muslims as best friends would never visit non-Muslims.

Table 7.16: Relationship Between Friendship-Affiliation and Performing the Daily Prayers

Best friends	How often do you pray?					Total (%)
	Regularly, five times a day Muslim (%)	All prayers except morning prayer (%)	Occasionally (%)	Never (%)	No answer (%)	
Muslim	137 (69.2)	22 (11.1)	35 (17.7)	3 (1.5)	1 (0.5)	198 (80.2)
Non-Muslim	11 (25.0)	9 (20.5)	16 (36.4)	7 (15.9)	1 (2.3)	44 (17.8)
No answer	2 (40.0)	1 (20.0)	2 (40.0)	–	–	5 (2.0)
Total	150 (60.7)	32 (13.0)	53 (21.5)	10 (4.0)	2 (0.8)	247 (100.0)

Table 7.16 illustrates that there is also a significant difference between those who choose non-Muslims and those who choose Muslims as best friends in terms of performing daily prayers ($P = 0.00 < 0.01$). According to this data, anglicized Muslims have less inclination towards the practice of religion as compared to others. Although such a finding may be regarded as an inevitable outcome of our way of defining the initial categories, it is not merely a case of circular reasoning. For it does highlight a degree of incompatibility between the culture of Britishness – or at least a leaning towards that which is perceived as British culture – and the formal practices of Islam. It could be argued, for example, that there is no essential incompatibility between the two, the first being a culture, the second, a religion, and that the first can be superimposed upon the second, or vice versa. But our findings indicate, on the contrary, that an explicit orientation towards British culture will act as an obstacle in the way of taking the formal prescriptions of religion.

The percentage of the respondents who perform the regular daily prayers and who choose Muslims as best friends (69.2%) is significantly higher than the percentage of those who choose non-Muslims as best friends (25%). As is to be expected, the percentage of those who never carry out daily prayers have chosen a higher number of non-Muslims as best friends (15.9%) in contrast to the number of their close friends who are Muslims (1.5%). In this light, it can be expressed that the number of Muslims who choose non-Muslims as best friends can be taken as an indicator of Anglicization and distancing from the practice of religious ritual such as prayer.

7.7. Hybrid Identity

The concept of hybridity is a result of the paradigmatic shift in theory from modernism to postmodernism. The shift is motivated by anti-essentialist, anti-integrationist zeal (Werbner, 1997: 1). As Hutnyk (1997: 118) has suggested: 'Hybridity, diaspora and postcoloniality are now fashionable and even marketable terms.' Werbner believes that cultural hybridity becomes routine in the context of the globalization era. From this perspective, hybrid identity is not necessarily the result of diasporic culture only; it will be a dominant trend within every culture that is engaging with world culture through mass production of goods and ideas, transnational satellite TV programmes, global tourism, the global music industry and internet networking.

According to Cohen & Kennedy (2000: 363): 'Hybridity refers principally to the creation of dynamic mixed cultures.' Sociologists and anthropologists who use the expression 'syncretism' to refer to such phenomena, have long observed the evolution of commingled cultures from two or more parent cultures. Lull (2000) points out that hybridity is a result of 'transculturalization'. For Lull, transculturalization refers to 'a process whereby cultural forms literally move through time and space, where they interact with other cultural forms and settings, influence each other, produce new forms, and change the cultural settings' (Cohen & Kennedy, 2000: 242). Hybrid culture therefore with its accompanying identity 'is not a simple impregnating of one culture with the contents of another' but involves an ambivalence in regard to both of the original cultures, and this results in a sense of 'freedom, nomadism ... even opportunism' (Naficy 1993: 127).

Kaur & Kalra (1996: 229) argue that hybridity is inherent in all identifications involving the two terms British and Asian. For them 'There might be at least two levels of debate: one that clings to an essential nature of an exclusivist category, and the other that opens up to form new possibilities of alliances.'

Young (1995: 23) suggests that: 'Today the notion is often proposed of a new cultural hybridity in Britain, a transmutation of British culture into a compounded, composite mode.' According to him (Young, 1995: 25) hybridity 'works simultaneously in two ways: "organically", hegemonizing, which creates new spaces, structures, scenes, and "intentionally", diasporizing, intervening as a form of subversion, translation and transformation.'

Hutnyk (1997) emphasizes the role of technology in the hybridization of diasporic culture and postcolonial consciousness. He has attempted to examine, by way of example, the recent work of Paul Gilroy (1993) who notes that: 'The musical components of Hip-hop are a hybrid form nurtured by the social relations of the South Bronx where Jamaican sound system culture was transplanted during the 1970s, placed in this local setting in "conjunction with specific technological innovations" and able to "flaunt and glory in its own malleability" enough to become "transnational in character'" (Hutnyk, 1997: 123).

One can argue that there are two types of hybridity; *institutional hybridity* and *globalized hybridity*. Institutional hybridity is the result of immigration and face-to-face interaction between the original culture and the new culture, i.e. the culture of the host society. This hybrid identity is embodied in diasporic culture in the immigrant society. This hybridity is institutional because individuals are located between two strong socially and politically established institutions. One institution arises from the language, political, educational and media institutions of the host country; and the other institution is rooted in the sense of belonging properly to the family, together with the linguistic, cultural and civilizational adherence to the original country.

Globalized hybridity is basically a common type of identity that is a result of the process of globalization and transculturalization. It is important to notice that one individual can be regarded as an example of both institutionalized and globalized hybridity. While British Muslims are an example of institutional hybridity in terms of being born in Britain and being brought up in a British environment, they can obviously also be an example of globalized hybridity, because of their interaction with transnational/non-British culture such as American and other European cultures.

British Muslim identity in essence is a sort of hybrid identity, but while being British Muslims, they can be dominantly orientated towards one particular culture rather than another, i.e. to present themselves as Islamists, traditionalists, or nationalists, etc.

Amongst Muslim youth in Britain, one can also notice a sizeable minority that belong to two or more identities without discernible priority given to one culture or another. They can be said to belong to the category of *hybrid identity*. They tend to oscillate between two or more cultures, living on the margins that divide cultures. *Institutionalized hybrid identities* are in essence identities that have been influenced equally by two major factors. From one side they are affected by the deep-rooted attachment to everything that has been passed, from one generation to the next, throughout history. This dimension of identity is shaped and moulded, traditionally, within the environments of home, school, mosque and the general cultural domains that were important to the individual. In the past, one's religious personality was the outcome of these factors. To a very limited extent, in the present these factors also play a part; but they now compete with the factors arising out of the new environment that one lives in, and struggles with on a daily basis.

This kind of identity can be seen within the migrant communities, especially among the young generations. They have adapted to today's mixed cosmopolitan cultures, a mixture of *the original* and *the new culture,* which are neither purely one nor the other. One can categorize the term 'hybrid identity' as the identity of those who have an orientation towards both the original culture and the new culture.

7.7.1. *No Firm Orientation towards the Original Culture*

In today's consumer-based societies some of the consumers who exercise the 'power to choose'[1] have done so in such a way that the choices made have become hybridized, convoluted, vague or ambivalent. From this flows the hybrid personality (in particular amongst the migrant community). This type of personality is prone to two main tendencies stemming from the two different cultures: the relatively fixed and constant factors associated with the home culture; and secondly, the dynamically changing factors of the 'new culture', the new environments at school, clubs, places of entertainment, and so on.

Table 7.17 shows a contradictory phenomenon, namely, migrants who have not assimilated well within British society feel nonetheless nostalgic about Britain when they travel back to their motherlands, and wish to return (8.2%).

---

1. See views of Bauman (1990: 107–24) regarding the relationship between Power and Choice in his book: *Thinking Sociologically.* For him power is the ability to act, which is an enabling capacity. 'The more power people have, the wider is their range of choice ... to have power is to be able to act more freely' (Bauman, 1990: 113).

*Table 7.17: Comparison Between Views of Respondents About British Society
and the Country that They Eventually Wish to Live in*

How do you feel about British Society?	Country that eventually you wish to live in				Total (%)
	All the same no specific feeling (%)	You are happy to be where you are (%)	You wish to quickly return to England (%)	No answer (%)	
Happy	46 (36.5)	41 (32.5)	36 (28.6)	3 (2.4)	126 (51)
Not happy	37 (33.6)	61 (55.5)	9 (8.2)	3 (2.7)	1 1 0 (44.5
No answer	4 (36.4)	4 (36.4)	1 (9.1)	2 (18.2)	11 (4.5)
Total	87 (35.2)	106 (18.6)	46 (18.6)	8 (3.2)	2 4 7 (100.0)

This brings us back to Chapter 1 and the argument put forward by Featherstone (1990). He suggested that one of the consequences of changes caused by globalization was that more and more people were inclined to be involved with more than one culture, thus increasing the practical problems of intercultural communication and creating a type of hybrid identity. More on this will be discussed in the conclusion.

7.7.2. No Primacy for the New Culture (British Culture)

In Table 7.18, 7.9% of the respondents who said that they were content to be a part of British society, showed favourable inclinations towards their parent's homeland. This percentage also includes those who affirmed their happiness with British society, but at the same time had indicated their desire to live in the United States (7.9%) or any other country other than Britain (6.3%) ($P =$ 0.00 <0.01. It is important to realize that, whilst all the respondents were born (and presently live) in Britain, 44.5% of them do not feel happy in this country. This indicates that either the British society is an inconvenient environment for them to live in; global diversity and expansion of cultural and social choices have made them unhappy about their current situation or that they are simply more oriented (and feel a sense of 'longing') towards their motherland.

*Table 7.18: Views of Respondents on British Society and the Country that They
Eventually Wish to Live in*

How do you feel about British Society?	Country in which you wish to live in permanently				Total (%)
	Permanently in UK (%)	Return to my parents' homeland (%)	United States (%)	Other (%)	
Happy	98 (77.8)	10 (7.9)	10 (7.9)	8 (6.3)	126 (51)
Not happy	62 (56.4)	29 (26.4)	18 (16.4)	1 (0.9)	110 (44.5)
No answer	4 (36.4)	3 (27.3)	3 (27.3)	1 (9.1)	11 (4.5)
Total	164 (66.4)	42 (17)	31 (12.6)	10 (4.0)	247 (100.0)

One may suggest that one of the many attractions of the so-called 'original culture' can be linked to the perceived rejection of the immigrants by British society (the new culture); and this rejection, in turn, could be due to some British young Muslims not accepting the standards of British society.[1]

Nazem and Yagob have mentioned precisely this rejection by the new culture. Although they were born in Britain, they do not consider Britain as their natural homeland:

No, I feel Britain has never accepted me. (Nazem, aged 31)

No I don't consider Britain to be my home country even though I think it is the best place to be in order for us to understand the modernist culture and to utilize the best elements of it into the Islamic revival.
(Yagob, aged 19)

Asad who has a Sufi background gave another, somewhat contradictory answer:

Yes and No, a home can be considered anywhere. A person has to create an atmosphere of a home around him. (Asad, aged 28)

---

1. See The Runnymede Trust's report (1997) on media coverage that misleads public opinion about Muslims around the world and racial, cultural and religious attacks against British Muslims.

7.8. Undetermined Identity

Undetermined identity can be considered as another aspect of hybrid identity. While hybrid identity represents that group of people who are more inclined to have an affinity towards diverse cultural values and role models, undetermined identity on the other hand represents more of a rejection of the diverse cultures with which the individual is confronted. This is a type of hybridity that Young (1995: 25) calls 'raceless chaos', which 'produces no stable new form but rather something closer to Bhabha's restless, uneasy, interstitial hybridity: a radical heterogeneity, discontinuity, the permanent revolution of forms.' A lack of trust of both the motherland and the new culture characterizes this type, together with a low degree of acceptance of such a type within both cultures.

This is the phenomenon that several sociologists have referred to as hybridity, vagrancy and disorder. Friedman (1994: 233) insists that we live in an 'era of disorder, even of increasing disorder. The disorder is of a global nature, but experience of that disorder is highly personal for most people.' Robertson (1996: 131) also holds that we are living in a period of confusion and uncertainty. Pieterse (1995: 56–60) suggests that hybrid culture as a result of differences between home culture (matching the culture of origin) and outdoor culture (matching the culture of residence), is a combination of educational, social, cultural and political characteristics, which create a type of identity represented by 'Muslim in the daytime, disco in the evening' and secular in social and political practice. Pieterse sees cultural hybridization as a phenomenon that refers to the mixing of Asian, African, American and European cultures: hybridization is the making of global culture as a global melange. Hybridity is used as an expression of the difference between the categories, forms and beliefs that go into the mixture. Yet the very process of hybridization shows the difference to be relative and, with a slight shift of perspective, the relationship can also be described in terms of an affirmation of similarity.

Globalization creates confusion as to what is important in life. A significant proportion of the new generation cannot choose and decide with certainty what direction their life should take. In Falk's view (1992: 48) one of the consequences of the globalization of Western cultural influence, including its commitment to modernization, is a world order crisis of multiple dimensions; nuclearism, industrialism, materialism and consumerism.

This type of identity pertains exclusively to the young generations, especially that of modern youth. One way of gauging the proportion of those with an undetermined identity is by referring to the figure mentioned in Table 7.14, relating to those who said that they were confused about their identity, as such confusion is one of the key ingredients – whether as a cause or a consequence – of undetermined identity: 9.7% of the respondents, or 24 out of 247, said that they were confused about their identity. Now while those having a hybrid identity might also be included in this category, a distinction between the two types of identity must be maintained, as will be seen below, and in the conclusion.

Another definition of undetermined identity could be given according to the transformationalists' theory that has already been discussed earlier in Chapter 1. This discusses the way in which the process of globalization has created a slippery surface for those actively and dynamically intent on conforming to and having a religious identity. In particular, according to relativists such as Robertson, in the globalization age religious values have lost their absoluteness and have been turned into relative concepts. This in turn has led to the generation of extreme conflicts between religion and other by-products of cultural globalization.

Table 7.19: Are British Muslims in General, and the Youth in Particular, Focused and Clear About Their Muslim Identity?

View	Frequency	Percentage
Yes	86	34.8
No	158	64.0
Don't know	3	1.2
Total	247	100.0

As Table 7.19 shows, the majority of respondents (64%) affirmed that Muslims and youths in particular had no clear perception about their Islamic identity.

Over one-third of the respondents that were questioned believe that this lack of clarity is the result of a 'cognitive change' (leading to an absence of religious understanding), which brings uncertainty into the role of religion and belief through the process of transformation from a traditional society to that of a modern society. In view of the new circumstances at hand, everything is subject to change, even long-standing and deep-rooted beliefs, as part of the mainstream flow of massive diversification. In the age of transformation, generations who may have been the mediators or originators of such change will be confronted with more than one interpretation of events owing to the fact that, while they still cling to their old identity, or at least some aspects of it; they are at the same time confronted with baffling new forms of modernity and now postmodernity.

Table 7.20: What Could Be the Cause of Identities' Ambiguity?

View	Frequency	Percentage
People's perception of religion has changed	90	36.4
Religious centres have failed to give guidance	29	11.7
Lack of permanence and stability in principles and beliefs	45	18.2
Parents do not care about Islamic identity any more	13	5.3
Western media	70	28.3

A group of respondents (11.7%) believe that ambiguity arises as a result of lack of guidance from religious organizations. They have not adapted themselves to the new society, therefore they cannot give insight to others, and still less, guidance to their followers. The third group of respondents (18.2%) believe that the lack of permanence and stability in religious principles and belief is the main reason for ambiguity amongst the new Muslim generation.

In this study, 5.3% of the British Muslims surveyed indicated that their parents do not consider religious identity as a serious consideration in their children's upbringing. While this is a small percentage, it undoubtedly contributes to the confusion experienced by those who are not clear about their religious identity. A substantial percentage of respondents (28.3%) believe that the 'Western media' plays an important role in creating ambiguity for British Muslims, particularly in relation to their origin and identity.

Abul Rahman, Sara, Rizwan and Nadia believe that the vagrancy of identities among British Muslims is basically a result of Americanization:

Americanization has confused the British Muslim identity.
(Abul Rahman, aged 22)

Some people may feel lost because they cannot or do not want to modernize according to Western norms and standards, in particular American values, and yet find it difficult to keep entirely to Islam. (Sara, aged 17)

Americanization has caused many Muslims to be confused consequently many have been led astray. Islamic identity for many is still there, but

Americanization and globalization is having a huge impact on the British Muslim identity. (Rizwan, aged 18)

Sara holds very clear views about the concept of 'undetermined identity' – those who do not have a 'dominant inclination' either to the American or to Islamic cultures. This is also one of the central points that has been raised by The Frankfurt School – that mass culture will lead to anarchy (see Lowenthal, 1961), thus bringing an end to cultural and social authority, and will create self-alienation of individual identities in the religious and nationalistic contexts.

7.8.1. Hopelessness and Rootlessness

The sense of hopelessness and rootlessness that one feels when one is subjected to change on a huge scale[1], as well as the impact of monotonous daily activities, and conflicting or contradictory role models, leads to the phenomenon of dual personality. The ambiguity arising out of such an environment is compounded by the severing of deep-rooted historical ties, all of which leads to despondency and ultimately to an undetermined identity (see views of Baudrillard; 1983, Robertson, 1992 and Ashley 1994 in Chapter 2). The further diversification of sources of authority on values, the diminution of religious activities and of overtly religious or pious conduct, also add a further strain on one's search for identity, leading to further confusion and uncertainty.

Within traditional societies, as discussed earlier, factors that influenced people's identity were very limited and few. In contrast, contemporary societies manifest a dizzying multiplicity of factors and sources, each having a direct or indirect influence on the individual's search for identity.

The consequence of such a condition is the feeling of hopelessness and nostalgia as well as loneliness. Once one is subjected to such an environment it would be extremely difficult, if not impossible, for one to believe in one particular system or follow one specific path. One finds one's determination and resolve weakened when faced with such overwhelming pressures.

---

1. According to what we discussed in the first chapter, the speed of change within the globalization age has made man incapable of making decisions and denies him the time needed for reflection. Consequently, religious and cultural values have lost their absolute character and turned them into relative issues. The pace of change is so fast that people no longer possess any permanent values in their lives. As a matter of fact, there seems to be a breakdown in the majority of social relations. This in turn means that we do not have an 'anchor' in our lives, and all our attachments are short-lived. In such an environment one's mind is constantly moving from one issue to the next and from one picture to another. The closeness and proximity of cultures and religious thinking have made the process of decision-making more difficult.

Table 7.21: Privileged Identity and Ideal Home

As a British Muslim, how do you regard yourself primarily?	I wish to live in UK because:						Total (%)
	I don't belong here, but there is no other choice (%)	I feel that I belong here (%)	For educational advantages (%)	The economic and social system suits me (%)	The family and friends are here (%)	Other (%)	
As British	1 (2.8)	22 (61.1)	4 (11.1)	6 (16.7)	2 (5.6)	1 (2.8)	36 (14.6)
As Muslim	34 (18.4)	49 (26.5)	45 (24.3)	18 (9.7)	34 (18.4)	5 (2.7)	185 (74.9)
As being confused	12 (50.0)	3 (12.5)	4 (16.7)	2 (8.3)	2 (8.3)	1 (4.2)	24 (9.7)
No answer	1 (50.0)	–	1 (50.0)	–	–	–	2 (0.8)
Total	48 (19.4)	74 (30.0)	54 (21.9)	26 (10.5)	38 (15.4)	7 (2.8)	247 (100.0)

The sense of detachment that can be implicit in settling down within an alien culture is a very serious issue, in particular among those who have migrated to Western countries. As can be seen from the table, 61% of those who regard themselves as British rather than anything else feel that they 'belong' in Britain; this percentage is significantly higher than those who prefer to call themselves Muslims rather than British (26.5%).

Some of the respondents (9.7% of the total) had no clear views on the matter; half of this group felt excluded from the British way of life; 30% of the respondents felt that they belonged in Britain. The majority of these respondents (49 out of 74) had identified themselves as Muslims whilst 22 out of 74 respondents expressed a sense of being 'British'. In contrast, 3 out of 74 of the respondents were confused about their identity. Interestingly, the majority (34 out 48) of those who felt that they did not belong here (and had no other choice in residing elsewhere) also defined themselves primarily as Muslims. There was hardly anyone with a British identity who felt a sense of alienation.

7.8.2. Confusion about Religious Belief

Table 7.22 illustrates certain viewpoints of those who did not manifest any clear perceptions or give any primacy to a number of key religious principles. In particular, it focuses on how this group relate to residence in England and their original homeland.

Table 7.22: Comparison Between Those Who Are Confused About Religious Belief and Views of Respondents on Their Cultural Attachment

Those who did not show any clear perception – for or against – the following principles	You go on a holiday to where your parents are from, how do you feel about England?		
	All the same no specific feeling %	You are happy to be where you are %	You wish you were back in England quickly %
Hijab is compulsory for all women	62.5	6.3	31.3
Jihad is a duty of all Muslims	42.9	–	57.1
Islamic law is applicable even in contemporary societies	27.3	9.1	63.6
Sexual relations before marriage is not legitimate	80	20	–

The majority of the respondents who were confused about some of the religious issues expressed no specific feeling about their motherland, i.e. those who have no idea about the necessity of *hijab* (62.5%) and the illegitimacy of sexual relations before marriage (80%). The majority of those who pointed out that they would wish to go back to England indicated that they have no firm ideas about *jihad* (57.1%) or the applicability of Islamic law in modern and postmodern society (63.6%). This shows that, on the one hand the degree of confusion among those who have a firm orientation towards their motherland is lower, and on the other hand that the degree of confusion among those who have no specific feeling about 'home' is substantially higher than others.

In this chapter the main concentration has been on the different types of British Muslim identity that were established as a result of the process of heterogenization, owing to induced fragmentation of identities. In relation to the heterogenization of religious identities, the main argument was that the original culture of many of the immigrants to Britain was steeped in the norms of traditional society. It was thus insular, with the indigenous culture leaving little 'space' for the impact of other cultural influences. For the children of these immigrants, and for the immigrants themselves, now designated as 'British Muslims', the process of globalization has vastly extended the consumer's 'power of choice'. This has meant that they have been exposed to many non-familiar cultures, civilizations, religions, norms and values. As individuals consumed new cultural products, their responses and ways of assimilating what they were consuming differed. Therefore the diversification of cultural possibilities, ranging from local to transnational, has itself induced a process of fragmentation of identity.

On the basis of our findings, we arrived at the categorization of British Muslim identity in terms of eight different types. These types, taken in conjunction with Castells' theory, can be further subdivided into three different groups:

1. The first group, those possessing 'resistance identity', includes those we have called traditionalists, Islamists and the nationalists; these types of identity certainly existed before the advent of the global age, but in the globalization age they differ in certain key respects. First of all, these categories have to be qualified by the fact that the environment within which the individuals possessing such identity traits is that of advanced industrial societies. They attend secular schools and universities, they live within a secular culture, with all its attendant social and political institutions. Accordingly, their adherence to given traditional Islamic values has to go side by side with the presence of other cultural elements within the framework of a liberal democratic society. Therefore they all show support for the original values of religious identity, i.e. they all hold fast to the rudiments of Islam and oppose Western culture whenever there is a fundamental conflict between the two. Their responses are, on the whole, reactionary and antagonistic in relation to globalization. (Castells, 1997: 65–7). The result of this backlash is that some fragments of the previous identity – psychological, cultural, emotional – are awakened, perhaps radicalized and intensified; the other dimensions of specifically religious identity will thus be conditioned by the radicalism brought about by this reversion to previous aspects of identity. It must also be stressed that the radicalization of those elements is as a result of the acuteness of the contact between 'original' and 'global' culture; Islamic orientation emerges very much as a consequence of the clash between these two dimensions of culture. The form taken by this orientation is either traditionalist, Islamist or nationalist, depending upon the specifics of each individual case.

2. The identity of the second group – 'legitimizing identity' – is formed as a result of adaptation within the social, political and cultural norms of

271

Western society. This group harmonizes its attitudes, values and behaviour with the dominant culture or what we called 'the new culture'. Under this umbrella, the anglicized, secularist and modernist identities were discussed. Again, it should be noted that the identity of this group is the result of contemporary cultural norms, such as they have been impregnated by globalization; therefore they differ markedly from those referred to as modernists or secularists in the past.

3. The third group can be categorized as having a 'projective identity'. This group in turn comprises two subgroups: the first shows an inclination towards both *the original culture* and *the new culture*, i.e. it constitutes a kind of hybrid identity; the second arises out of the rejection of both *the original culture* and *the new culture*, i.e. it forms an 'undetermined identity'. The existence of these two groups is the direct consequence of the globalization process, which has been described by many sociologists as 'identity crises".

---

1. As Cvetkovich & Kellner (1997) explained, under pressure of the dialectics of the global and the local, human identity has extended to diverse components from the global, national, regional and local, as well as the specificities of gender, race, class and sexuality. For Cvetkovich & Kellner (1997: 12): 'This situation is highly contradictory with reassertions of traditional modes of identity in response to globalization and a contradictory melange of hybrid identities – and no doubt significant identity crises – all over the world.'

EIGHT

Conclusion

The main aim of this research was to examine the responses of the British Muslim community to the process of globalization, in order to evaluate the nature of the impact of globalization on the identity of British Muslims. We began this study by analysing the different theories of and approaches to cultural globalization; this analysis revealed a range of conflicting and often different views on the relationship between religious identity and globalization. Of all the theories put forward in this regard, it has been Robertson's theory of 'glocalization' which provided the best overarching framework within which the insights of other conceptual schemas – such as those of the relativists, reproductionalists, post-structuralists and transformationalists – could best be aligned and tested by the empirical findings of this research. In terms of glocalization theory, the tensions between global and local forces; between universalism and particular cultures; between the 'world at large' and specific places – such as the Borough of Brent – is given the greatest prominence. The determinants of culture, in such a view, cannot be reduced either to global factors or to local factors alone; rather it is the 'glocal' nature of cultural reality today that determines such fundamentals as identity of self, 'other' and the relationship between the two. This relationship, together with all the social relationships which form the matrix of individual identity, is the outcome of the tensions arising out of the dichotomy between the global and the local. Therefore this interaction has created a new 'glocal' culture, the specific nature of which can only be assessed through close analysis of the particularities of each local culture in its concrete relationship with global forces – and not all global forces, but those which have a particular, discernible impact on the local cultural situation.

Hence, no theorist can know in advance what the outcome of 'globalization' will be with regard to particular places and cultures. The process is in a fluid state, forming, unforming and reforming from moment to moment. So the focus must be specific, while keeping open one's conceptual framework to accommodate the ever-changing nature of the influences that have become global in nature.

In terms of this theoretical openness, we are able to accommodate the contradictory processes of simultaneous homogenization and heterogenization, both of which can be seen as concomitants of the overall process of globalization. In other words, just as there are tensions between the local and the global forces, so within the global forces themselves, one has to take note of the fact that both sets of processes are actively involved, one tending towards homogenizing global culture, the other tending towards the differentiation of cultures – on both the global level and the local level.

Brent was selected as the locality in which to undertake this analysis, for, as noted in Chapter 4, its multicultural make-up, with a large and significant presence of Muslims – themselves from diverse backgrounds – make it an ideal place for a study of British Muslim identity. In order to understand British Muslim identity in Brent, further insight was needed in relation to Muslim identity throughout the history of Islam. This is due to the fact that no local Muslim identity can, or should, exist in isolation. Therefore my theoretical and empirical perspective needed to locate this religious identity both in the context of unsettling and transforming contemporary global changes and in the context of longer-term historical trends and forces. We would certainly uphold what Cantwell Smith (1957: 47) stated in such a bold fashion, in the citation made earlier in Chapter 4: 'The fundamental malaise of modern Islam is a sense that something has gone wrong with Islamic history. The fundamental problem of modern Muslims is how to rehabilitate that history, to set it going again in full vigour, so that Islamic society may once again flourish as a divinely-guided society should and must'.

It is clear that no account of the role of global or glocal dynamics in the construction of contemporary Muslim identity can ignore the importance of history. While Cantwell Smith may be accused of attributing to Muslims a greater sense of their own history than they actually possess, the objective truth of his assertion seems to be proven by the contortions and distortions through which so many of today's so-called Muslim movements are passing.[1] In our

---

1. See in this regard the analysis of Nasr (1989) in his *Traditional Islam in the Modern World*, where a critique is made of the secular assumptions underlying modern militant Islamist movements. See also the chapter 'From Sufism to terrorism: the distortion of Islam in the political culture of Algeria' by R. Shah-Kazemi (1997: 160) where he argued that 'Islam in the political culture of Algeria has been reduced from its intrinsic nature as an all-encompassing religion to the status of a narrowly-conceived ideology, from a lived reality of faith comprising legal, moral, and social duties, to a contrived programme of external action dictated by the exigencies of power politics.'

findings, it was clear that the respondents' views of their own history as Muslims was rather abstract, though in terms of religious praxis, their relationship towards the religious tradition in its earliest historical phase was more concrete. This conforms to both Habermas' theory on 'the end of the history' and Giddens' prediction on intensification of the process of returning to the 'tradition'. Habermas (1975) argued that new circumstances created totally new social and cultural structures and a fundamental shift has been experienced by new generations. This has affected the 'historical consciousness' of the consumers of modern liberal culture of the West. For Giddens (1999), religious tradition will be clearer as a result of the acuteness of the contrast provided by the elements and forces of globalization. Whatever the actual degree of historical influence on contemporary Muslims, it cannot be denied that the history of Muslim communities is of considerable relevance, both for outsiders wishing to see how Muslims in the past have expressed their identity, and for Muslims themselves who, even if unconsciously, are the products of their history. They are subject to an on-going historical process. This is a dialectical process defined by, on the one hand, the specific and relatively stable sources of Islamic identity as expressed in the fundamental beliefs and ritual practices of the faith; and, on the other hand, by the changing configuration of local, cultural, national and linguistic factors. The main difference, of course, is that, whereas in the past this configuration of local culture was also itself relatively stable, in today's globalized and continually globalizing world, the local/glocal culture is in a state of rapid and continuous development. Nonetheless, it is necessary to view the outcome of the local/global dialectic against the backdrop of the historical continuum of Muslim identity, rather than divorced from this history. Further, according to Ansari (2000: 92) identity, ethnicity, religion, class and gender are susceptible to the historical processes as well as the 'internal and external' factors that have been 're-imagined' in this context. This is exactly what reproductionalists put forward in their theory on the interaction between the local and the global cultures, which enhanced the 'reproductional glocal identity'.

In Chapter 3, our discussion of the historical dimensions of Muslim identity clearly demonstrated that this identity has continuously evolved from its earliest formation, and that it has never been a static and immutable phenomenon. Rather, the specifically Islamic element has always had to be synthesized with local culture in order to take root within any setting. The globalized world of today does not change this dialectical pattern in its essence, but it does radically transform the parameters of what is 'local' culture; now, it might be said, the entire globe has become localized, and thus the formal Islamic element within Muslim identity is having to be accommodated within a much wider framework than ever before. Therefore we find that the twin phenomena of homogenization and heterogenization make their impact on Muslim identity in complex, contradictory and challenging ways. Muslim identity is, in one respect, heterogenized through the multiplicity of inputs from the global environment; and in another respect it is homogenized, in that particular modes of identity will become globally entrenched, that is globalized. But even this homogenization, largely to be understood as the ideologization of Islam, can be seen as part of the process of fragmentation, since it is only one mode of Muslim identity and one with which not all Muslims will identify themselves.

8.1. *Impact of Globalization on the Main Elements of Muslim Identity*

With regard to the main elements of British Muslim identity, we have discussed four different aspects of religious identity:
1. understanding of religious principles
2. the observance of religious practices
3. the adherence to religious beliefs
4. religiosocial relationships.

Each of these components of religious identity has been examined in relation to the process of globalization. Some major changes have taken place in the arenas of religious understanding and practices; everyday life in the British cultural and ideological milieu has challenged these two aspects in a marked way. For example, our statistical data show that the absolutism of religious truth has to some extent given way to a more pluralistic concept of religious values; and, on the level of observance, certain of the more social or collective aspects of religion have diminished in importance, such as congregational prayers in general and Friday prayers in particular. On the other hand, the social and political dimensions of the globalization process, together with the domestic sociocultural parameters, have clearly had a significant impact on religious identity, creating a reactionary[1] resistance to 'glocal forces', as they are perceived as inherently Western, and therefore they result is an intensification of religiopolitical identity.

---

1. Ansari (2000: 96–7) has pointed out that British Muslim identity 'has developed in response or in reaction to the negative interactions with this (British) society'. This is due to the fact that 'power to decide policy, to distribute resources and to arrange the various affairs of society rests in the hands of the majority community' – native British – consequently 'Muslims have suffered from the rejection, disadvantage and exclusion'.

As regards religious beliefs, the findings of the research have shown insignificant changes in such fundamental articles of belief as the existence of God, life after death and the prophethood of Muhammad. These fundamental principles of the Islamic faith have remained largely unaltered; and this is evidence of the persistence of inner faith as a key determinant of identity. However, as regards the implications of these principles, their concomitants and their consequences for individual and social life, the research has shown that there is a high degree of variation. Some respondents see these principles as being entirely of an individual order, without requiring any external expression, others insist on the necessity of Islam as a way of life encompassing all aspects of existence, individual and collective, cultural and political. The influence of the local culture – liberal, secular and cosmopolitan – is clear here, but it must be remembered that its impact has been greatly strengthened by the influx of the same elements of liberalism from the global dimension; here we have a clear example of 'glocalization'.

Although Turner (1994) has mentioned that such shifts in religious orientation and the transformation of religious behaviour is not based on 'cognitive' reasoning, the result of this research indicates that a significant change in the thought processes and ways of understanding Islam have in fact gone hand in hand with changes in behaviour. It may well be that the main factor in both sets of changes is, as Turner argues, the daily environment in which the individual lives, as opposed to being the result of carefully thought-out rational positions. However, even if the reason for the change is not initially cognitive, the impact of the environment upon the thinking of the individuals in question cannot be overlooked: there is a real cognitive change as a result of the environmental influences. Also, these influences themselves carry with them not just habits, images and products. Ideas, concepts, theories and ideologies are also transmitted from the environment, and these cannot but have an impact on the religious orientation of the individual. So even if our data confirm that the new lifestyles of Muslims in Britain 'displace' the influences of religion in their everyday lives, it is also the case that particular ideas – such as the necessity of establishing an Islamic state to combat the forces of Western imperialism – will be part of the message received by young Muslims. Thus, a secularizing influence as regards lifestyle in day-to-day affairs may well go hand in hand with a politicizing influence as regards the ideological dimension of religious identity. This paradoxical combination of influences, giving rise to a mode of 'secular/militant' Muslim identity, was clearly seen as a possibility, given the types of responses recorded in the data-analysis.

Another important conclusion in this part of the research is that social relationships among Muslims cannot be analysed in isolation from religious thought, understanding and belief. The process of secularization and liberalization, which is a major component of the process of globalization, has seriously affected social relationships among British Muslims. In contrast to what was the case in traditional Muslim societies, the majority of Muslims in this survey no longer consider religion as a fundamental criterion for social relationships in their everyday lives. According to the statistical data of this research, religion does not play a determining role in the choice of friends. On the other hand, religion is still of great importance as regards choice of marriage partners.

It should also be stressed that day-to-day issues have been substantially influenced by transnational factors, and that these everyday features of life in Britain have in turn changed basic elements of religious identity in a variety of (sometimes contradictory or paradoxical) ways. The findings indicate that such factors as role models provided by American film stars, together with the cinema industry (as a whole), the 'McDonalds'-style of life, dress-codes (even if unwritten), Western cultural patterns, behavioural norms and the material standards of life have all combined to influence the expectations, orientations, and processes of identity-construction of Muslims in Britain, taking our sample group as indicative of the general population of British Muslims. All of these changes can be attributed to one basic reality: the *power of choice* has been increased. *Local choice* is increasingly interlinked with *global choice* or *transnational choice*. This expanded choice is not restricted to material goods that are bought and sold on the international market, but, more importantly, extends into the realm of lifestyle, cultural orientation and even ideological and philosophical values. This diversification of choice together with the sheer variety of attitudes, ideas and responses, has been clearly observed in the research findings of this dissertation.

8.2. British Muslim Identity and Global Culture

The very concept of British Muslim identity has been discussed in relation to the notion of 'British identity', which was itself put into question by Paxman (1999), Marr (2000), Alibhai-Brown (2000) and Parekh (2000). They argued that, with the impact of globalization, whatever was left of British identity was in the process of gradually exhausting itself. Whatever the actual degree to which this hypothesis is true, the fact remains that the concept of 'Britishness' is undergoing severe strain. Apart from language and geography, it is difficult to identify any particular elements that might differentiate Britishness from many other cultural characteristics in Western countries. This unity of culture is even more pronounced when one takes into consideration the acute contrast between identifiably 'Western' culture and non-Western cultures, even though, under the weight of globalization, the pockets of Western culture in the rest of the world are rapidly expanding also, hence the very term globalization. In the British milieu, British Muslim identity was differentiated from other Muslim identities elsewhere by reference to such straightforward, objectively verifiable factors as one's birthplace, place of up-bringing, and language; and by more subjective factors such as sense of belonging, self-definition, and so on. In this discussion different perspectives of respondents in relation to defining elements of Muslim identity were also examined.

The points of view of respondents with regard to British society as a local force, together with the nature of identity as fixed or relative – considered both in terms of British identity and as a response to the process of globalization – were also examined. The results reveal a situation that contains elements reflecting both the *relativist* and the *Islamist* approach. Some of the respondents believed that transformation from a *fixed identity* to a *relative identity* was inevitable due to the diversification and multiculturalization of all aspects of life. Others believed that Muslim identity should be fixed and firm. One explanation for this can be due to the diversification of identity, which can induce fragmentation and the disunity of Muslims. This fragmentation holds out the bleak prospects referred to earlier in our discussion of Durkheim's theory of the role of religion as the basic cement of community formation. Just as Durkheim (1976) feared the consequences of a diminished role for formal religion in modern industrial society, it is clear that these consequences in a postmodern, global society are even more fundamentally challenging the institutions of religion, while dispersing, through global channels, attitudes and ideas that are not only indifferent to religion, but also counter to religion.

The globalization of culture, in the sense of the spreading of the Western consumerist ethic is not the only threat to religious identity; the impact of heterogenization can be seen even within the framework of religion itself, and in this research the fragmentation of religious identity within the Islamic community of Britain is very clear, as is the emergence of hybrid and undetermined forms of cultural identity. If the present fragmentation of identity continues in this manner within the Muslim community in Britain, the likelihood of gaining recognition as a distinct religious community will diminish; the differences of opinion and clashes over fundamental orientations will certainly reduce the ability of the Muslims in this country to act in a unified manner over concrete issues and thus win recognition, status and respect.

A significant part of our studies highlighted the process of globalization more specifically in relation to citizenship and British Muslim identity within the Borough of Brent. As part of this survey we utilized statistical information backed up with qualitative data. These results indicated that the respondents differentiated between the notion of 'home' and that of citizenship of an alien country. Citizenship here implied a different connotation to one's native homeland. Although the respondents considered themselves as citizens of Britain, they did not harbour any great affinity with Britain as being their natural homeland.

The findings of this survey indicated that, in the majority of British Muslims, the sense of cultural and spiritual belonging was strikingly absent. In essence the realization of living in an alien culture yet belonging to another can be the direct consequence of the globalization process which paves the way for the greater movement of peoples between national boundaries.

One can conclude that this type of migration that occurs mainly on socioeconomic grounds to, usually, the richer Western countries, not only does not loosen people's connection to their native roots but on the contrary it increases the sense of belonging to the land of their origin. As a result the majority of British Muslims surveyed in this research showed no empathy towards the pains and problems of British society, for example in times of war they showed a marked reluctance to fight as soldiers for Britain, citing religion as being a critical factor in their decision. By the same token, with regard to sporting events, such as a football game, where there were no religious overtones, the respondents again indicated their support in such a scenario for the native team that represented the motherland. Therefore they reinforced their patriotism for the motherland. This is in line with Giddens's theory (1999), which posits the crystallization of tradition on one hand, and on the other hand the 'detraditionalization' of identities in response to the process of globalization.

Our findings have also indicated that in today's modern age the sense of belonging to one's motherland has been relatively subdued with the advent of new and diverse cosmopolitan societies creating new nostalgic attachments with no notion of patriotism or sense of belonging to any particular land. In relation to this, 33.5% of the respondents surveyed said that they felt attached to all lands alike. This type of sentiment does not tally with the slogan of nationalism or the banner of Islamists – rather it indicates feelings of emptiness and bewilderment as a result of a self-identity crisis or hybrid identity.

8.3. Homogeneity of British Muslim Identity

The dichotomy between homogenization and heterogenization as two concomitant phenomena of globalization was then addressed. According to our research it has been observed that the impact of the globalization trend has intensified the fragmentation of identities. In Albrow's (1996: 144) terms, 'Globalization restores the boundlessness of culture and promotes the endless renewability and diversification of cultural expression rather than homogenization.' In fact, as Ritser (1998: 86) argued, it is homogenization that tends to bring forth heterogenization as a response to it. However, globalization has not operated in a single dimension, nor is it a process that has altered in a uniform manner every discernible tendency in culture and society.

In relation to the process of Americanization, it was observed that, on the one hand, resistant Muslim movements were established as a result of the process of homogenization. On the other hand, there is homogenization viewed as the McDonaldization or Hollywoodization of cultures, more commonly referred to as Americanization. Therefore, the study of homogenization can be viewed in a dualistic manner, one being the Americanization or globalization process through which the wider Muslim identity can be studied, and the tide of Muslim resistance against the globalizing forces which has become very apparent according to Barber (1996). The notion of *jihad* is the direct response to the forces of McDonaldization. In the past, the opponents of Islam, such as the Crusaders, waged military campaigns against the Muslims; and this had the effect of uniting the Muslims in the face of a common adversary. In the contemporary era, Americanization has created a backlash amongst the Muslims; and this has provoked a range of different types of resistance in global terms: some unifying and others disunited and somewhat chaotic.

However, it can clearly be seen that, just as homogenization can be considered as a global phenomenon that transcends local boundaries, so the movement or tendency that is defined as the inverse of the dominant trend of globalization, i.e. 'reverse globalization', likewise transcends local boundaries, serving as a mirror-image of what it opposes. The resistance movements of Islamists or 'jihadists' throughout the world fall into this category of groups tending towards 'reverse globalization', but doing so in a 'globalized' manner themselves.

While to a large extent British Muslims have been heterogenized, not only through the process of globalization, but also as a result of denominational differences, a considerable number of British Muslims still seek the reestablishment of a global 'Muslim *umma*'[1]. The idea of establishing a Muslim *umma* seems to be an important motivating factor for British Muslims in their effort

---

1. For Muslims in Britain and all over the world, *umma* is an 'ideal global community', which, as Ansari defined (2000: 92) it, is a community that 'does not recognize national or racial differences'.

to establish unity in diversity. This recalls Durkheim's concept of a 'collective consciousness': in the present context, the recognition that collective Muslim consciousness is fragmenting itself gives rise to efforts to safeguard what is left of it – either through traditional/conservative preservation, or through Islamist agitation. In both cases, what we observe is a local response to the perceived global reality of a disunited and increasingly fragmented *umma* or collective Muslim consciousness, therefore a 'glocal' dichotomy of identity: conservative Muslim versus militant Muslim, both reacting to the same perceived state of global Muslim affairs in radically different ways.

In relation to the process of Americanization, another phenomenon has appeared which can be regarded as *the Dialectical identity in the age of globalization*. From the Frankfurtian point of view *the global cultural industry* has had a great impact on local identities, resulting in Westernization and adaptation with American culture. On the other hand the process of Americanization has itself intensified the resistance against domination of American culture; therefore the result of this trend is dichotomous.

In fact what they said was different to their actions. On the one hand, they criticized the domination of American culture but, on the other hand, when asked about their dietary habits in relation to what types of foods they favoured and the types of films and news that they watched, the majority of them were inclined to favour American fast foods, Hollywood cinema and the news channel of choice was the CNN. These findings indicate that there was not a significant degree of differentiation between the views of the religious and the non-religious, or the nationalists and the Islamists in relation to the consumption of American products, which have become, in truly global terms, ubiquitously available.

From the above findings we can outline a different theory – one that considers that the multitude of product diversity that has resulted from the Americanization of culture has led to the creation of 'transreligious' values. This implies that religious tendencies do not influence the consumption of Western products except in some cases where religion has explicitly endorsed certain limitations, such as drinking alcohol, in which case there is a discrepancy between the religious and non religious factions. Consequently there exists a paradoxical mode of behaviour of actions and thoughts, which somehow in this theoretical approach is dissolved.

8.4. Heterogeneity of British Muslim Identity

As regards to heterogeneity of identity, the findings of this research have also shown that any exact and precise definitions of identity are elusive, and that any attempt to make neat distinctions between different types of identities is problematic and complicated. The process of globalization has juxtaposed many cultural products of a variety of cultures and nations, which has entailed the heterogeneity of previously integrated cultures and identities not only in the periphery but also in the centre[1]. Therefore cultural exchange as well as sociopolitical and economic interaction between different cultures and, in particular, the domination of Western and specifically American culture, has reproduced identities. These factors have relativized or diluted the strength of values that were formerly more binding, consequently modifying many elements of traditional identities.

For the children of these immigrants, and for the immigrants themselves, now designated as 'British Muslims', the process of globalization has vastly extended the consumer's 'power of choice'. This has meant that they have been exposed to many non-familiar cultures, civilizations, religions, norms and values. As individuals consumed new cultural products, their responses and ways of assimilating what they were consuming differed. Therefore the diversification of cultural possibilities, ranging from local to transnational, has itself induced a process of fragmentation of identity.

The following two boxes demonstrate the types of identity-formation that have emerged out of the analysis of this data. The first box focuses on the specific combinations of the two elements 'political Islam' and 'traditional Islam'. In the earlier discussion of religious identity, many more factors were discussed than just these two. These two have, however, been used as the basis for this appraisal of identity types because they appear to be the most fundamental distinguishing factors in defining contemporary religious identity among British Muslims, both in our sample group and in the country at large, to the extent that this group can be taken as indicating dominant traits in the wider British Muslim community. In this table, the intention is to bring out the religious aspect of identity, by setting it in the context of the principal elements raised in the questions and responses of the subjects of the research. The second box focuses on the cultural aspect of identity, and demonstrates the way in which the local and transnational elements combine to form identity; here, the foundation of the approach is the theory of 'glocalization'.

---

1. Jean Franco (1996: 261–72) in his paper: 'Globalization and the crisis of popular' has discussed that destabilization and fragmentation of identities in the age of globalization cannot simply be left to the periphery, but it is also crucial that intellectuals at the centre should begin the process of dismantling their own position of privilege.

Box 8.1: Islamic Orientation: Islamist/Traditionalist/Modernist/Secularist

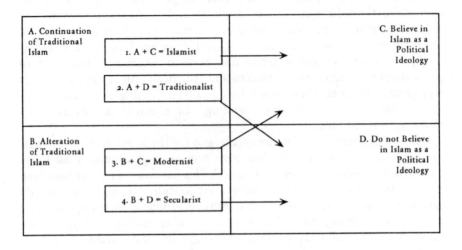

Box 8.2: Glocalization Model for Identity Development

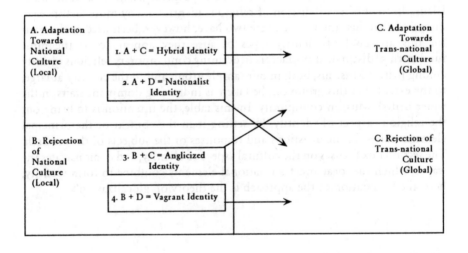

The two boxes have been formulated in this way for the sake of analytical purposes, to highlight the key factors involved; but it is clear that the elements in question cannot be separated in actual reality. Since the focus of the research is on British Muslim identity, the two critical elements – Islamic orientation and local vs transnational culture – cannot be divorced from each other. The complex flow of relationships between the different elements produces a variety of possible configurations of identity, to which we will return, after highlighting what appears to be the principal types that have emerged from the data analysis. Eight types thus emerge out of the combinations of the four sets of variables. The following are the simplified descriptions of the categories, which we have explained in more detail in Chapter 7.

1. The first category consists of those who believe Islam as a political ideology and who also support the continuation of traditional Islam. This type of identity has been characterized as 'Islamist'.
2. The second category consists of those who combine their belief in Islam as a political ideology with support for a radical alteration of traditional Islam. This type of identity has been characterized as 'modernist'.
3. The third category consists of those who do not believe in Islam as a political ideology, and support the continuation of traditional Islam. This type of identity has been characterized as 'traditionalist'.
4. The fourth category consists of those who do not believe in Islam as a political ideology nor in the continuation of traditional Islam. This type of identity has been characterized as 'secularist'.
5. The fifth category consists of those who have a tendency towards both national and transnational culture. This type of identity has been characterized as 'hybrid'.
6. The sixth category consists of those who are oriented towards national culture and simultaneously reject transnational culture. This type of identity has been characterized as 'nationalist'.
7. The seventh category consists of those who reject national culture and support adaptation of transnational culture (Westernized identity). This type of identity has been characterized as 'Westernized'.
8. The eighth category consists of those who do not accept national as well as transnational culture. They are facing crises of identity or what we may characterize as 'vagrant'.

These categories must be further nuanced, however, to accommodate the facts of the Islamic communities in this country. When, for example, national culture is rejected, the culture in question is that of Britain; but it does not necessarily mean a rejection of the local culture within Britain, which may in fact be a hybrid culture, formed out of the original culture of the parents' national homeland abroad, on the one hand, and elements of British culture that have shaped this imported culture on the other hand. We have referred to this earlier in connection with the 'culture of the home' as opposed to the dominant culture in the external environment.

Similarly, as regards the category of 'undetermined identity', which has also been referred to as a 'crisis of identity', this equation can only be sustained if the rejection of the national culture (together with transnational culture) implies the rejection of the home culture also. Only in this case can one refer to such an identity as being in a state of crisis. It can also be the case that the rejection of national and transnational culture produces a kind of 'vagrant' identity, the result of an Islamist or modernist orientation. A number of those who reject the two forms of Western culture – both in its national and in its transnational expressions – do so out of a rejection of secularism, and a belief in Islam as a totalist ideology. Here, it is significant to note that a high proportion of the respondents fall into the category of 'Islamist', that is they regard Islam as a total way of life, to be integrated into every aspect of thought and action. However, one must note that this important finding does not necessarily reflect the attitudes within the wider Muslim community in Britain. This is because 45% of the respondents in our sample group went to Muslim schools, the remainder being drawn at random. It is from the random group that wider generalizations can legitimately be drawn: in this group; there was a considerably lower percentage of respondents who could be characterized as Islamists. This group can be considered as a more accurate reflection of the proportion of those with identifiably 'Islamist' tendencies in the British Muslim community at large.

Although some types of identities such as traditionalist, Islamist and even nationalist cannot be considered as completely 'new' identities, they can nonetheless be considered as new in terms of the radicalization of the core content of each identity. That is, such key elements as tradition, political Islam and national culture gain a new dimension as a result of the forces of globalization. Tradition, for example, has come to mean something quite different for those who adopt their tradition as the key guiding force in their lives; it is now sharply contrasting with the modern environment against which the conception of 'tradition' is now viewed. As Giddens remarks, in the past, 'tradition' was not challenged, its continuity was taken for granted. In the globalized context, the challenge to traditional modes of thought and action results, on the one hand, in the weakening of these ways of thinking and acting, and, on the other hand, has acted as a catalyst for the reproduction of traditional identity in a form that cannot be regarded as a simple extension of past traditional identities, but as crystallizing around different responses to the global environment. In some cases this response will be militant, in which traditional 'conservative' identity will flow in the direction of radical Islamist identity, thus blurring the distinction between the two types of identity. In other cases, the previously traditionalist mentality, in which the notion of nationalism was either weak or non-existent, will develop in the direction of a conservative stress on nationalism, that of the country in which one lives, rather than the land of one's origins, as a means of maintaining the essential elements of one's culture in the new environment. The resulting mode of identity will be a combination between national and traditional types of identity.

All elements of identity become to some extent radicalized in the new environment. Although this is clearer in the case of the militant reaction of Muslims to the impact of alien culture – transnational culture – it is not necessarily less real in the case of secular, nationalist/anglicized, undetermined and hybrid identities. For the latter types – undetermined and hybrid – they can be regarded as altogether new identities, arising out of the radicalization of the previous elements of identity, this process having gone so far that confusion rather than clarity is attached to the notion of 'identity'. Whilst sociologists have noted that alienation and weakening of identity are the observed results of the process of modernization and industrialization, what has been perceived in the global age is a significant intensification of this development. The result is the kind of vagueness and rootlessness that has been noted in this research, leading us to formulate the identity-type 'vagrant'; and the heterogeneous self-concept that led us to formulate the identity-type 'hybrid'. These types are, as mentioned above, not to be regarded as water-tight categories; they are analytical tools to help us to identify key trends, tendencies, and facets; the types are distinguished on the basis of the responses given by the subjects of this research and can be considered as a means of gaining a deeper understanding of the nature of Muslim identity in Britain. We are well aware of the danger of mistaking preconceived categories and 'ideal types' with the complex realities that they are supposed to help us to understand. The categories emerging in this study, however, are empirically derived and are not *a priori* notions that determine in advance the results and conclusions of the research.

It is also important here to stress that identity-formation processes are very much in a state of flux, and this reflects the overall state of societal change in the constantly changing global age. Just as the pressure of multiple forces on society has resulted in a clear pattern of fragmentation, differentiation, and heterogenization, likewise, the individual and his or her identity manifest a high degree of fragmentation, so that it is difficult to be altogether definitive about the types that have been identified. What we have tried to show here, however, is the predominant characteristics and qualities that emerge out of this highly differentiated pattern of variables.

Finally, what must be stressed is the following point: more concrete, in-depth studies of Muslims in particular localities (or 'glocalities') and regions of Britain are needed if we are to arrive at empirically realistic analyses of the nature, dimensions and implications of British Muslim identity. As has become clear through this research project, any attempt to predict in advance the precise configuration of elements comprised within British Muslim identity will be fraught with problems. Theoretical postulates and assumptions must be critically subjected to the test of empirical data; it is such data that ought to be the basis of any typology of identity, and such a typology may in turn be the basis for making theoretical predictions of future trends and possibilities. But the value of the typology and its accompanying ramifications will be more in terms of its explanatory capacity. Taking into account the fact that the very notion of 'British Muslim identity' is contestable, and far from having a clearly defined referent, we hope, in this research, to have formulated at least a preliminary typology of British Muslim identity that accurately reflects the diversity and fluidity of the perceptions that Muslims have of themselves, their religion, their environment – both local and global, hence *glocal* – and the complex interplay between all these factors. For it is out of this complex matrix of perceptions that the sense and the notion of 'British Muslim identity' arises; a notion that may be singular in linguistic terms, and which may be conceived as singular in theoretical terms also, but that turns out, on closer empirical inspection, to be an internally differentiated phenomenon, the precise nature of which can only be gauged in concrete studies of particular Muslim individuals and groups living in Britain.

Bibliography

Abrahamian, E. (1982) *Iran and Modernism: The Iranian Revolution of 1906*, London, I.B.Tauris.

Abramson, A. (1998) The invention of television, in: A. Smith & R. Paterson (eds) *Television: An International History*, Oxford, Oxford University Press.

Abu-Rabi, I. M. (1998) Globalization: a contemporary Islamic response? *American Journal of Islamic Social Sciences*, 15; 3.

Abu-Zahra, N. (1998) Islamic history, Islamic identity and the reform of Islamic law, in: J. Cooper, R. Nettler & M. Mahmoud (eds) in *Islam and Modernity: Muslim Intellectuals Respond*, London and New York, I. B. Tauris.

Adorno, T. W. & Horkheimer, M. (1977) *The Culture Industry: Enlightenment*, London, Verso.

Ahmad, A. S. (1988) *Discovering Islam: Making Sense of Muslim History and Society*, London and New York, Routledge & Kegan Paul.

Ahmad, A. S. (1992) *Postmodernism and Islam*, London and New York, Routledge.

Ahmad, A. S. & Donnan, H.(1994) Islam in the age of postmodernity, in: A. S. Ahmad & H. Donnan (eds) *Islam, Globalization and Postmodernity*, London and New York, Routledge.

al-Azmeh, A. (1993) *Islam and Modernities*, London and New York, Verso.

Albrow, M. (1996) *The Global Age*, Cambridge, Polity Press.

Alibhai-Brown, Y. (2000a) *Muddled Leaders and the Future of the British National Identity*, Political Quarterly Publishing, Oxford, Blackwell Publishers, pp. 26–30.

Alibhai-Brown, Y. (2000b) *Who Do We Think We Are? Imagining the New Britain*, Allen Lane, The Penguin Press.

Ameli, S. R. (2000) Cultural globalization and Muslim identity, in: M. S. Bahmanpour and H. Bashir (eds), *Muslim Identity in the 21ˢᵗ Century: Challenges of Modernity*, London, BookExtera.

Amin, S. (1989) *Eurocentrism*, USA, Monthly Review Press.

Andrews, D. L. (1998) The (Trans) National Basketball Association: American commodity-sign culture and global-local conjuncturalism', in: A. Cvetkovich & D. Kellner (eds), *Articulating the Global and the Local: Globalization and Cultural Studies*, United Kingdom, Westview Press, pp.72–101.

An-Nisa Bulletin Election Supplement (1998) *The Muslim Vote*, London, An-Nisa Society.

Bibliography

An-Nisa Society (2000) *Brent's Muslim Community*, London, An-Nisa Society.

An-Nisa Society (2000) *Annual Report*, London, An-Nisa Society.

Ansari, K. H. (2000) Negotiating British Muslim identity, in: M. S. Bahmanpour & H. Bashir (eds) *Muslim Identity in the 21ˢᵗ Century: Challenges of Modernity*, London, BookExtra, pp. 89–100 .

Appadurai, A. (1990) Disjunction and difference in the global cultural economy, in: Mike Featherstone (ed.) *Global Culture: Nationalism, Globalization and Modernity*, London, Sage. pp. 295–310.

Arkoun, M. (1994) *Rethinking Islam: Common Questions, Uncommon Answers*, Boulder, San Francisco and Oxford, Westview Press.

Arnold, T. W. (1935) *The Preaching of Islam*, Darf Publishers Ltd.

Axtamann, R. (1997) Collective Identity and the Democratic Nation-State in the Age of Globalization, in: A. Cvetkovich & D. Kellner (eds), *Articulating the Global and the Local: Globalization and Cultural Studies*, United Kingdom, Westview Press.

Babbie, E. (1995) *The Practice of Social Research*, London, Wadsworth Publishing Company ITP.

Balio, T. (ed.) (1990) *Hollywood in the Age of Television*, London, Boston, Unwin Hyman.

Barber, B. R. (1996) *Jihad vs. McWorld: How Globalism and Tribalism are Reshaping the World*, New York, Ballantine Books.

Barker, C. (1997) *Global Television: An Introduction*, USA, Blackwell Publishers.

Barker, C. (1999) *Television, Globalization and Cultural Identities*, Buckingham and Philadelphia, Open University Press.

Baudrillard, J. (1983) *Simulation*, translated by Paul Foss, Paul Patton & Philip Beitchman. New York: Semiotext.

Baudrillard, J. (1993) *Symbolic Exchange and Death*, London, Thousand Oaks and New Delhi, Sage.

Bauman, Z. (1990) *Thinking Sociologically, the Great Britain*, Oxford: Basil Blackwell.

Beck, U. (1992) *Risk Society: Towards a New Modernity*, London, Sage.

Beck, U. (1997) *The Reinvention of Politics*, Cambridge, Polity Press.

Becker, H. (1963) The culture of a deviant group: the jazz musician, in: Ken Gelder & Sara Thornton (eds) (1997) *The Subcultures Reader*, London and New York, Routledge.

Bell, D. (1979) *The Cultural Contradictions of Capitalism*, London, Heinemann.

Bellah, R. N. (1968) *International Encyclopedia of Social Sciences*: Vol. 13, United States, The Macmillan Company & The Free Press.

Bellah, R. N. (1973) *Emile Durkheim: on Morality and Society*, Chicago, University of Chicago Press.

Belyaev, E. A. (1969) *Arabs, Islam and the Arab Caliphate in the Early Middle Ages*, USA & UK, Praeger Pall Mall.

Berger, P. & Luckmann, T. (1967) *The Social Construction of Reality*, London, Allen Lane, Penguin Press.

Berger, P. (1969) *The Social Reality of Religion*, London, Faber.

Berger, P. (1994) Social sources of secularization, in: J. C. Alexander & S. Seidman (eds), *Culture and Society: Contemporary Debates*, United States, Cambridge University Press.

Berlin, I. (1969) *Two Concepts of Liberty*, Oxford, Oxford University Press.

Beyer, P. (1990) Privatization and the public influence of religion in global society, in: M. Featherstone (ed.) *Global Culture*, London, Sage, pp. 373–96.

Beyer, P. (1994) *Religion and Globalization*, London, Sage.

Beyer, P. (1998) Globalizing system, global culture, models and religion(s). *International Sociology*, 13; 1: 79–94.

Bif News (1994) *The Voice of Brent's Muslim Community*, Brent Islamic Forum, an Umbrella Organization for Muslims in the London Borough of Brent.

Boddy, W. (1998) The beginnings of American television, in: A. Smith & R. Paterson (eds) *Television: An International History*, Oxford, Oxford University Press.

Boyed-Barrett, O. (1977) Media imperialism: towards and international framework for the analysis of media systems, in: J. Curran, M. Curevitch & J. Woollacott (eds), *Mass Communication and Society*, Great Britain, Edward Arnold.

Brent and Harrow Refugee Survey (1995) *Brent & Harrow Health Agency Brent & Harrow Refugee Groups. Northwest London Training and Enterprise Council in Partnership*, London, Brent & Harrow Health.

Brent Eid Festival (1997) *Souvenir Brochure, Bridge Par Complex, Harrow Road and Wembley*, published by Brent Crescent.

Brener, L. (1993) Constructing Muslim identities in Mali, in: B. Louis (ed.), *Muslim Identity and Social Change in Sub-Saharan Africa*.

Burayidi, M. A. (1997) *Multiculturalism in a Cross-National Perspective*, Lanham, New York and London, University Press of America.

Cassell, P. (1993) *The Giddens Reader*, London, Macmillan.

Castells, M. (1994) European Cities, the Informational Society, and the Global Economy, *New Left Review*, 204.

Castells, M. (1996) *The Information Age: Economy, Society and Culture Volume I: The Rise of the Network Society*, Oxford, Blackwell Publishers.

Castells, M. (1997) *The Information Age: Economy, Society and Culture Volume II: The Power of Identity*, Oxford, Blackwell Publishers.

Castells, M (2000) Materials for an examploratory theory of the network society, in: *British Journal of Sociology*, 51; 1: 5–24.

Chambers, I. (1987) Maps for the metropolis: a possible guide for the postmodern *Cultural Studies*, 1: 1.

Chaernaik, W., Deegan, M. & Gibson, A. (eds) (1996) *Beyond the Book: Theory, Culture, and the Politics of Cyberspace*, London, The Centre for English Studies, University of London.

Chorafas, D. N. (1992) *The Globalization of Money and Securities: The New Products, Players, and Markets*, Chicago, IL: Probus.

Cohen, R. & Kennedy, P. (2000) *Global Sociology*, London, McMillan Press Ltd.

Coleman, S. (1991) Faith which conquers the world: Swedish fundamentalism and the globalization of culture, *Ethos*, 1–2: 6–18.

Colley, L. (1992) *Britons: Forging the Nation 1707–1837*, New Haven and London, Yale University Press.

Cox, H. (1965) *The Secular City: Urbanization and Secularization in Theological Perspective*. New York: Macmillan.

Cramer, D. (1994) *Introducing Statistics for Social Research*, London and New York, Routledge.

Crone, P. (1996) The rise of Islam in the world, in: F. Robinson (ed.), *Cambridge Illustrated History: Islamic World*, Cambridge, Cambridge University Press.

Cvetkouich, A & Kellner, D. (1997) Introduction: thinking global and local, in: A. Cvetkovich & D. Kellner (eds) *Articulating the Global and the Local: Globalization and Cultural Studies*, United Kingdom, Westview Press, pp. 1–30.

Danesi, D. (1994) *Cool: The Signs and Meanings of Adolescence*, Toronto, Buffalo and London, University of Toronto Press.

De Vaus, D. A. (1994) *Surveys in Social Research*, London, UCL Press.

Dorfman, A. & Mattelart, A. (1975) How to read Donald Duck: imperialist ideology, in: *The Disney Comic*, New York, International General.

Dunning, J. H., Koght, B. & Blomstrom, M. (1990) *Globalization of Firms and the Competitiveness of Nations*, Lund, Institute of Economic Research, Lund University Press.

Dunning, J. H. (1993) *Multinational Enterprises in a Global Economy*, New York, Addison-Wesley.

Durkheim, E. (1976) *The Elementary Forms of the Religious Life*, London, Macmillan.

Durkheim, E. (1984) *The Division of Labour in Society*, New York, Free Press.

Dussel, E. (1998) Beyond eurocentrism, in: F. Jameson & M. Miyoshi (eds) *The Cultures of Globalization*, Durham and London, Duke University Press.

Dworking, R. (1981) What is equality? Part II: Equality of resources. *Philosophy and Public Affairs*, 10; 4: 283–345.

Dyer, C. H. (1993) EcoCultures: global culture in the age of ecology, in: *Journal of International Studies*, 22; 3: 483–501.

Eade, J. (1997a) Introduction, in: J. Eade (ed.) *Living the Global: Globalization as Local Process*, London and New York, Routledge.

Eade, J. (1997b) Roots and routes: Bangladeshis in Britain and narratives of home, in: S. Weil (ed.) *Ethnicity & Migration in Global Perspective*, Jerusalem, Hebrew University Magnes Press.

The Economist (1998) 12 September 1998.

Evans, E. D. & Potter, T. H. (1970) Identity crisis: a brief perspective, in: E. D. Evans (ed.) *Adolescents Readings in Behavior and Development*, United States, The Dryden Press Inc.

Esposito, J. L. (1994) *Islam: the Straight Path*, Oxford and New York, Oxford University Press.

Ezzati, A. (1976) *Introduction: Shi'i Islamic law and Jurisprudence*, Pakistan, Ashraf Press Lahore.

Ezzati, A. (1978) *An Introduction to the History of the spread of Islam*, London, News and Media Ltd.

Falaturi, A. (1993) *A Guide to the Presentation of Islam in School Textbooks*, Cologne, CSIC.

Falk, R. (1992) *Explorations at the Edge of Time: the Prospects for World Order*, Philadelphia, Temple University Press.

Falk, R. (1999) The monotheistic religions in the era of globalization, in: *Global Dialogue* no. 1.

Featherstone, M. (1990) Global culture: an introduction, in: M. Featherstone (ed.) *Global Culture: Nationalism, Globalization and Modernity*, London, Thousand Oaks and New Delhi, Sage

Featherstone, M. (1991) *Consumer Culture and Postmodernism*, London, Sage.

Featherstone, M. (1995) *Undoing Culture: Globalization, Postmodernism and Identity*, London, Thousand Oaks and New Delhi, Sage.

Ferguson, M. (1992) The mythology about globalization. *European Journal of Communication*, 7.

Fox, E. (1992) *Cultural Dependency Thrice Revisited*, UCD Photocopy Collection.

Foster, R. J. (1991) Making national cultures in the global ecumene. *Annual Review of Anthropology*, 20; 235–60.

Franco, J (1996) Globalization and the crisis of popular, in: Ton Salman (ed.) *The Legacy of the Disinherited*, Amsterdam, CEDLA Publication, pp. 261–72.

Friedman, J. (1994) *Cultural Identity & Global Process*, London, Thousand Oaks and New Delhi, Sage.

Frith, S. (1980) Formalism, realism and leisure: the case of punk, in: K. Gelder & S. Thornton (eds) (1997) *The Subcultures Reader*, London and New York, Routledge.

Frith, S. & Horne, H. (1987) *Art into a Pop*, London, Methuen.

Gadamer, H. G. (1998) *Reason in the Age of Science*, Cambridge and London, The MIT Press.

Gadamer, H. G. (1999) *Truth and Method*, London, Sheed & Ward.

Gary, G. (1999) *McLuhan and Baudrillard: the Master of Implosion*, London, Routledge.

Geaves, R. (1996) *Sectarian Influences Within Islam in Britain: with Reference to the Concepts of 'Ummah' and 'Community'*, Leeds, Department of Theology and Religious Studies, University of Leeds.

Geertz, C. (1973) *The Interpretation of Culture*, New York, Basic Books.

Gellner, E. (1992) *Postmodernism, Reason and Religion*, London and New York, Routledge.

Giddens (1972) *Emile Durkheim: Selected Writings*, New York and Cambridge, Cambridge University Press.

Giddens, A. (1989) *Sociology*, Cambridge, Polity Press.

Giddens, A. (1990) *The Consequences of Modernity*, Stanford, Stanford University Press.

Giddens, A. (1991) *Modernity and Self-Identity: Self and Society in the Late Modern Age*, Standford, Stanford University Press.

Giddens, A. (1994) Living in a post-traditional society, in: U. Beck, A. Giddens & S. Lash (eds) *Reflexive Modernization: Politics, Tradition and Aesthetics in the Modern Social Order*, Standford, Stanford University Press, pp. 56–109.

Giddens, A. (1998) *The Third Way: the Renewal of Social Democracy*, Cambridge, Polity Press.

Giddens, A. (1999) *Runaway World: How Globalization is Reshaping our lives*, London, Profile Books.

Gillespie, M. (1995) *Television, Ethnicity and Cultural Change*, London and New York, Routledge.

Glasner, P. E. (1977) *The Sociology of Secularization*, London, Routledge & Kegan Paul Ltd.

Glock, C. & Stark, R. (1965) *Religion and Society in Tension*, USA, Rand McNally & Company.

Gordon (1991) *Islam World Religions*, New York and Oxford, Facts on File.

Grunebaum, G. E. V. (1970) *Arabs, Islam and the Arab Caliphate in the early Middle Ages* (translated from the Russian by Adolphe Gourevitch), London, Allen & Unwin.

Habermas, J. (1975) *Legitimization Crisis*, Boston, Beacon Press.

Harding, S., Phillips, D. & Fogarty, M. (1986) *Contrasting Values in Western Europe*, London, Macmillan.

Hall, S. (1991) The local and the global: globalization and ethnicity, in: A. D. King (ed.) *Culture, Globalization and the World System: Contemporary Conditions for the Representation of Identity*, Binghamton, Suny Press, pp. 20–39.

Hall, S. (1992) The question of cultural identity, in S. Hall, D. Held & T. McGrew (eds) *Modernity and Futures*, Cambridge: Polity, pp. 274–316.

Halliday, F. (1997) Nationalism, in: J. Baylis & S. Smith (eds), *The Globalization of World Politics: an Introduction to International Relations*, Oxford, Oxford University Press.

Halliday, F. (1999) Review article: Islamophobia. *Ethnic and Racial Studies*, 22; 5: 892–902.

Hargrove, B. (1979) *The Sociology of Religion: Classical and Contemporary Approaches*, Illinois, AHM Publishing Corporation.

Harvey, D. (1989) *The Condition of Postmodernity*, Oxford, Blackwell.

Haynes, J. (1998) *Religion in Global Politics*, London and New York, Longman.

Haynes, J. (1999) *Religion, Globalization and Political Culture in the Third World*, Houdmills and London, Macmillan Press Ltd.

Held, D., McGrew, A., Goldblatt, D. & Perraton, J. (1999) *Global Transformations: Politics, Economics and Culture*, Cambridge, Polity Press.

Herman, E. S. and McChensney, R. W. (1997) *The Global Media: The New Missionaries of Corporate Capitalism*, London and Washington, Cassell.

Hetata, S. (1998) Dollarization, fragmentation and God, in: F. Jameson & M Miyoshi (eds) *The Cultures of Globalization*, Durham and London, Duke University Press.

Hirst. P. & Thompson, G. (1996) *Globalization in Question: The International Economy and the Possibilities of Governance*, Cambridge, Polity Press.

Hobden, S. & Wyn Jones, R. (1997) World-system theory, in: J. Baylis & S. Smith (eds) *The Globalization of World Politics: an Introduction of International Relations*, Oxford, Oxford University Press.

Hodgson, M. G. S. (1974) *The Venture of Islam: Conscience and History in a World Civilization, Vol. I: The Classical Age of Islam*, Chicago and London, The University of Chicago Press.

Hodgson, M. G. S. (1974) *The Venture of Islam: Conscience and History in a World Civilization, Vol. II: The Expansion of Islam in the Middle Periods*, Chicago and London, The University of Chicago Press.

Hodgson, M. G. S. (1974) *The Venture of Islam: Conscience and History in a World Civilization, Vol. III: The Gunpowder Empires and Modern Times*, Chicago and London, The University of Chicago Press.

Huntington, S. P. (1996) *The Clash of Civilizations and the Remaking of World Order*, New York, Simon & Schuster.

Bibliography

Hutnik, N. (1985) Aspects of identity in multi-ethnic society. *New Community*, 12; 2: 198–309.

Hutnyk, J. (1997) Adorno at Womad: south crossovers and the limits of hybridity-talk, in: P. Werbner & T. Modood, *Debating Cultural Hybridity: Multi-Cultural Identities and the Politics of Anti-Racism*, London & New Jersey, Zed Books.

Ibrahim, A. (1991) The ummah and tomorrows world. *Futures*, 26; 302–10.

IHRC (2000) *Anti-Muslim Discrimination and Hostility in the United Kingdom*, London.

Iqbal, Wahhab (1989) *Muslims in Britain: Profile of a Community*, London, The Runnymede Trust.

Irwin, J (1970) Notes on the status of the concept subculture, in: K. Gelder & S. Thornton (eds) (1997) *The Subcultures Reader*, London and New York, Routledge.

Jacobson, J. (1998) *Islam in Transition: Religion and Identity Among British Pakistani Youth*, London and New York, Routledge.

Jafarian, R. (1994) *Caliphate Period*, Qum, Dar al Hoda.

Jameson, F. (1998) Globalization as philosophical issue, in: F. Jameson & M. Miyoshi (eds), *The Cultures of Globalization*, Durham and London, Duke University Press.

Janoski, T. (1998) *Citizenship and Civil Society: A Framework of Rights & Obligations in Liberal, Traditional, and Social Democratic Regimes*, Cambridge, Cambridge University Press.

Jay, M. (1996) *The Dialectical Imagination: A History of The Frankfurt School and the Institute of Social Research 1923–1950*, Berkeley, Los Angeles and London, University of California Press.

Johansen, J. (1995) Sufis in politics, in: J. Sposito (ed.) *The Oxford Encyclopedia of Modern Islamic World*, Oxford, Oxford University Press.

Kalberge, S. (1993) Cultural foundations of modern citizenship, in: B. S. Turner (ed.) *Citizenship and Social theory*, London, Thousand Oaks and New Delhi, Sage.

Kamali, H. (1989) *Principles of Islamic Jurisprudence*, Cambridge, Islamic Texts Society.

Kamenka, E. (ed.) (1976) *Nationalism*, London, Arnold.

Kamilapour, Y. R. (ed.). (1994) *The U.S. media and the Middle East: Image and Perception*, Westport, CT, Greenwood Press.

Kaur, R. & Kalra, V. S. (1996) New paths for South Asian identity and musical creativity, in: S. Sharma, J. Hutnyk & A. Sharma (eds), *Dis-Orienting Rhythms*, London and New Jersey, Zed Books.

Kearney, H. (2000) The importance of being British. *Political Quarterly Publishing*, Oxford, Blackwell Publishers, pp. 26–30.

Keddie, N. R. (1995) *Iran and the Muslim World: Resistance and Revolution*, London, Macmillan.

Kenneth Jones, R. (1978) Paradigm shifts and identity theory, in: Hans Mol (ed.) *Identity and Religion: International, Cross-cultural Approaches*, London, Thousand Oaks and New Delhi, Sage.

Kellner, D. (1995) *Media Culture, Cultural Studies, Identity and Politics between Modern and Post-modern*, London and New York, Routledge.

Khan, S. (1998) *The Development of Muslim Reformist (Jadid) Political Thought in the Emirate of Bukhara (1870–1924) with particular reference to the writings of Ahmad Donish and Abdal Rauf Fitrat*, Thesis (PhD) SOAS, University of London.

King, A. (1990) Architecture, capital and the globalization of culture, in: M. Featherstone (ed.), *Global Culture: Nationalism, Globalization and Modernity*, London, Sage, pp. 397–411.

King, A. D. (1990) *Global Cities: Post-Imperialism and the Internationalization of London*, London and New York, Routledge.

King, A. D. (1991) *Culture, Globalization and the World System: Contemporary Conditions for the Representation of Identity*, Binghamton, Suny Press.

King, R. (1995) Migrations, globalization and place, in: D. Massey and P. Jess (eds), *A Place in the World: Places, Cultures and Globalization*, New York, Oxford University Press.

Kisubi, A. T. (1997) Ideological Perspectives on Multiculturalism, in: M. A. Burayidi (ed.), *Multiculturalism in a Cross-national Perspective*, Lanham, New York and London, University Press of America.

Konrad, G. (1984) *Anti-politics Intellectuals and Rise of New Class*, London, Macmillan.

Kroes, R. (1996) *Europeans and American Mass Culture*, Urbana and Chicago, University of Illinois Press.

Kubey, R. & Csikazentmihalyis (1990) *Television and the Quality of Life: How Viewing Shapes Everyday Experience*, Lawrence Erlbaum.

Lapidus, Ira M. (1988) *A History of Islamic Societies*, USA, Cambridge University Press.

Lash, S. & Urry J. (1994) *Economies of Signs and Space*, London, Sage.

Lechner, F. J. (1985a) Fundamentalism and socio-cultural revitalization in America: a sociological interpretation. *Sociological Analysis*, 46: 243–60.

Lechner, F. J. (1985b) Modernity and its discontents, in: J. C. Alexander (ed.) *Neofunctionalism*, Beverly Hills, Sage, pp. 157–78.

Lee, C. (1980) *Media Imperialism Reconsidered*, Beverly Hills, London, Sage Publications.

Legenhausen, M. (1999) *Islam and Religious Pluralism*, Great Britain, al-Hoda.

Lewis, L.M. (1966) *Islam in Tropical Africa*, London.

Lewis, P. (1994) *Islamic Britain: Religion, Politics and Identity among British Muslims*, London, I. B. Tauris.

Lewisohn, L. (1995) *Beyond Faith and Infidelity: the Sufi and Teachings of Mahmud Shabistari*, Richmond (Surrey), Curzon Press.

Lidz, V. M. (1979) *Religious Change and Continuity: Secularization, Ethical Life, and Religion in Modern Societies*, San Francisco & Washington and London, Joseey-Bass Publishers.

Lings, M. (1992) *The Book of Certainty: the Sufi Doctrine of Faith, Vision and Gnosis*, Cambridge, Islamic Text Society.

Lowenthal, L.(1961) *Literature, Popular Culture and Society*, Palo Alto, Pacific Books.

Lowy, R. F. (1995) Eurocentrism, ethnic studies, and the New World order: toward a critical paradigm. *Journal of Black Studies*, 25: 6; 712–36.

Lull, J. (2000) *Media, Communication, Culture: a Global Approach*, Cambridge, Polity Press.

Madsen, R. (1997) Global mono-culture, multiculture, and polyculture. *Social Research*, 60; 3; 493–511.

Mann, M. (1986) *The Social Sources of Power: Volume 1, A History of Power from the Beginning to A.D. 1760*, Cambridge, Cambridge University Press.

Mann, M. (1996) Has globalization ended the rise and rise of the nation-state? Paper presented at the *Directions of Contemporary Capitalism Conference*, University of Sussex, April 1996.

Mardin, S. (1989) *Religion and Social Change in Modern Turkey: The Case of Bediuzzaman Said Nursi*, Albany, State University of New York Press.

Martin, V. (1989) *Islam and Modernism, the Iranian Revolution on 1906*, London, I. B. Tauris.

Marr, A. (2000) *The Day Britain Died: The Subject of a Major BBC TV Series*, London, Profile Books.

Mathews, G. (2000) *Global Culture, Individual Identity: Searching for Home in the Cultural Supermarket*, London and New York, Routledge.

Mazrui, A. A. (1998) Globalization, Islam, and the West: between homogenization and hegemonization. *American Journal of Islamic Social Sciences*, 15; 3: 2–13.

McLuhan, M. (1964) *Understanding Media*, London, Routledge.

McGrew, A. G., Lewis P. G. *et al.* (1992) Global politics: globalization and the nation-state, in: A. G. McGrew, P. G. Lewis *et al*, *Global Politics*, Cambridge, Polity.

McMichael, P. (1996) Globalization: myths and realities, in: J. T. Roberts & A. Hite (eds) (2000) *From Modernization to Globalization*, Oxford, Blackwell Publishers.

Merrill, J. C., Lee, J. & Friedlander, E. J. (eds) (1994) *Modern Mass Media*, USA, Harper Collins College Publishers.

Meyer, J. W. (1994) Rationalized, in: W. R. Scott & J. W. Meyer *et al.* (eds) *Institutional Environments and Organizations: Structural Complexity and Individualism*, London, Sage.

Mignolo, W. D. (1998) Globalization, civilization processes and the relocation of languages and cultures, in: F. Jameson & M. Miyoshi, *The Cultures of Globalization*, Durham and London, Duke University Press.

Mlinar, Z. (1992) Individuation and globalization: the transformation of territorial social organization, in: Z. Mlinar (ed.), *Globalization and Territorial Identity*, Aldershot, Brookfield , Singapore and Sydney, Avebury.

Modood, T., Beishon, S. & Virdee, S. (1994) *Changing Ethnic Identities*, London, Policy Studies Institute.

Modood, T. (1997) Culture and identity, in: T. Modood *et al.* (eds), *Ethnic Minorities in Britain: Diversity and Disadvantage*, London, Policy Studies Institute.

Mol, H. (1976) *Identity and the Sacred: a Sketch for a New Social-Scientific Theory of Religion*, Oxford, Basil Blackwell.

Morley, D. & Robins, K. (1995) *Spaces of Identity: Global Media, Electronic Landscapes and Cultural Boundaries*, London and New York, Routledge.

Moyser, G. (1991) Politics and religion in the modern world: an overview, in: G. Moyser (ed.), *Politics and Religion in the Modern World*, London, Routledge, pp. 1–27.

Morteza, S. J. (1995) *Al Sahieh Men Serat a Nabi al Azam*, Lebanon, Dar al Hoda.

Mowlana, H., Gerbner, G. & Schiller, H. I. (eds). (1992) *Triumph of the Image: the Media's War in the Persian Gulf: a Global Perspective*, Boulder, CO, Westview Press.

Mowlana, H. (1996) *Global Communication in Transition: the End of Diversity?*, London, Thousand Oaks and New Delhi, Sage.

Mowlana, H. (2000) Covering Islam: media and its impact on Muslim identity, in: M. S. Bahmanpour & H. Bashir (eds), *Muslim Identity in the 21ᵗ Century: Challenges of Modernity*, London, Book Extra.

Muir, S. W. (1892) *The Caliphate: its Rise, Decline and Fall*, London, Oxford Horace Hart, Printer to the University.

Mulhall, S. & Swift A. (1996) *Liberals & Communitarians*, Oxford UK & Cambridge USA, Blackwell.

Mumtaz Ali, M. (1996) *The Muslim Community in Britain: an Historical Account*, Malaysia, Pelanduk Publications.

Munjee, A. (1986) *The Rape of a Noble Ideology: U.S.A. In Perspective 1783–1985*, California USA, First Amendment Publishers.

Muqtedar Khan, M. A. (1998) Constructing identity in global politics. *American Journal of Islamic Social Sciences*, 15; 3: 81–106.

Nachmias, C. F. & Nachmias, D. (1992) *Research Methods in the Social Sciences*, London, Edward Arnold.

Naficy, H. (1993) *The Making of Exile Cultures*, Minneapolis, University of Minnesota Press.

Nak-chung, P. (1998) Nations and literatures in the age of globalization, in: F. Jameson & M. Miyoshi (eds) *The Cultures of Globalization*, Durham and London, Duke University Press.

Nasr, S. H. (1993) *A Young Muslim's Guide to the Modern World*, Cambridge, The Islamic Texts Society.

Nasr, S. H. (1998) *Islamic-Christian Dialogue-Problems and Obstacles to be Pondered and Overcome*, Washington, DC., Center for Muslim–Christian Understanding.

Nasr, S. H. (1991) *Islamic Spirituality, Vols I & II*. New York, State University of New York Press.

Nasr, S. H. (1987) *Traditional Islam in the Modern World*, London, KPI.

Niyazi, B. (1964) *The Development of Secularism in Turkey*, Montreal, McGill Press.

Nicholson, R. A. (1930) *Literary History of the Arabs*, England, Curzon Press.

Nielsen, R. S. (1988) Muslims in Britain, in: T. Gerholm & Y. G. Lithman (eds) *The New Islamic Presence in Western Europe*, London and New York, Mansell Publishing Limited.

Nielsen, R. S. (1995) in: J. L. Esposito (ed.) *The Oxford Encyclopaedia of the Modern Islamic World*, Vol. 2, New York and Oxford, Oxford University Press.

Nobutaka, I. (1997) The information age and globalization of religion, in: I. Nobutaka (ed.) *Globalization and Indigenous Culture*, Tokyo, Institute for Japanese Culture and Classics, Kokugakuin University.

O'Brien, O. (1994) Ethnic identity: gender and life cycle in North Catalonia, in: *The Anthropology of Europe: Identities and Boundaries in Conflict*, USA, Berg.

Ohmae, K. (1995) *The End of the Nation State*, New York, Free Press.

Panikkar, R. (1984) The dialogical dialogue, in: *Frank Whaling: The World's Religious Traditions*, Edinburgh, T. & T. Clark Ltd.

Parekh, B. (1990) *Britain and the Social Logic of Pluralism in Britain: a Plural Society*, London: Commission for Racial Equality.

Parker, D. (1995) *Through Different Eyes: the Cultural Identities of Young Chinese People in Britain*, Hong Kong, Singapore and Sydney, Avebury.

Parsons, T. (1970) *The Social System*, London, Routledge & Kegan Paul Ltd.

Paxman, J. (1999) *The English: a Portrait of a People*, London, Penguin Books.

Peach (1990) The Muslim population of Great Britain. *Journal of Ethnic and Racial Studies*, 13; 3: 411–19.

Philo, G. (1990) *Seeing & Believing: the Influence of Television*, London & New York, Routledge.

Pieterse, J. N. (1995) Globalization as hybridisation, in: M. Featherstone *et al.* (eds) Global Modernities.

Price, M. E. (1995) *Television, the Public Sphere and National Identity*, Oxford, Clarendon Press.

Q-Circle (1997) Nationality means nothing: Islam is trans-national, in: *Q-News*, 274: 16–17.

Rahman, F. (1982) *Islam & Modernity: Transformation of an Intellectual Tradition*, Chicago & London, The University of Chicago Press.

Ramadan, T. (1999) *To be a European Muslim*, Leicester, The Islamic Foundation.

Randell, K. (1994) *Luther and the German Reformation 1517–55*, Hodder & Stoughton.

Raza, M. S. (1993) *Islam in Britain: Past, Present & Future*, Leicester, Volcano Press Ltd.

Razwy, S. A. A. (1997) *A Restatement of the History of Islam and Muslims*, USA, The World Federation of SIM.

Reece, J. E. (1984) Outmoded nationalism and emerging patterns of regional identity in contemporary Western Europe, in: P. Boerner (ed.) *Concepts of National Identity: an Interdisciplinary Dialogue*, Germany, Novos Veragsgesellschaft, Band-Baden.

Ritzer, G.(1988), *Sociological Theory*, New York, McGraw-Hill Publishing Company.

Ritzer, G. (1993) *The McDonaldization of Society*, Thousand Oaks, London and New Delhi, Pine Forge Press.

Ritzer, G. (1998) *The McDonaldization Thesis: Explorations and Extensions*, London, Thousand Oaks and new Delhi, Sage.

Robbins, T. & Robertson, R. (1987) *Church–State Relations: Tensions and Transitions*, New Brunswick, Transaction Books.

Robinson, F (1999) Secularization, Weber and Islam, in: T. Huffed (ed.) *Weber and Islam*, New Brunswick NJ, Transaction Books.

Robertson, R. (1987) Globalization and societal modernization: a note on Japan and Japanese religion. *Sociological Analysis*, 47: 35–42.

Robertson, R.(1989a) Internationalisation and globalisation. *University Centre for International Studies Newsletter*, University of Pittsburgh (Spring): 8–9.

Robertson, R. (1989b) Globalisation, politics, and religion, in: J. A. Beckford & T. Luckmann (eds) *The Changing Face of Religion*, Beverly Hills: Sage, pp. 10–23.

Robertson, R. (1990) After nostalgia? Wilful nostalgia and the phases of globalization, in: B. S. Turner (ed.) *Theories of Modernity and Post-Modernity*, London, Sage.

Robertson, R. (1991) Social theory, cultural relativity and problem of globality, in: D. A. King (ed.) *Culture Globalization and the World-System*, Malaysia, Macmillan.

Robertson, R. (1992a) *Globalization: Social Theory and Global Culture*, London, Sage.

Robertson, R. (1992b) Globality, global culture and images of world order, in: H. Haferamp & N. Smelser (eds), *Social Change and Modernity*, Berkeley, University of California.

Robertson, R. (1994) Religion and the global field. *Social Compass*, 41; 1: 121–35.

Robertson, R. (1995) Glocalization: time-space and homogeneity-heterogeneity, in: S. Featherstone, S. Lash & R. Robertson (eds), *Global Modernities*, London, Thousand Oaks and New Delhi, Sage.

Robertson, R. (1996) Globality, globalization and trans-disciplinarity, in: *Theory, Culture & Society*, London, Thousand Oaks and New Delhi, Sage, pp. 127–33.

Robertson, R. & Chirico, J. (1985) Modernization, globalisation, and worldwide religious resurgence: a theoretical exploration. *Sociological Analysis*, 46: 219–42.

Robertson, R. & Garrett, W. R. (eds) (1991) *Religion and Global Order*, New York, Paragon House Publishers.

Rorty, R. (1988) The priority of democracy to philosophy, in: M. D. Peterson & R.C. Vaughan (eds) *The Virginia Statute on Religious Freedom*, Cambridge, Cambridge University Press.

Runnymede Trust (1997) *Islamophobia a Challenge for Us All: Report of the Runnymede Trust Commission on British Muslims and Islamophobia*, London, Runnymede Trust.

Russell, B. (1946) *History of Western Philosophy*, London, Allen and Unwin

Said, E. W. (1981) *Covering Islam: How the Media and the Experts Determine How We See the Rest of the World*, New York, Pantheon Books.

Said, E. W. (1993) *Culture and Imperialism*, London, Chatto and Windus.

Samad, Y,(1994) *Imagining a British Identification*, Warwick University.

Samuel, R. (1989) *See Patriotism: the Making and Unmaking of British Identity*, London & New York, Routledge.

Sani Umar, M. (1988) The role of European imperialism in Muslim countries. *The Islamic Quarterly*, 32; 2: 77–98.

Saunders, P (1993) Citizenship in a liberal society, in: B. S. Turner (ed.) *Citizenship and Social Theory*, London, Thousand Oaks and New Delhi, Sage.

Sahifeh Nour (1986) *Collection of Ayatollah Khomeini's Speech*, Tehran, Ministry of Islamic Guidance.

Samuel, Paphael (1989) *Patriotism: The Making and Unmaking of British Identity.*

Sasscn and Portcs (1993) Miami: a new global city? *Contemporary Sociology*, 22; 4: 271–477.

Sayyid, B. S. (1997) *A Fundamental Fear: Eurocentrism and the Emergence of Islamis*, London & New York, Zed Books Ltd.

Shaban, M. A. (1970) *The Abbasid Revolution*, Cambridge, London, New York and Melbourne, Cambridge University Press.

Shaban, M. A. (1971) *Islamic History: A New Interpretation*, Cambridge, New York, New Rochelle, Melbourne and Sydney, Cambridge University Press.

Shah-Kazemi, R. (1997) From Sufism to terrorism: the distortion of Islam in the political culture of Algeria, in: *Algeria: Revolution Revisited*, London: Islamic World Report, pp. 160–93.

Shariati, A. (1979) *Civilization and Modernization*, Aligarh, Iranian Students Islamic Association.

Shepard, W. E. (1978) Islam and ideology: towards a typology, *Middle East Studies*, 19: 307–36.

Shiller, H. (1976) *Communication and Cultural Domination*, New York, International Arts and Sciences Press.

Shils, E. & Harry, M. (1968) Ideology, in: *The International Encyclopedia of Social Sciences Vol. 7*, London: Macmillan Company & The Free Press, pp. 66–85.

Shotter, J. (1993) Psychology and citizenship: identity and belonging, in: B. S. Turner (ed.) *Citizenship and Social Theory*, London, Thousand Oaks and New Delhi, Sage.

Smart, N. (1998) *The World's Religion*, Cambridge, Cambridge University Press.

Smith, A. D. (1991) *National Identity*, London, Penguin Group.

Smith, M. (1997) Overcoming racial stereotypes through multicultural education: a native American perspective, in: M. A. Burayidi (ed.), *Multiculturalism in a Cross-national Perspective*, Lanham, New York and London, University Press of America.

Smith, M. A. & Kolloc, P. (eds) (1999) *Communities in Cyberspace*, London & New York, Routledge.

Smith, C. (1957) *Islam in Modern History*, New York, New American Library, Mentor.

Sommerville, C. J. (1992) *The Secularization of Early Modern England: from Religious Culture to Religious Faith*, New York and Oxford, Oxford University Press.

Soroush, A. (2000) *Reason, Freedom, and Democracy in Islam*, Oxford, Oxford University Press.

SPSS (1990) *SPSS: Advanced Statistics, User's Guide*, Chicago, Marija J. Norusis/SPSS Inc.

Spuler, B. (1969) *The Muslim World: a Historical Survey: Part I – The Age of Caliphs*, Leiden (Netherlands), E. J. Brill.

Spuler, B. (1969) *The Muslim World: a Historical Survey: Part II – The Mongols*, Leiden (Netherlands), E. J. Brill.

Stalker, P. & Rienner, L. (2000) *Workers without Frontiers; the Impact of Globalization on International Migration*, Pub. Inc, New Cloth.

Stam, R. (1995) Eurocentrism, polycentrism, and multicultural pedagogy: film and the quincentennial, in: R. D. L. Campa, E. A. Kaplan & M. Sprinker (eds), *Late Imperial Culture*, London & New York, Verso.

Stivers, R. L. (1991) Evangelicals in Transition, *Theological Education* 27: 33–50.

Sztompka, P. (1993) *The Sociology of Social Change*, Oxford UK & Cambridge, Blackwell.

Taji-Farouki, S. (1996) *A Fundamental Quest: Hizb al-Tahrir and the Search for the Islamic Caliphate*, London, Grey Seal.

Thomas, C. (1997) Globalization and the south, in: C. Thomas & P. Wilkin (eds) *Globalization and the South*, USA, St. Martin's Press.

Thomas, G. M., Meyer, J. W., Ramirez, F. O. & Boli, J. (1987) *Institutional Structure: Constituting State, Society and the Individual*, London, Sage.

Thornton, S. (1995) The social logic of subcultural capital, in: K. Gelder & S. Thornton (eds) (1997) *The Subcultures Reader*, London and New York, Routledge.

Tiryakian, E. A. (1986) Sociology's great leap forward: the challenge of internationalisation. *International Sociology* 1; 2.

Tomlinson, J. (1991) *Cultural Imperialism: a Critical Introduction*, London, Printer Publishers.

Tomlinson, J. (1999) *Globalization and Culture*, Chicago, The University of Chicago Press.

Tunstall, J. (1977) *The Media are American: Anglo-American Media in the World*, London, Constable.

Turner, B. S. (1983) *Religion and Social Theory*, London, Heinemann Educational Books.

Turner, B. S. (1993) Contemporary problems in the theory of citizenship, in: B. S. Turner (ed.) *Citizenship and Social theory*, London, Thousand Oaks and New Delhi, Sage.

Turner, B. S. (1994) *Orientalism, Postmodernism and Globalism*, London, and New York, Routledge.

United Nations (1996) *Globalization and Liberalization: Effects of International Economic Relations on Poverty*, New York and Geneva, United Nations.

Vertovec, S. (1996) Muslims, the State, and the public sphere in Britain, in: G. Nonneman, T. Niblock & B. Szajkowski (eds) *Muslim Communities in the New Europe*, Lebanon, Garnet Publishing Limited.

Vertovec, S. & Peach, C. (1997) Introduction: Islam in Europe and the politics of religion and community, in: S. Vertovec & C. Peach (eds) *Islam in Europe: The Politics of Religion and Community*, London, Macmillan Press Ltd.

Voll, J. O. (1982) *Islam: Continuity and Change in the Modern World*, USA, Westview Press, Inc.

Wahhab, I. (1989) *Muslims in Britain: Profile of a Community*, London, The Runnymede Trust.

Wehr H. (1976) *Arabic-English Dictionary*. 3rd edn. Spoken Languages Service.

Whelan, G. T. (1994) *Values and Social Change in Ireland*, Ireland, Gill & Macmillan.

Wallerstein, I. (1991a) *Unthinking Social Science: The Limits of Nineteenth-Century Paradigms*, Cambridge, Polity Press.

Wallerstein, I. (1991b) The national and universal: can there be such a thing as world culture? in: A. D. King, *Culture Globalization and the World-System*, Binghamton, Macmillan.

Wallerstein, I. (1995) *After Liberalism*, New York, New Press.

Ward, K. (1989) *Mass Communication and the Modern World*, London, Macmillan.

Waters, M. (1995) *Globalization*, London and New York, Routledge.

Waters, M. (2000) *Globalization* (2nd edn), London and New York, Routledge.

Werbner, P. (1997) Introduction: the dialectics of cultural hybridity, in: P. Werbner & T. Modood, *Debating Cultural Hybridity: Multi-Cultural Identities and the Politics of Anti-Racism*, London & New Jersey, Zed Books.

Wiggershaus, R. (1995) *The Frankfurt School: its History, Theories and Political Significance*, Cambridge, Polity Press.

Winter, T. J. (1999) Islam in England: strands for the splicing. *Q-News*, 306: 22–7.

Wriston, W. (1992) *The Twilight of Sovereignty*, New York, Charles Scribners Sons.

Young, R. J. C. (1995) *Colonial Desire: Hybridity in Theory, Culture and Race*, London and New York, Routledge.

Index of Concepts

Index of Names